PRINCIPLES OF ECONOMICS

TAMIKA STEWARD
Tarrant County College

Kendall Hunt
publishing company

Chapters 14, 16, and 19 are from *Principles of Macroeconomics: Understanding Our Material World,* 3E, by Fred Newbury, Dave Shorow, and Gus Herring.

Chapters 10 and 20 are from *An Applied Approach to Economics,* 3E, by Jack A. Chambless.

Chapter 11 is from *Economics: Principles and Applications,* 3E, by Rolando A. Santos.

Chapter 13 is from *Principles of Macroeconomics* by Ryan Amacher and Jennifer Pate.

Chapter 9 is from *Intro to Microeconomics* by Michael Snyder.

Kendall Hunt
publishing company

www.kendallhunt.com
Send all inquiries to:
4050 Westmark Drive
Dubuque, IA 52004-1840

ISBN 978-1-4652-2976-2

Printed in the United States of America

10 9 8 7 6 5 4 3 2 1

CONTENTS

CHAPTER 1	Getting Down to the Basics	1
CHAPTER 2	An Analysis of Supply and Demand	7
CHAPTER 3	How Responsive Are You to Elasticity?	21
CHAPTER 4	A Matter of Satisfaction: Utility	29
CHAPTER 5	The Cost of Running a Business	33
CHAPTER 6	Pure Competition	39
CHAPTER 7	Monopoly and Antitrust Policy	45
CHAPTER 8	Monopolistic Competition and Oligopoly	49
CHAPTER 9	Derived Demand	55
CHAPTER 10	Determining Wages	69
CHAPTER 11	The Market of Public Goods	95
CHAPTER 12	Gross Domestic Product	103
CHAPTER 13	Economic Growth Unveiled	109
CHAPTER 14	What Goes Up Must Come Down: The Business Cycle	135
CHAPTER 15	The Aggregate Nature of Economics	149
CHAPTER 16	Fiscal Policy	155
CHAPTER 17	Our Money	173
CHAPTER 18	Money Creation	177
CHAPTER 19	Monetary Policy	183
CHAPTER 20	International Trade	199

Getting Down to the Basics

WHY STUDY ECONOMICS

Have you ever turned on the news and thought to yourself: 'why am I watching this? I don't understand anything they are saying at all,' 'why are the politicians debating issues such as immigration, health care, and international affairs?' 'Why should I care about monetary policy or fiscal policy?' 'What is that anyway?' 'Why are gas prices always rising?' 'How do they expect me to pay my bills if I have to use all of my income on gas for my vehicle?' If you've asked yourself any of these questions or questions similar in meaning, keep reading. In this chapter, we will explore the basic concepts of economics. Upon completing this chapter, you will have a better understanding of the following topics:

- Microeconomics versus macroeconomics
- Positive versus normative statements
- Key economic ideas
- The economic goal and problem

DEFINITION OF ECONOMICS

Economics is a social science that examines decisions made for individuals, businesses, and the economy. Economics consists of two major branches: macroeconomics and microeconomics. *Macroeconomics* examines decisions made for the whole economy. Gross domestic product, fiscal policy, unemployment, and the business cycle are concepts of macroeconomics. *Microeconomics* examines decisions made for individuals

Microeconomics	Macroeconomics
Dr. Pepper introduces a new flavor	The Japanese Yen appreciates in value
Apple was charged with violating an antitrust policy	The United States deficit increased from last quarter
Sears introduced the self-checkout kiosk in some locations	The unemployment rate in Texas increased
University of Oklahoma enters the final four in basketball	The Federal Reserve increased the money supply

and businesses. Determining a consumer's demand for goods or services, examining the costs of resources for a business, and establishing the level of satisfaction are concepts of microeconomics.

Your Turn: On the lines below, write down three things considered microeconomics and three things considered macroeconomics.

____

____

____

____

____

POSITIVE AND NORMATIVE STATEMENTS

A *positive statement* is a statement of fact. Positive statements express occurrences in the economy backed up by evidence and proof. A *normative statement* is a statement of opinion.

Positive Statements	Normative Statements
The sky is blue.	Everyone should go to college.
An increase in prices will decrease demand for goods and services.	Everyone should eat a vegetarian diet.
The economy is experiencing a recession.	The government should increase minimum wage.
Starbucks is located on every corner of the street.	Retailers should lower the prices of goods so everyone can afford the goods.

SCIENTIFIC METHOD

Economists use models to analyze issues occurring in the world. The economic models are used to answer questions. Remember the scientific method from high school? Economists use the same steps from the scientific method to answer questions. The steps include the following:

1. Make an observation
2. Form a hypothesis
3. Test the hypothesis
4. Accept or reject it
5. If reject, continue to retest

KEY ECONOMIC IDEAS

Three key topics encompass the world of economics: people are rational, people respond to incentives, and people think on the margin. Let's look at each of these topics in detail.

Rational Behavior

Economists assume that individuals are rational. Is this always the case? Suppose you lost your job several months ago. You've depleted your savings account. You have bills to pay and a family to feed. What should you do? A person thinking rationally will look for another job. A person thinking irrationally will spend large sums of money, increase debt, or even rob a bank. We will have further discussions on rational behavior in upcoming chapters.

People Respond to Incentives

Economists believe people respond to incentives. Do you believe people respond to incentives? Why are you pursuing a college degree? Do you want a better paying job or do you desire a promotion at your current job? Higher pay or promotion is an incentive to pursue a college degree.

Marginal Analysis

Every decision a business owner makes is critical to the success of the organization. The business owners must not only consider the costs and benefits associated with running a business, they must also consider the extra cost and extra benefit of running the business. Considering the extra cost and benefit is known as thinking on the margin. *Marginal cost* is the extra cost incurred from creating another unit of a good or service. *Marginal benefit* is the extra benefit gained from creating another unit of a good or service. Let's take a look at an example. Suppose Jennifer owns a clothing boutique. She hires workers to crochet sweaters. One worker can make four sweaters. Two workers can make ten sweaters. How many extra sweaters were created by hiring the second worker? The marginal benefit of hiring the second worker is six sweaters. Later in this book, we will explore how producers produce the optimal quantity by equating marginal benefit with marginal costs.

SCARCITY, OPPORTUNITY COSTS, AND PRODUCTION POSSIBILITIES

What is the difference between a want and a need? A need is something you have to have to survive. A want is an unlimited desire. Our needs are food, clothing, and shelter. Our wants are endless. If you are a parent, you have heard your child say that he just has to have that new Beyblade he just saw on TV. Is the Beyblade a true need? No it is not; it is a want. Create a mental list of everything you want. Can you have it all? No, your wants are unlimited. Now, let's examine the concept of scarcity. Scarcity exists because wants exceed resources. As stated before, wants are unlimited desires. Make a mental note of three things you really want. What do you have to do to obtain the three wants? Do you have to give something up? Do you have all of the resources to obtain those wants? Individuals, businesses, and society as a whole cannot satisfy all of their wants. All entities have limited resources. What are economic resources?

Economic resources are also known as factors of production. Listed below are the four factors of production:

- Land. Gifts of nature. All natural resources fall under the category of land.
- Labor. Individuals working. Any effort applied to the production of goods and services qualify as labor.

- Capital. Capital contains two categories: physical capital and human capital. Physical capital consists of property and equipment. Human capital consists of education and training.
- Entrepreneurial Ability. An entrepreneur is a risk-taker; he makes things happen in his business. He uses a combination of resources (the factors of production) to operate his business.

So far, we established that wants exceed resources. Would you agree that we all make choices? In economics, we call choices opportunity costs. An opportunity cost is a trade-off. It is the next best alternative. Think about it. What could you do today instead of read chapter one of the economics textbook? You could go to the movies, enjoy some time with your family, or read another book for entertainment purposes.

Suppose John has ten hours in his day. He can spend his time watching TV or he can go to work. The table below shows the choices for his ten hour day.

Watch TV	Go to Work
10	0
8	2
6	4
4	6
2	8
0	10

The table shows John can watch ten hours of TV and spend zero hours working. He could watch zero hours of TV and work for ten hours. Let's take the example a step further. Examine the following graph. The graph denotes John's combination of choices for watching TV or going to work.

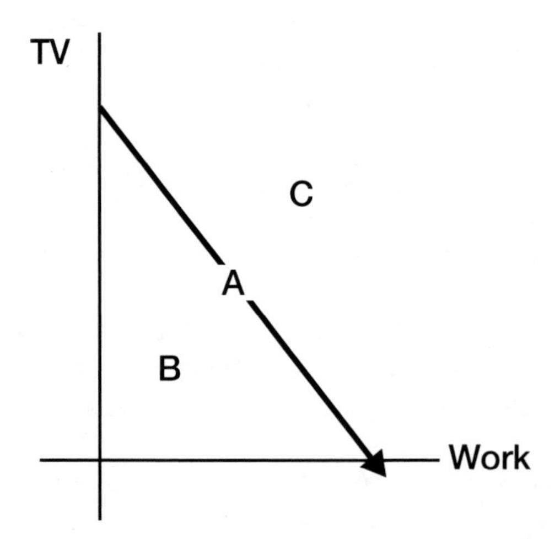

The production possibilities frontier shows the combination of goods or services produced with the efficient use of resources. Let's explore the points on John's production possibilities frontier.

- Point A: Efficiency line. Point A denotes efficient use of the resources. Ideally, the individual should produce at one of the points on the efficiency line.

- Point B: Point B denotes an inefficient use of resources. If John used all of his resources wisely, he could attain all of the points on the line. Points located inside of the line are inefficient but attainable.
- Point C: Unattainable. The individual used too much of the resources.

Assumptions of the PPF

A variety of things can affect the output in an economy. Consider the following assumptions:

1. The individual or firm produces only two goods or services.
2. Resources and technology are fixed.
3. The individual or firm operates at full employment.

Shifts in PPF

The production possibilities curve can shift to the left or the right. The following things cause a change in the production possibilities curve:

1. Economic growth or decay. The curve will shift to the left if the economy is experiencing a recessionary time period. The curve will shift to the right if the economy is experiencing an expansionary time period.
2. Changes in resources or technology. Advancements in technology can cause the PPF to shift to the right.
3. Unemployment. An increase in the unemployment rate will cause the PPF to shift to the left.

Types of PPF

Next, we must consider two types of production possibilities frontiers: straight-line and bowed.

Straight-Line PPF The straight-line PPF exhibits constant opportunity costs. Let's revisit the TV and work example. If John increased his work time from zero hours to two hours he gives up two hours of TV time. If John increases his work day from two hours to four hours he gives up two hours of TV time. John gives up two hours of TV time every time he increases the amount of hours worked in the day.

Bowed PPF The bowed PPF exhibits increasing opportunity costs. As the individual or firm produces more units of one good, the opportunity cost of producing the other good increases. Examine the following chart for increasing opportunity costs.

Books	DVDs
0	500
100	450
200	350
300	200
400	100
500	0

The opportunity cost of producing DVDs increases as the production of books increases. When the production of books increases from 0 to 100, the opportunity cost of DVDs is 50 (500–450). When the production of books increases from 100 to 200, the opportunity cost of producing DVDs is 100 (450–350).

KEY TERMS

Macroeconomics	Normative statement	Production Possibilities Frontier
Marginal analysis	Opportunity cost	Resources
Microeconomics	Positive statement	Scarcity

An Analysis of Supply and Demand

Have you ever wondered why we experience price increases and decreases? Have you ever wondered why sometimes an overstock of a good exists and sometimes not enough of the good exist? The answer is supply and demand.

DEMAND

Demand is from the perspective of the consumer. To establish a demand, the consumer must be willing and able to purchase the good or service.

Quantity Demanded: The amount of a good or service an individual plans to purchase at a specified price and time period. Do you drink Starbucks coffee? The typical mocha grande is $5.00 per cup. Suppose you purchase one cup of coffee a day for a year. Your quantity demanded for coffee is 365 cups of coffee in one calendar year at $5.00 per cup.

Law of Demand: An increase in the price of a good will decrease the quantity demanded of a good, ceteris paribus. A decrease in the price of a good will increase the quantity demanded of a good, ceteris paribus. If the Starbucks coffee increased to $7.00 a cup, quantity demanded for the coffee would decrease. Three effects show why the law of demand holds true:

- Substitute effect: An increase in the price of a good will lead individuals to substitute that good for something else.
- Income effect: A decrease in the price of a good will cause the individual to experience an increase in money income.
- Law of diminishing utility: As an individual consumes more of a good, his level of satisfaction begins to decrease.

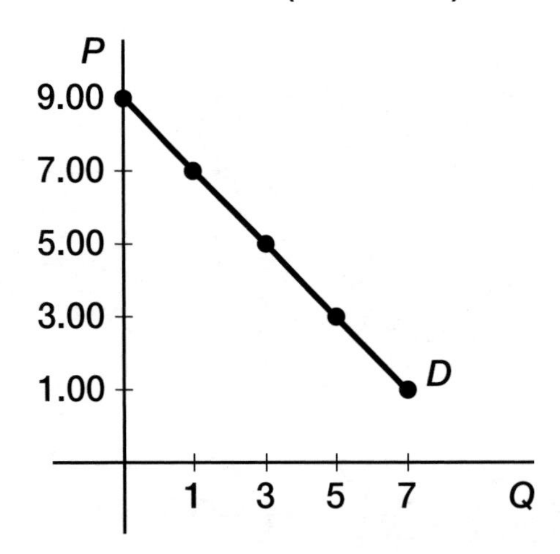

Price	Quantity
$1.00	7
$3.00	5
$5.00	3
$7.00	1
$9.00	0

Shown above is the demand schedule for ice cream. The demand schedule measures price on the vertical axis and quantity on the horizontal axis. The graph represents an individual's demand curve. According to the law of demand, as the price of ice cream increased, the quantity demanded decreased.

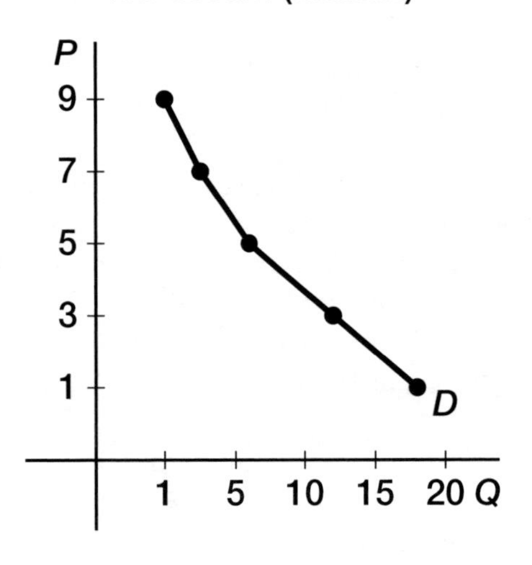

Individual Demand Curve versus Market Demand Curve

Now let's examine the market demand curve for ice cream. The market demand curve represents the collective amount of a good demanded at the same price. Just like individual demand, an increase in the price of ice cream decreases the collective amount demanded. Examine the following table. The quantity demanded of three individuals is listed. To arrive at the market quantity demanded, simply add the three quantities demanded together. The market demand curve will contain the prices and the market quantity demanded.

Price	$Quantity_1$	$Quantity_2$	$Quantity_3$	$Quantity_C$
$1.00	7	6	5	18
$3.00	5	4	3	12
$5.00	3	2	1	6
$7.00	2	1	0	3
$9.00	1	0	0	1

Changes in Demand: A change in demand is signified by a shift in the demand curve. An increase in demand shifts the demand curve to the right and a decrease in demand will shift the curve to the left. Let's examine the things that can cause a change in demand.

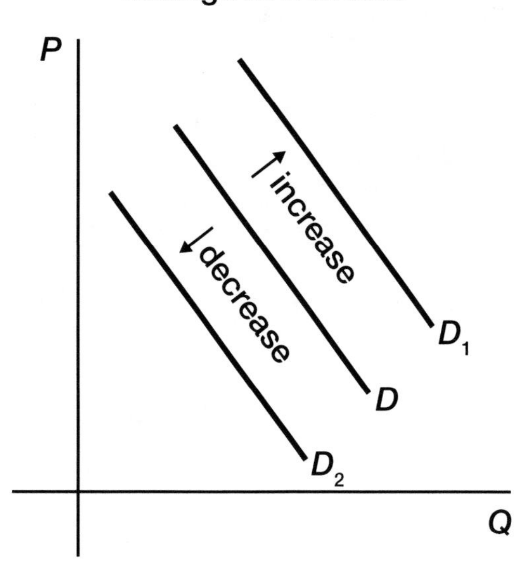

Five things cause a change in demand:

- Prices of related goods. Prices of related goods fall under two categories: substitutes and complements. Substitutes are goods used in place of the good. Complements are goods that go with the good.
  - Substitutes. If the price of hamburgers increases, what happens to the demand for hot dogs? The demand for hot dogs increases. An increase in the price of hamburgers leads to a decrease in the quantity demanded of hamburgers. Consumers will find a substitute, hot dogs, for the hamburgers.
  - Complements. If the price of hamburgers decreases, what happens to the demand for French fries? The demand for French fries increases. If the price of hamburgers

decreases, more consumers will purchase hamburgers. What do consumers eat with hamburgers? French fries. An increase in quantity demanded of hamburgers will increase the demand for French fries.

- Income. Money income is what a consumer earns in the form of salaries or wages. Money income is used to purchase goods and services. Goods are classified as normal or inferior.
  - Normal Goods: If the consumer experiences an increase in income, an increase in demand for the normal good will occur. If the consumer experiences a decrease in income, a decrease in the demand for normal goods will occur. If the consumer's income increases, what happens to the demand for steaks? The demand for steaks increases. If the consumer's income decreases, the demand for steaks decreases as well.
  - Inferior Goods: Inferior goods are also known as generic or off-brand goods. If a consumer experiences an increase in income, a decrease in the demand for inferior goods will occur. If a consumer experiences a decrease in income, an increase in the demand for inferior goods will occur.
- Expected future prices. Suppose today the price of gas is $3.50. You heard that the price of gas will decrease to $1.00 for one day. What will happen to the demand for gas today? What about tomorrow? The demand for gas today will decrease and tomorrow will increase.
- Population. If the population of a particular area increases, the demand for goods will increase as well. If the population of the state of Texas decreases, what will happen to the demand for groceries? Less people in the state of Texas will decrease the demand for groceries.
- Preferences. Preferences are also known as consumer tastes. DC shoes were in style last summer. According to the fashion critics, Chucks are in style this summer. What will happen to the demand for DC shoes this summer? The demand for DC shoes will decrease. Consumers will purchase more Chucks since the Chucks are now in style.

CHANGES IN DEMAND VERSUS A CHANGE IN QUANTITY DEMANDED

A change in demand causes a shift in the demand curve. A change in quantity demanded causes a movement along the curve. If the price of ice cream increases, what happens to the demand for chocolate syrup? The demand for chocolate syrup decreases. The following graph shows the change in demand for the syrup.

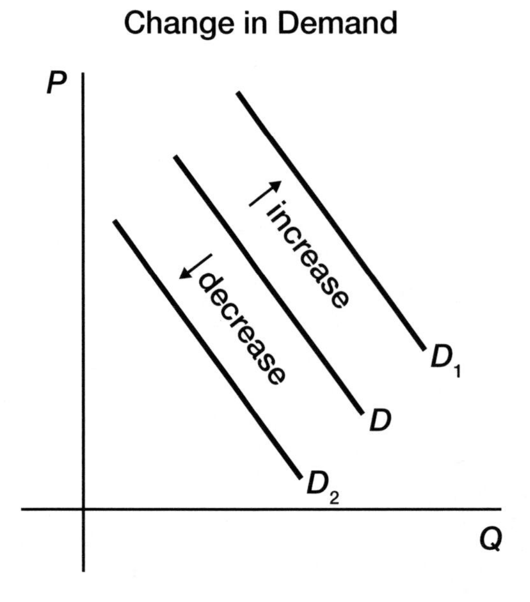

If the price of ice cream increases from $1.00 to $3.00, the quantity demanded decreases from seven to five ice creams. The decrease is shown on the following graph.

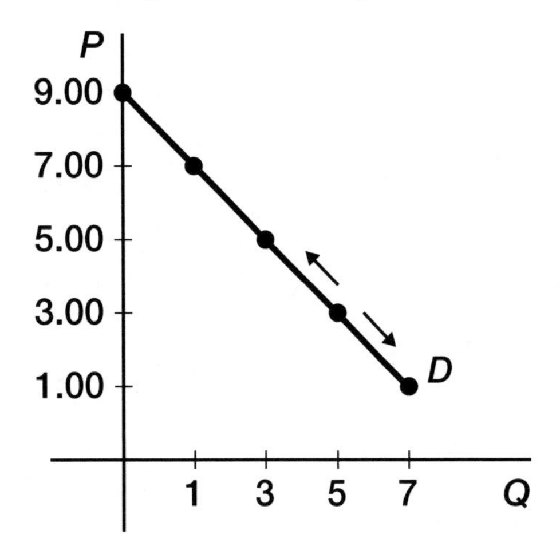

True or False: A change in preferences causes a movement along the demand curve? False: A change in preferences causes a shift of the demand curve. A change in *quantity demanded* causes a movement along the demand curve.

Supply

Supply is the perspective of the producer. The producer is willing and able to sell a good or service.

Quantity Supplied: The amount of a good a producer plans to sell at a specified price and time period. The Starbucks employee will sell the coffee at the designated price and time period.

Law of Supply: The law of supply shows an increase in the price of the good will lead to an increase in the quantity supplied, ceteris paribus. A decrease in supply will lead to a decrease in the quantity supplied, ceteris paribus. How is that possible? The price affects the producer's revenues. The higher the price set for the food, the greater the revenue generated.

Ice Cream (Individual)

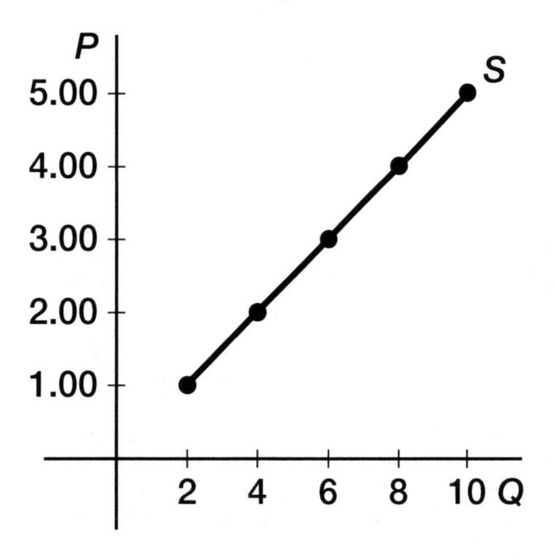

Price	Quantity
$1.00	2
$2.00	4
$3.00	6
$4.00	8
$5.00	10

Shown is the individual supply curve for a producer selling ice cream. As the price increases, the producers are willing to sell more ice cream. The supply curve is upward sloping. Now, let's examine the market supply curve for ice cream.

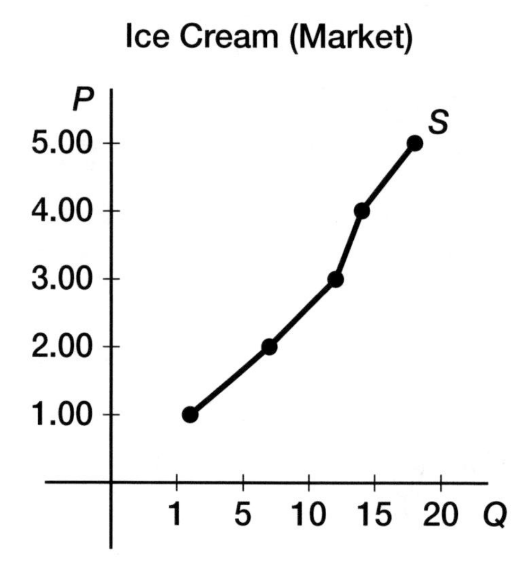

P	Q1	Q2	Q3	QM
$1.00	0	1	1	2
$2.00	2	3	2	7
$3.00	3	4	5	12
$4.00	4	5	5	14
$5.00	5	6	7	18

The market supply curve is comprised of the quantities producers are willing to sell at the same price. Add the three quantities together to arrive at the market quantity. The graph shows the market supply curve for ice cream.

Change in Supply versus Change in Quantity Supplied

Changes in Supply: A change in supply is shown by a shift in the supply curve. An increase in supply is shown by a rightward shift of the supply curve. A decrease in supply is shown by a leftward shift in the supply curve. True or False: An increase in supply shifts the curve upward. False: An increase in supply actually shifts the curve downward. Always say left or right when referring to increases and decreases. The following graph shows an increase and decrease in supply. Let's examine the things that cause a change in supply.

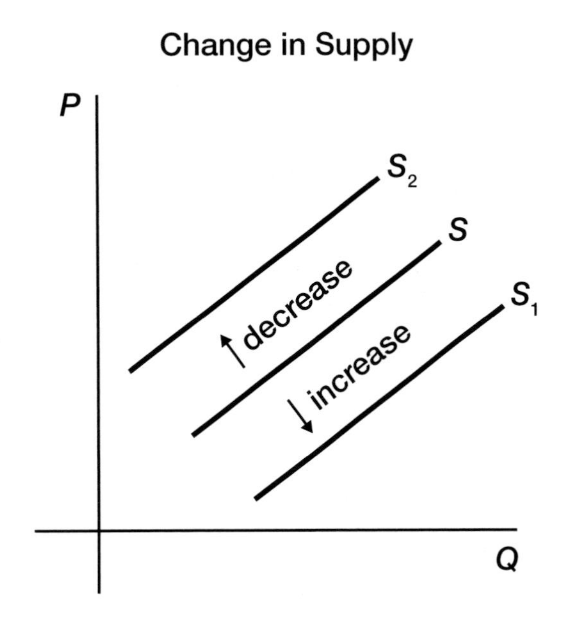

Six things cause a change in supply:

- Prices of inputs. Inputs are the factors of production. Suppose minimum wage increases. How will the increase affect supply? An increase in wages will increase the producer's cost of production. If the producer experiences an increase in the cost of production, supply will decrease.
- Prices of other goods produced. Other goods produced are substitutes and complements in production.
  - Substitutes
  - Compliments
- Expected future prices. The producers of XBOX know Black Friday occurs next week. The price of the XBOX will be $150 on that special shopping day. Normally, the price of the unit is $299. What will happen to the supply of the XBOX on Black Friday? Producers will supply less because revenues will decrease.
- Technology. The producers purchased new processors which are expected to help the XBOX run more efficiently. The improvement in technology will increase the supply of the unit.
- Number of suppliers. If more suppliers of the XBOX enter the market, the number of XBOX units available will increase.
- Taxes and subsidies. If the suppliers are imposed higher tariffs on exporting the XBOX units, the supply of the unit will decrease for foreign trade.

A change in quantity supplied chases a movement along the supply curve. Remember the ice cream example? What happened when the price of ice cream increased from $1.00 to $2.00? The quantity supplied increases from **two** to **four** ice creams. The curve did not shift. We moved from one point to another point on the same line.

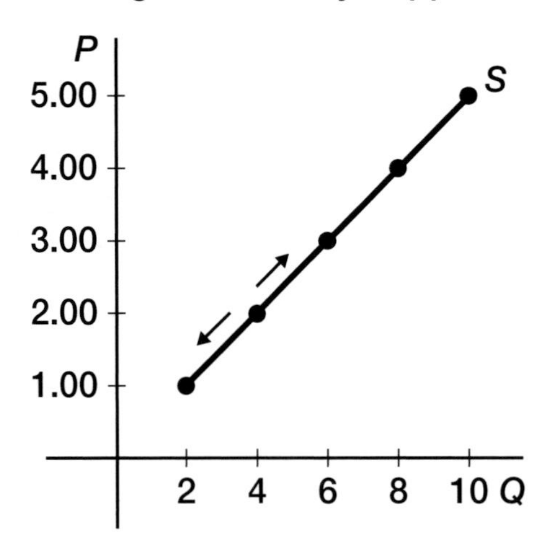

EQUILIBRIUM

Now that the concepts of supply and demand were explained, let's focus our attention on equilibrium. The term equilibrium means something is balanced. In the case of supply and demand, quantity demanded equals quantity supplied at the same price. The following chart displays equilibrium.

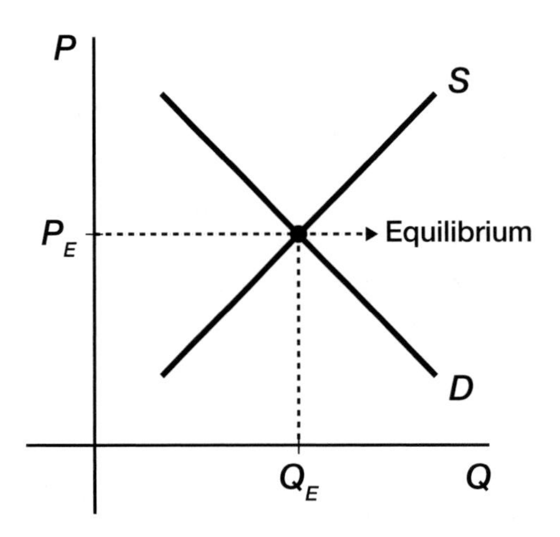

Consumers and producers are happiest at the equilibrium price. What happens if equilibrium is not achieved? Let's take a look.

Price	Quantity Demanded	Quantity Supplied
$100	300	100
$150	250	150
$200	200	200
$250	150	250
$300	100	300
$350	50	350

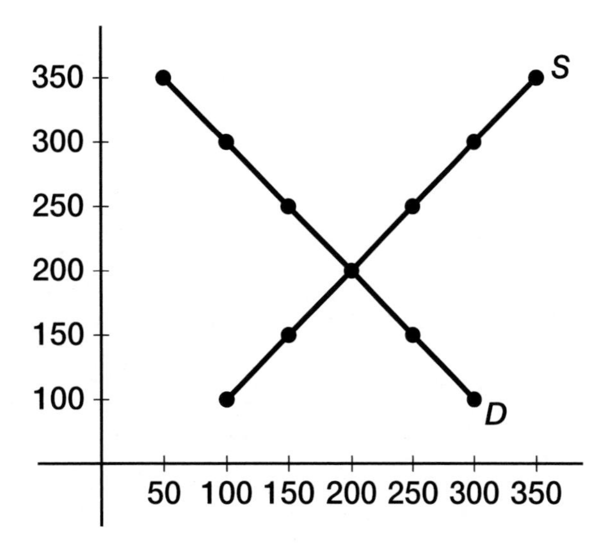

The graph shows the supply and demand curve for the XBOS. At a price of $200, 200 consumers have a demand for the unit and 200 producers have a supply of the unit. We have achieved equilibrium. What happens if the price of the XBOX is $150? There are 250 consumers with a demand and 150 producers with a supply of the XBOX. The quantity demanded exceeds the quantity supplied by 100 units. To decrease the demand of the good, producers must increase the price of the good. The goal is to arrive at the equilibrium price. When the quantity demanded exceeds quantity supplied a shortage occurs. A shortage will occur below the equilibrium price. The following graph displays a shortage of the XBOX.

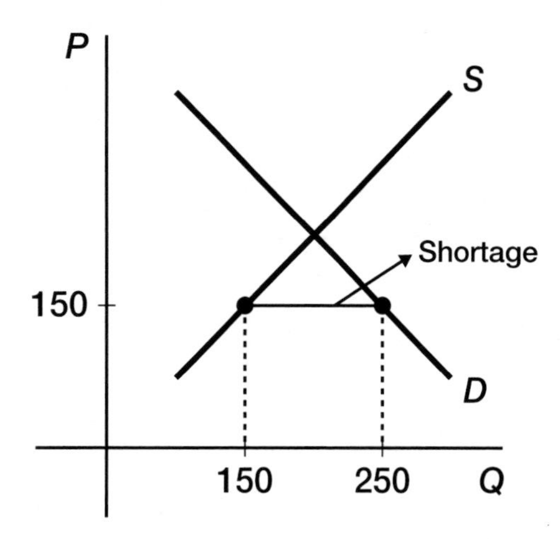

What happens if the price of the XBOX is $300? The producer is willing to sell 300 units and the consumers established a demand of 100 units. Quantity supplied exceeds quantity demanded by 200 units. To increase the demand of the XBOX, the producers must decrease the price. The goal is to arrive at equilibrium. If quantity supplied exceeds quantity demanded a surplus occurs. A surplus occurs above the equilibrium level. The following graph displays a surplus of the XBOX.

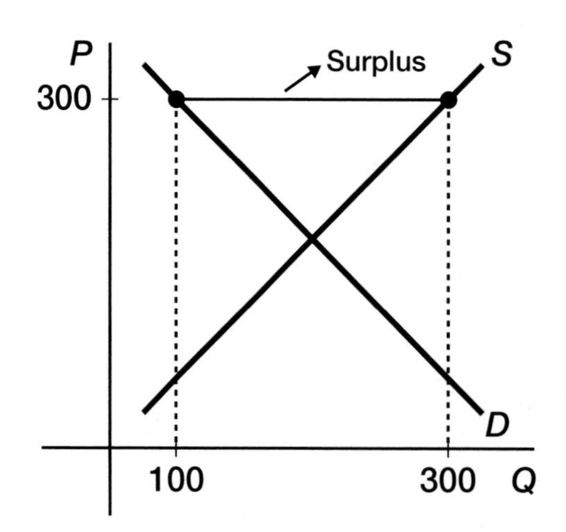

Your Turn: Use the table below to plot supply and demand curves for economics textbooks.

Price	Quantity Demanded	Quantity Supplied
$50	160	25
$75	140	80
$100	120	120
$125	75	140
$150	50	160
$200	25	180

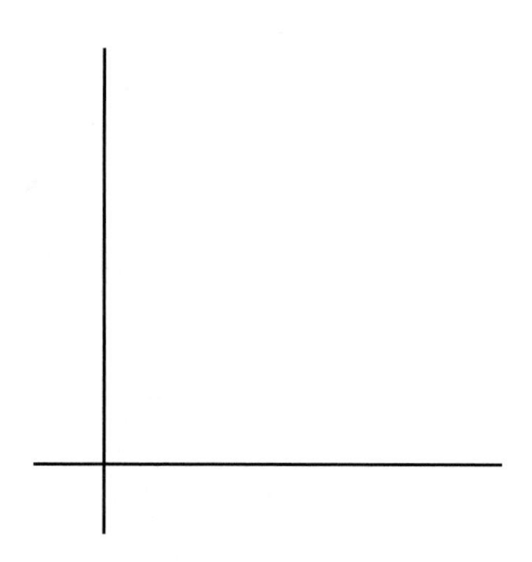

a. What is the equilibrium price and quantity? ______________________________

b. At a price of $50, does a surplus or shortage occur? What is the amount?

____

c. At a price of $150, does a surplus or shortage occur? What is the amount?

____

SIMULTANEOUS CHANGES IN SUPPLY AND DEMAND

So far, we have examined changes in supply and demand separately. Now, let's see what happens when supply and demand change at the same time.

1. Increase in supply and demand. If supply and demand increases at the same time, the equilibrium quantity will also increase. The equilibrium price can increase, decrease, or remain the same. The effect on equilibrium price depends on the magnitude of the change; therefore, equilibrium price is indeterminate.
2. Decrease in both supply and demand. If supply and demand both decreases, the equilibrium quantity will also decrease. The equilibrium price is indeterminate because the price can increase, decrease, or remain the same depending on the magnitude of the change.
3. Increase in demand accompanied by a decrease in supply. If demand increases and supply decreases, the equilibrium price will increase. The equilibrium quantity can increase, decrease, or remain the same depending on the magnitude of the change in supply and demand. The equilibrium quantity is indeterminate.
4. Decrease in demand accompanied by an increase in supply. If demand decreases and supply increases, the equilibrium price decreases. The equilibrium quantity can increase, decrease, or remain the same depending on the magnitude of the change.

HELPFUL HINT:

If supply and demand moves in the same direction, the equilibrium price is indeterminate. If supply and demand moves in opposite directions, the equilibrium quantity is indeterminate.

Event	Effect on Equilibrium Price	Effect on Equilibrium Quantity
Demand increases, supply constant	Increases	Increases
Demand decreases, supply constant	Decreases	Decreases
Supply increases, demand constant	Decreases	Increases
Supply decreases, demand constant	Increases	Decreases
Demand and supply increases	Indeterminate	Increases
Demand and supply decreases	Indeterminate	Decreases
Demand increases and supply decreases	Increases	Indeterminate
Demand decreases and supply increases	Decreases	Indeterminate

Use what you know about supply and demand to answer the following question regarding the diamond-water paradox: Why are diamonds more expensive than water?

____

____

____

____

____

PRICE CONTROLS

At times, the government must intervene and establish price controls. What are the effects on equilibrium if price controls are established by the government? Let's take a look.

Price Ceiling

If the government establishes a price ceiling, the producer cannot set a price above that price. A classic example of a price ceiling is rent control. Say, for example a three bedroom apartment in a nice suburban area is $1200 a month. At $1200 a month, 500 individuals have a demand for the apartments and 500 apartments are available. What happens if the government steps in and establishes a price ceiling of $300 a month for the same apartment? Take a look at the following graph.

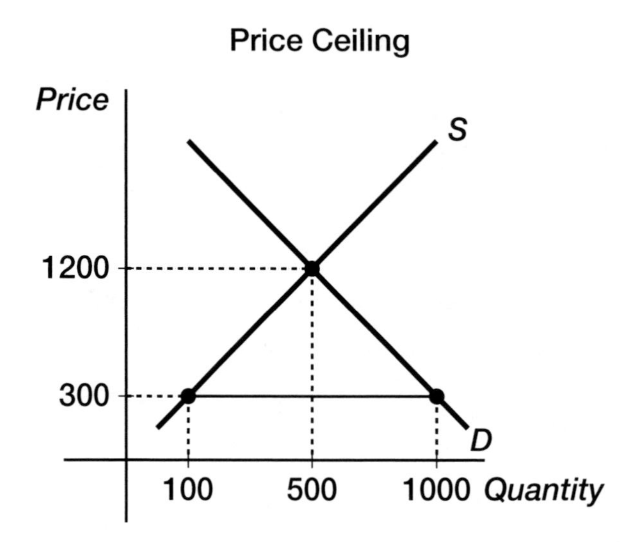

If the price is $300 a month for rent, 1000 individuals would want to move into the apartments; however, only 100 apartments are available. The use of price ceilings creates a shortage. In the case of rent control, a shortage of 900 apartments exists. Take a few minutes and think about the current gas price situation occurring in the economy. Write down your thoughts to the following question: What would happen if the government imposed a price ceiling on gas prices? Use an economic model to explain your reasoning.

____

____

____

____

____

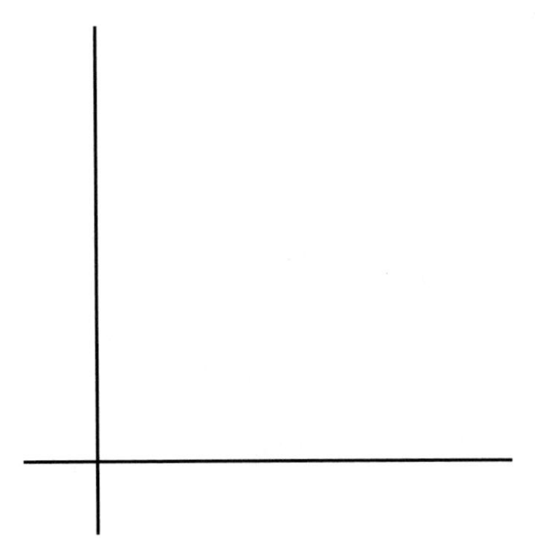

Price Floor

A second government imposed price control is a price floor. A price floor is the minimum price established by the government. An example of a price floor is minimum wage. Currently, minimum wage is $7.50 an hour. Employers cannot pay employees less than that hourly rate. What would happen if minimum wage increased from $7.50 an hour to $15.00 an hour? Let's take a look at the following graph.

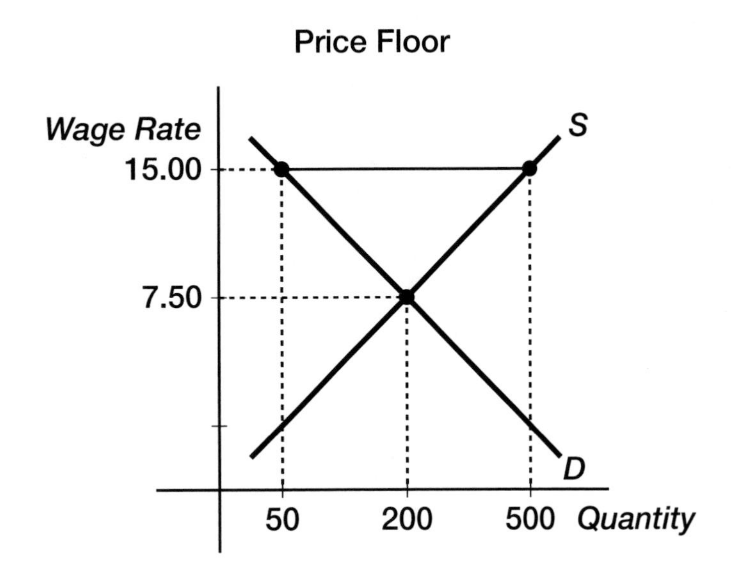

If minimum wage increases to $15.00 an hour, 500 individuals are willing to supply their labor and 50 jobs are available to workers. Imposing a price floor creates a surplus. In the case of minimum wage, a surplus of 450 individuals searching for jobs exists. Use the lines below to explain why a price floor creates a surplus.

____

____

____

____

____

KEY TERMS

Demand
Equilibrium
Law of demand
Law of supply
Price ceiling
Price floor
Quantity demanded
Quantity supplied
Shortage
Supply
Surplus

How Responsive Are You to Elasticity?

PRICE ELASTICITY OF DEMAND

Have you ever wondered how producers establish a price for some goods and services? Do you believe that a factor other than supply and demand comes into play? The producers must examine how consumers will respond to a change in the price of a good or service. This chapter contains the following objectives:

- Calculate price elasticity of demand
- Understand the various levels of elasticity
- Examine the determinants of price elasticity of demand
- Understand the relationship between price elasticity of demand and total revenue

Price elasticity of demand measures how consumers will respond to a change in the price of a good or service. Before we get into the definition of elasticity, let's examine how to calculate that figure. The calculation can occur in three steps:

1. Find the average
2. Find the change
3. Find the elasticity

Suppose Burger King changed the price of the Whopper from $2.50 to $3.75. The quantity demanded went from 250,000 to 200,000. What is the price elasticity of demand? Let's break it down to the steps listed above.

1. Find the average price and quantity demanded.

$$2.50 + 3.75/2 = 3.125$$
$$250000 + 200000/2 = 225000$$

2. Find the change in price and quantity demanded. To find the change, subtract the two numbers provided and divide it by the average:

   2.50 − 3.75/3.125 = −.40
   250000 − 200000/225000 = .22

3. Find the elasticity of demand: %ΔQD/%ΔP

   .22/−.40 = −.55

According to the law of demand, an increase in price will decrease quantity demanded or a decrease in price will increase quantity demanded, ceteris paribus. Since price and quantity demanded move in the opposite direction, the price elasticity of demand is always negative. The absolute value of −.55 is .55. What does this number mean? Let's define a few terms.

HELPFUL HINT:

When finding the price elasticity of demand, you must take the absolute value of the elasticity.

Elastic. A good or service is elastic if the percentage change in quantity demanded is greater than the percentage change in price. Elasticity is greater than one. A consumer will respond to a change in the price by finding a substitute for the good or service.

Inelastic. A good or service is inelastic if the percentage change in quantity demanded is less than the percentage change in price. Elasticity is less than one. A consumer will not respond to a change in the price. He will continue to purchase the good.

Unit elastic. A good or service is unit elastic if the percentage change in quantity demanded is equal to the percentage change in the price. Elasticity is equal to one. The consumer is indifferent to a change in the price.

Is the figure .55 elastic, inelastic, or unit elastic? Since the figure is less than 1, it is inelastic. Changing the price of the Whopper from $2.50 to $3.50 will not have a big impact on consumers. Consumers will continue to purchase the Whopper.

The following graph shows the levels of elasticity on the demand curve. The top portion of the demand curve is elastic, the middle portion is unit elastic, and the bottom portion of the demand curve is inelastic.

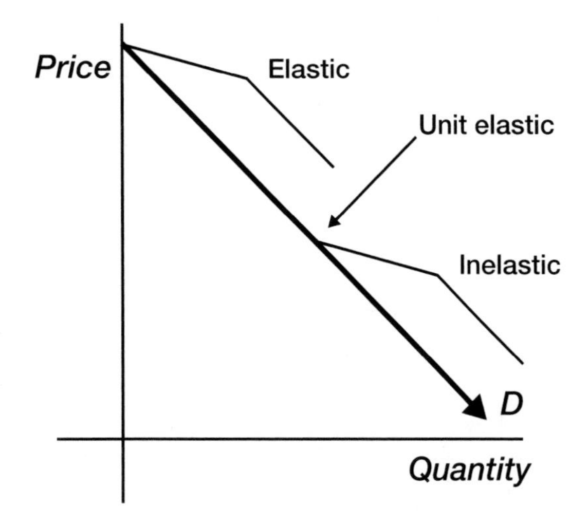

Your Turn:
The movie theater changed the price of the morning matinee from \$5.00 to 7.50. The quantity demanded changed from 300,000 to 100,000. What is the price elasticity of demand? Is the morning matinee elastic, inelastic, or unit elastic?

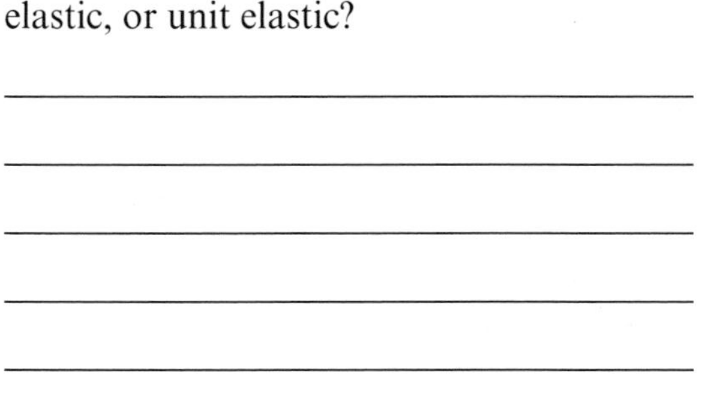

Suppose you were asked the following question: The quantity demanded of movie tickets for a matinee increased by 15 percent while the price of those tickets decreased by 12 percent. Are the movie tickets elastic or inelastic? What is the price elasticity of demand?

Let's take a look at the first question. As you read earlier, if the percentage change in quantity demanded is greater than the percentage change in price, the good is elastic. If the percentage change in quantity demanded is less than the percentage change in the price the good is inelastic. In the preceding question, the percentage change in quantity demanded is 15 percent and the percentage change in price is 12 percent. The movie tickets are elastic. To answer the second question, use the price elasticity of demand formula: $\%\Delta QD/\%\Delta P$.

$.15/-.12 = |-1.25| = 1.25$

Your Turn: The quantities demanded of tacos decreased by 8 percent while the price of tacos increased by 10 percent. What is the price elasticity of demand for the tacos? Are the tacos elastic or inelastic?

____

____

____

____

____

Two Extreme Cases

Two extreme cases exist for price elasticity of demand. *Perfectly elastic:* Consumers are infinitely responsive to a change in the price of a good or service. Say, for example, the professors of a major university had to purchase the white board markers used in the classroom. The price of the markers is the same at Wal-Mart and the university bookstore. Many of the professors will purchase the markers from the university bookstore because of convenience. What would happen if the price of the markers increased by 150 percent at the university bookstore? Many of the professors will stop purchasing the markers at the bookstore and purchase them at Wal-Mart. The graph for the demand curve for a good that is perfectly elastic is shown.

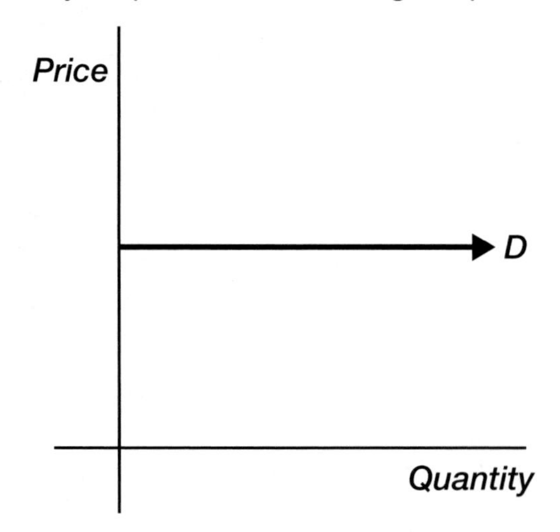

Perfectly inelastic: The change in quantity demanded remains constant when the price of a good or service changes. A perfectly inelastic good is a good that people require. Price is not a factor. For example, diabetics require insulin to survive. Insulin is perfectly inelastic. What other good may fall under the category of perfectly inelastic? The demand curve for perfectly inelastic is vertical. See the following graph.

Extreme Cases

Perfectly inelastic—When the quantity demanded remains constant when the price changes.

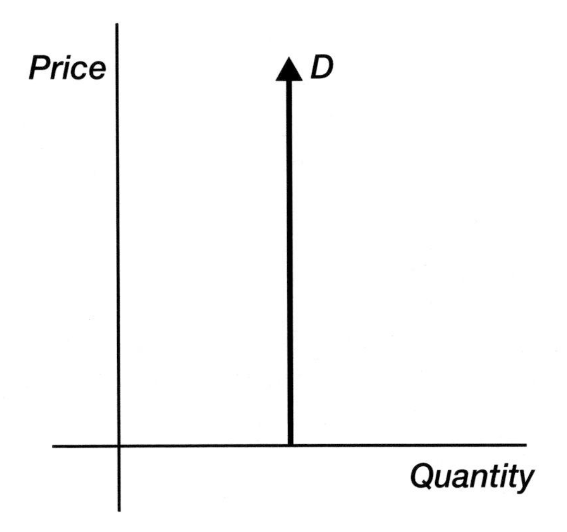

Total Revenue and Elasticity

As stated earlier, price elasticity of demand considers how consumers respond to a change in price. Now we must consider how the change in price will affect the producer's total revenue. Total revenue equals price multiplied by quantity. If the good is elastic, an increase in price will decrease total revenue or a decrease in price will increase total revenue. Total revenue and price move in opposite directions. If the good is inelastic, an increase in price will increase total revenue or a decrease in price will decrease total revenue. Total revenue and price move in the same direction. It the good is unit elastic, an increase or decrease in the price will not affect total revenue. Total revenue remains constant.

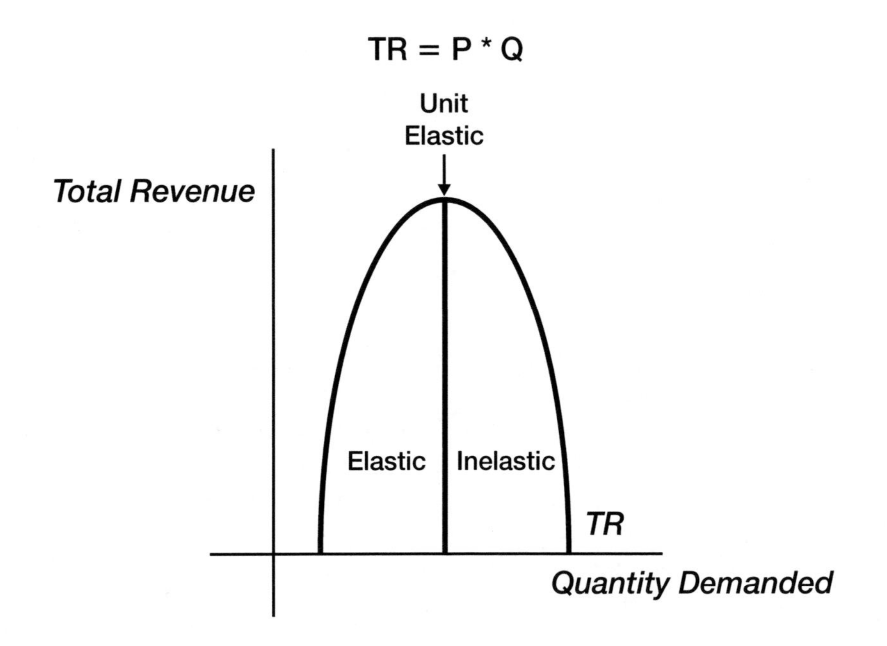

	Price	Total Revenue
Elastic	Increases	Decreases
Elastic	Decreases	Increases
Inelastic	Increases	Increases
Inelastic	Decreases	Decreases
Unit Elastic	Increases or Decreases	No change

Determinants of Price Elasticity of Demand

Substitutability. The more substitutes that are available for the good, the more elastic is the good. Classify the goods as necessities or luxuries. How many substitutes are available for necessities? Not very many substitutes exist for necessities. How many substitutes are available for luxuries? The substitutes available for luxuries are endless. Necessities are inelastic while luxuries are elastic. Let's take a look at the oil used in vehicles. How many substitutes are available for oil? Would you consider oil elastic or inelastic? There are no substitutes for oil. Vehicles require oil to operate. Oil is an inelastic good. What if we examined the various brands of oil available for vehicles? How many brands of oil are available for vehicles? Numerous brands are available, making oil in this context an elastic good.

Portion of Income Spent on the Good. The higher the amount of income spent on the good the more elastic is the good. Let's take a look at two goods: Reece's peanut butter cups and an economics textbook. If the price of the Reece's peanut butter cup increases from .75 cents to $1.00 will consumers continue to purchase the good or find a substitute for the good? If the price of the Economics textbook increased from $150 to $250, will students continue to purchase the textbook or find a substitute for the textbook? The increase in the price of the candy will not hurt consumers as much as the increase in the price of textbooks. The students will find alternatives to purchasing the textbook.

Your Turn: Create a list of ten goods. Classify the goods as elastic or inelastic and explain your reasoning for each by stating how many substitutes are available for the goods.

____

____

____

____

____

Cross Elasticity

Another form of price elasticity of demand is cross elasticity. Cross elasticity is used to measure how responsive consumers are to a change in the price of compliments or substitutes. It is important to pay attention to the sign with cross elasticity. If the sign is positive, the good is a substitute; and the sign is negative for a compliment. Let's look at a few examples. If the price of hamburgers increases, the quantity demanded of hot dogs increases, ceteris paribus. The price of hamburgers and the quantity demanded of hot dogs are moving in the same direction. The sign is positive and the goods are substitutes. If the price of hamburgers decreases, the quantity demanded of French Fries increases.

The price of hamburgers and the quantity demanded of French Fries are moving in opposite directions. The sign is negative and the goods are compliments.

Let's take a look at a numerical example. What is the cross elasticity of demand if the price of a DVD player increased from $150 to $200 and the quantity demanded of DVD's decreased from 300,000 to 100,000? Based on the sign, are the goods compliments or substitutes? First, calculate the cross elasticity of demand by using the same formula. This time, do not take the absolute value! The cross elasticity of demand is −3.44. Since the elasticity is negative, the two goods are compliments.

Income Elasticity

Income is important to the concept of demand. The level of demand for goods and services is determined by consumers' level of income. Let's review the demand curve and consider income. If consumers experience a decrease in income, the demand curve for a normal good will shift to the left and the demand curve for an inferior good will shift to the right.

Income elasticity measures how responsive consumers are when a change in income occurs. The formula is percentage change in quantity demanded divided by percentage change in income ($\%\Delta QD/\%\Delta I$). Use the same three steps to compute income elasticity. You must pay attention to the sign! If the sign is positive, the good is classified as a normal good. If the sign is negative, the good is classified as an inferior good. As you recall, an inferior good is also known as a generic good.

Price Elasticity of Supply

Price elasticity of supply examines how responsive producers are to a change in price. The sign for price elasticity of supply is always positive. Price and quantity supplied always move in the same direction (the supply curve is upward sloping). The formula for price elasticity of supply is percentage change in quantity supplied divided by percentage change in price. If the percentage change in quantity supplied is greater than the percentage change in price, the good is elastic. Elasticity is also greater than one. If the percentage change in quantity supplied is less than the percentage change in price, the good is inelastic. Elasticity is less than one. If the percentage change in quantity supplied is equal to percentage change in price, the good is unit elastic. Elasticity is equal to one.

Determinant of Price Elasticity of Supply

The determinant for price elasticity of supply is time. The longer it takes the producer to change the price of the good, the more elastic is the supply of the good.

- Short run: The producer does not have enough time to change the plant capacity. Plant size is fixed.
- Long run: The producer has enough time to change the plant size. The longer the time period the more elastic the good or service.
- Market period: The time immediately after a change in market price is too short for producers to respond to a change in price. Supply curve is vertical.

KEY TERMS

Cross elasticity	Inelastic	Total revenue
Elastic	Price elasticity of demand	Unit elastic
Income elasticity	Price elasticity of supply	

A Matter of Satisfaction: Utility

It's Friday night and a major storm just swept through the town. You are stuck in the house. To pass the time, you decide to watch The Final Destination Series. You also ordered a large pizza from your favorite restaurant. How many of The Final Destination movies can you watch before you become tired? How many pieces of pizza can you consume before you become full? How does your level of satisfaction of watching the movie series and consuming pizza affect producers? This chapter will provide an explanation of a consumer's level of satisfaction. Before considering a consumer's level of satisfaction, an examination of a consumer's budget must take place. Recall the determinants of demand: prices of related goods, income, expectations of future prices, population, and preferences. To establish a demand for a good or service, one must have the money to pay for the good.

Assumptions:

- Consumers will use rational behavior
- Consumers are constrained by budgets

Suppose Justin has $100 in money income. He decided he wants to use the money exclusively on books and DVDS. If a book is $10 and a DVD is $20, what combinations can he purchase with his $100 money income?

Books	DVDs
10	0
8	1
6	2
4	3
2	4
0	5

What happens if the price of books increases to $20?

Books	DVDs
5	0
4	1
3	2
2	3
1	4
0	5

What happens if income increases to $200 with books at $10 and DVDs at $20?

Books	DVDs
20	0
18	1
16	2
14	3
12	4
10	5
8	6
6	7
4	8
2	9
0	10

Did you notice the difference in the shifts in the curve?

TOTAL UTILITY

Total utility is the total level of satisfaction a consumer receives from consuming a good or service. Take a look at the table below. Sarah's total utility for pizza and movies is listed below. Total utility is the level of satisfaction the consumer places on the good.

Pizzas	Total Utility	Movies	Total Utility
0	0	0	0
1	50	1	65
2	80	2	115
3	105	3	160
4	120	4	190
5	130	5	210
6	138	6	226
7	145	7	234
8	150	8	237

Total utility is measured in utils. Total utility increases as consumption increases.

MARGINAL UTILITY

Marginal utility is the change in total utility that arises from consuming another unit of a good or service. Sarah's marginal utility is listed in the table below. As she increases her consumption of pizza from zero units to one unit her marginal utility is 50 utils. As she increases her consumption from one piece of pizza to two pieces of pizza her marginal utility is 30 utils.

Pizza	Total Utility	Marginal Utility	Movies	Total Utility	Marginal Utility
0	0	—	0	0	—
1	50	50	1	65	65
2	80	30	2	115	50
3	105	25	3	160	45
4	120	15	4	190	30
5	130	10	5	210	20
6	138	8	6	226	16
7	145	7	7	234	8
8	150	5	8	237	3

DIMINISHING MARGINAL UTILITY

What happens to marginal utility as Sarah consumes more pieces of pizza? Marginal utility decreases. Why? After consuming so many units of a good or service a consumer will become full. According to the law of diminishing marginal utility, as total utility increases marginal utility will begin to decrease.

CONSUMER EQUILIBRIUM

Suppose a slice of pizza is $4.00 and a movie is $8.00. Money income is $48. At what quantities will the individual reach consumer equilibrium? To find consumer equilibrium, calculate marginal utility per dollar spent (marginal utility divided by the cost of the good). Next, locate where marginal utility per dollar spent is equal for both goods. Finally, allocate the full amount of the money income between both goods. Consumer equilibrium is reached when the marginal utility per dollar spent for both goods is equal.

Here are the steps for consumer equilibrium:

1. Calculate marginal utility.
2. Calculate marginal utility per dollar spent.
3. Find where marginal utility per dollar spent is equal for both goods and see if consumer spent all of money income.

Take a look at the chart below. Let's calculate the marginal utility per dollar spent for one piece of pizza and one movie:

Pizza: MU $/cost of pizza = 50/4 = 12.5
Movie: MU $/cost of movie = 65/8 = 8.13

Now that you see how to calculate marginal utility per dollar spent, examine the chart to see where the marginal utility per dollar spent is equal for both goods. Once you find where marginal utility per dollar spent is equal for both goods, ensure the consumer spent all of the $48 money income: Pizza (4*4 = 16) Movie (4*8 = 32); therefore, $16 for the pizza plus $32 for the movie equals $48 altogether.

Pizzas	Total Utility	Marginal Utility	MU per Dollar Spent	Movies	Total Utility	Marginal Utility	MU per Dollar Spent
0	0	—	—	0	0	—	—
1	50	50	12.5	1	65	65	8.13
2	80	30	7.5	2	115	50	6.25
3	105	25	6.25	3	160	45	5.63
4	**120**	**15**	**3.75**	**4**	**190**	**30**	**3.75**
5	130	10	2.5	5	210	20	2.5
6	138	8	2	6	226	16	2
7	145	7	1.75	7	234	8	1
8	150	5	1.25	8	237	3	.375

KEY TERMS

Marginal utility

Marginal utility per dollar spent

Total Utility

The Cost of Running a Business

Would you like to own your own business? Have you ever wondered why some companies earn profits while other companies suffer losses? In this chapter, we will examine the cost associated with operating a business. The objectives of this chapter include:

- Understanding the different costs of production
- Calculating total revenue
- Differentiating between short-run and long-run

The goal of the firm is to generate a profit. Profit is determined by subtracting total costs from total revenue. Total revenue equals price multiplied by quantity. Let's examine costs.

EXPLICIT AND IMPLICIT COSTS

Economists consider explicit and implicit costs. Explicit costs are the costs associated with operating a business. Explicit costs include paying employees, paying utilities, and purchasing equipment and supplies. Implicit costs are the opportunity cost of operating a business. As explained in an earlier chapter, opportunity cost is a trade-off; it is the next best alternative. Implicit costs include the money the owner could have earned working somewhere else. To understand the cost of running a business, the business owner must consider the implicit and explicit costs.

PROFIT

Let's take a look at profit. Two types of profit exist: accounting profit and economic profit. Accounting profit subtracts explicit costs from total revenue. Economic profit subtracts explicit and implicit costs from revenue. Suppose Kendall's Candles sold 10000 candles at $5.00 per candle. Kendall paid her employees $1000 and paid $1500 for utilities. Kendall could have earned $5000 working at Sack and Save. What is Kendall's accounting and economic profit?

Total Revenue: 10000*5		50,000
Employee pay	1000	
Utilities	1500	
Total Explicit Costs	2500	−2,500
Total Accounting Profit		47,500
Sack & Save Pay	5000	
Total Implicit Cost	5000	−5,000
Total Economic Profit		42,500

PRODUCTION

Another important aspect of profitability is production. Business owners must consider how much of a good to produce to stay profitable. Let's examine the production process. The business owner must consider how many employees to hire and how much output the employees can produce. The quantity produced is known as total product or output. Marginal product is the extra units of output produced by hiring an additional worker. The formula for marginal product is change in total product divided by change in labor. Average product is the number of units produced divided by labor.

Suppose you owned a sweater company. If you hired one person, she could produce four sweaters. If you hired a second person, the two employees could produce six sweaters together. On average, the two employees could produce three sweaters (average product). When you hired the second worker, the employees were able to create an additional two sweaters (marginal product). The following chart contains the marginal and average product for sweaters.

Labor	Total Product	Marginal Product	Average Product
1	4	—	4
2	6	2	3
3	10	4	3.33
4	14	4	3.5
5	17	3	3.4
6	19	2	3.17
7	20	1	2.85

Take a look at marginal product. Initially, marginal product increases, but as we employ more workers MP begins to decrease. Why? As a firm hires more workers some workers become unproductive. The business owner should not hire anymore workers once marginal product begins to decrease. Diminishing marginal returns: as a firm increases its input (hires more workers) the additional output produced begins to decrease.

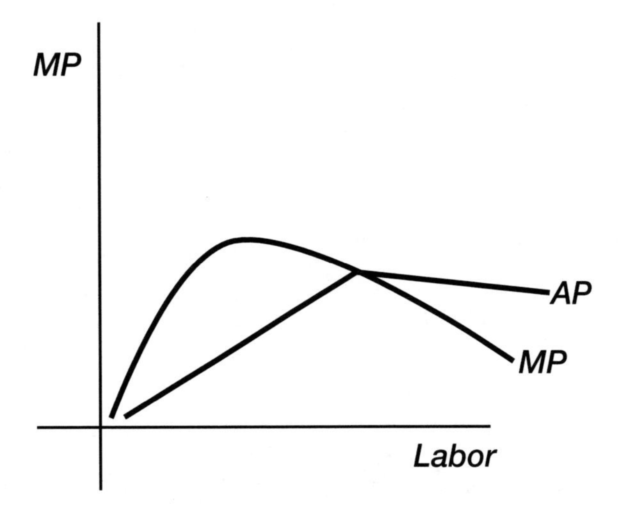

The preceding graph shows average product and marginal product for up to seven workers. As you can see, MP begins to diminish after the business owner hires the fourth worker.

SHORT RUN COST

In the short run, the business owner does not have enough time to change the size of the plant or warehouse. The short run contains at least one fixed input (plant size). Let's examine the costs associated with the short run.

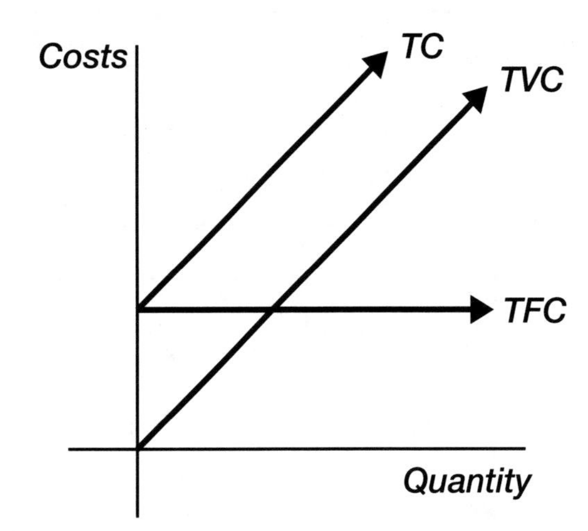

Every firm encounters unavoidable costs. The business owner must pay rent on a leased building. The unavoidable costs (fixed costs) do not change with additional levels of output. Variable costs change with every level of output. Variable costs include hiring workers, paying utilities, and ordering supplies. The short run contains fixed costs and variable costs. Total cost equals total fixed costs plus variable cost.

Next, we must examine average production. Average fixed cost equals total fixed cost divided by output. As output rises, average fixed costs decreases. Average fixed cost shows the business owner that increased output decreases fixed costs. Average variable cost is total variable cost divided by output. Average variable cost is an important figure to the business owner. If AVC declines, the business owner should increase output. Average total cost is computed by adding AFC to AVC or total cost divided by output.

Business owners should examine marginal costs to make more informed decisions. Marginal cost is the change in total cost resulting from producing additional output. Marginal cost tells the business owner whether producing the additional unit of output will create a profit or generate a loss.

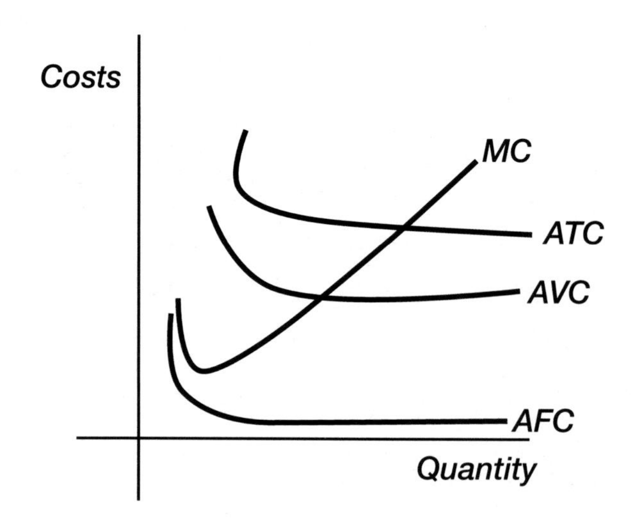

Please examine the following chart.

Labor	Output	MP	AP	TFC	TVC	TC	AFC	AVC	ATC	MC
0	0	—	—	45	0	45	—	—	—	—
1	4	4	4	45	100	145	7.5	16.67	24.17	50
2	6	2	3	45	155	200	4.5	15.5	20	13.75
3	10	4	3.33	45	195	240	3.21	13.93	17.14	10
4	14	4	3.5	45	215	260	2.65	12.65	15.3	6.67
5	17	3	3.4	45	240	285	2.37	12.63	15	12.5
6	19	2	3.17	45	270	315	2.25	13.5	15.75	30

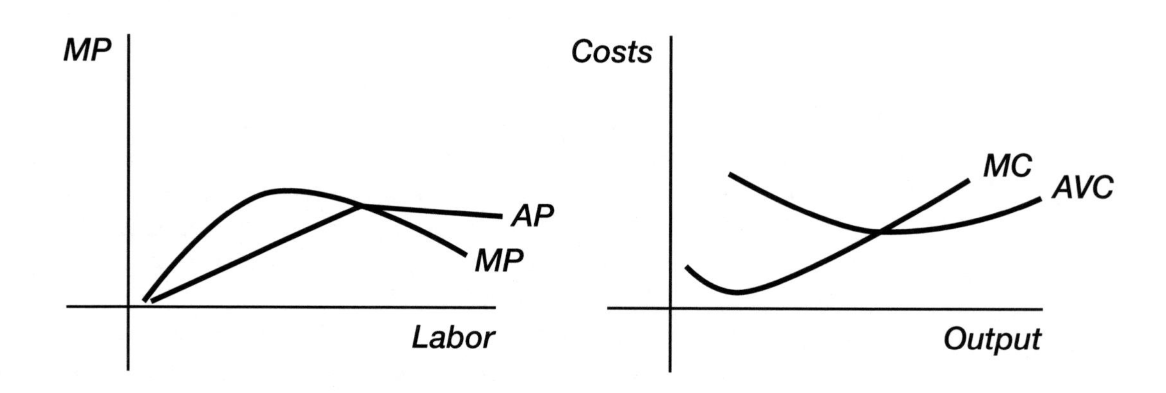

Important relationship to remember:

1. MP is at its maximum when MC is at its minimum.
2. When MP = AP, MC = AVC.

LONG RUN COSTS

The business owner has more control in the long run. In the long run, the business owner can increase or decrease the size of the plan and adjust costs. In the long run a firm can experience economies of scale, diseconomies of scale, and constant returns to scale. Economies of scale arise when a firm's average total costs decrease as output increases. Economies of scale occur because of labor and managerial specialization. Diseconomies of scale arise when a firm's average total cost increases as output increases. Constant returns to scale arises when a firm's average total cost remains constant as output increases.

KEY TERMS

Accounting profit
Average fixed costs
Average product
Average total costs
Average variable costs
Constant returns to scale
Diminishing marginal returns
Diseconomies of scale
Economic profit
Economies of scale
Explicit costs
Implicit costs
Marginal costs
Marginal product
Total costs
Total fixed cost
Total product
Total variable costs

CHAPTER SIX

Pure Competition

How do economists determine the market structure of a firm? Why are some firms profitable? We explored the costs of operating a business in the last chapter. Now, let's focus our attention on the market structures of the firm. The four market structures are pure competition, monopoly, monopolistic competition, and oligopoly. Let's examine pure competition. The characteristics of pure competition include:

- Many buyers and sellers
- Homogeneous products
- Free entry and exit
- Price takers

An example of a purely competitive industry is farming (agriculture). The market contains many farmers and a lot of consumers purchase goods from farmers. Farmers produce meats, fruits, and vegetables.

DEMAND CURVE

Firms operating under pure competition must take the price established by the industry. Have you ever noticed the price of a bundle of oranges falls within the same range at different stores? A consumer would not pay $10 at one store for the oranges if she knows she can purchase the same bundle of oranges for $5.00 at another store.

The industry determines the price for the firm in pure competition. Firms that do not have the ability to establish prices are price takers. The following graph shows the demand curve for the firm and the industry.

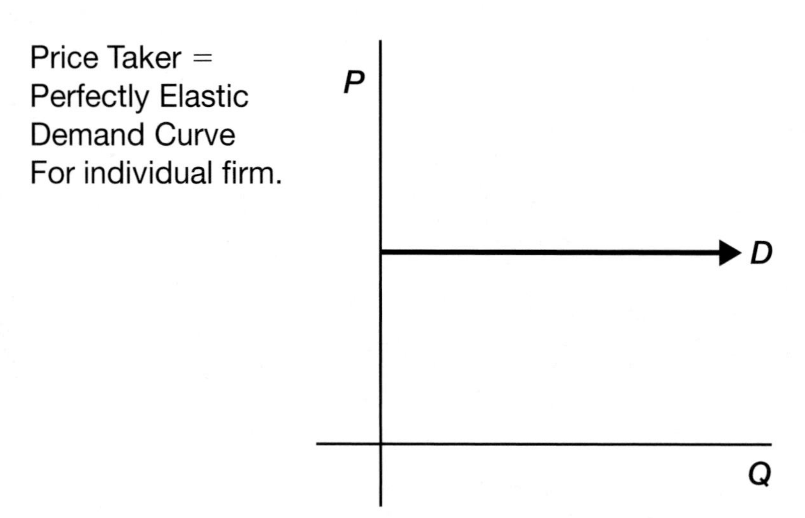

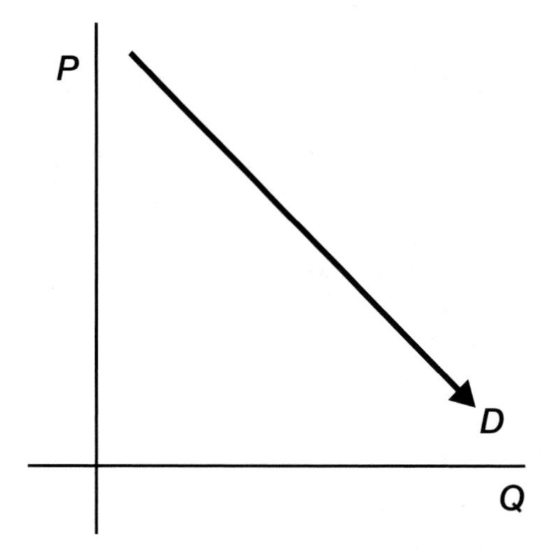

As you can see, the demand curve for the firm is horizontal (perfectly elastic) and the demand curve for the industry is downward sloping. Now let's explore profit in the short run for the purely competitive firm.

The firm must make two decisions:

1. Produce or shutdown
2. If producing, how many units should the firm produce

Suppose the industry says a producer can sell sweaters for $45 a sweater. How many units should the producer sell to earn the highest economic profit? To answer this question, we must examine revenue and costs.

To compute total revenue, multiply price and quantity. We must also consider marginal and average revenue. Marginal revenue is the additional revenue generated from the additional unit of output ($\Delta TR/\Delta O$). Average revenue is total revenue divided by output.

As stated in the previous chapter, total cost equals total fixed cost plus total variable costs. Average total cost is total cost divided by output. Marginal cost is the additional cost associated with the next unit of output ($\Delta TC/\Delta O$). Let's examine the following chart.

Output	Price	Total Revenue	Marginal Revenue	Average Revenue	Total Cost	Average Total Cost	Marginal Cost	TR-TC
0	45	0	—	—	50	—	—	−50
1	45	45	45	45	90	90	40	−45
2	45	90	45	45	120	60	30	−30
3	45	135	45	45	135	45	15	0
4	45	180	45	45	140	35	15	40
5	45	225	45	45	184	37	44	41
6	45	270	45	45	250	41.67	65	20
7	45	315	45	45	315	45	65	0
8	45	360	45	45	390	48.75	75	−30
9	45	405	45	45	490	54.44	100	−85

What did you notice about price, marginal revenue, and average revenue? Under pure competition, price will always equal marginal revenue and average revenue.

According to the chart, the firm achieves a normal profit (TR = TC) at three units and seven units. The firm achieves the highest level of economic profit (TR>TC) at five units. The firm should produce five units. Now let's examine the five units to see if it passes the profit maximizing rule.

Under the profit maximizing rule, we must compare marginal revenue and marginal cost. Marginal revenue is the extra revenue generated from producing one more unit of output. Marginal cost is the additional cost generated from producing another unit of output. The profit maximizing rule states the firm will produce the level of output where marginal revenue equals marginal cost as long as producing the unit is preferable to shutting down the operation. At five units of output, MC is approximately equal to MR and the firm earns an economic profit. Producing five levels of output is optimal under the profit maximizing rule.

SHUTDOWN CASE

As stated earlier, the producer must decide whether to produce or shut down the operation. The producer should shut down the operation if AVC is greater than the price. Take a look at that chart.

O	P	TR	TFC	TVC	TC	AFC	AVC
0	65	0	100	0	100	—	—
1	65	65	100	85	185	100	85
2	65	130	100	150	250	50	75
3	65	195	100	195	295	33.33	65
4	65	260	100	270	370	25	67.50

As you can see in the chart, the AVC is greater than the price for the quantities listed. The firm should shut down the operation.

LONG RUN

In the long run, the producer has enough time to change the size of the plant. Two things occur in the long run:

1. The firm can increase or decrease the size of the plant
2. Firms enter or leave the industry

The major focus of the long run is whether firms should enter or leave the industry. Firms operating under pure competition have identical costs. The entry and exit of firms do not affect the costs of the firm. Let's take a look at an example.

Suppose the industry states firms can sell 50,000 bundles of oranges for $50 each. The firms currently in the market are making an economic profit. Other firms see the economic profit and decide to enter the industry. The industry experienced an increase in the bundles of oranges available for sale. The industry says the firms can sell 60,000 bundles at $60 apiece. The firms earn a normal profit at $60 a bundle. The ability to earn a normal profit entices more firms to enter the industry. The industry now has 70,000 bundles of oranges available at $70 each. At $70, the firms begin to suffer losses. Firms begin to leave the industry because of the losses suffered. The industry now has 60,000 bundles available (number of bundles available decreased because firms left the industry). The firms sell the 60,000 bundles for $60 each. The firms experience a normal profit. Some firms leave the industry because of the normal profit. The industry has 50,000 bundles available for $50 each. The firms in the industry experience an economic profit. Because of the continuous entry and exit of firms, the firms only experience a normal profit in the long run.

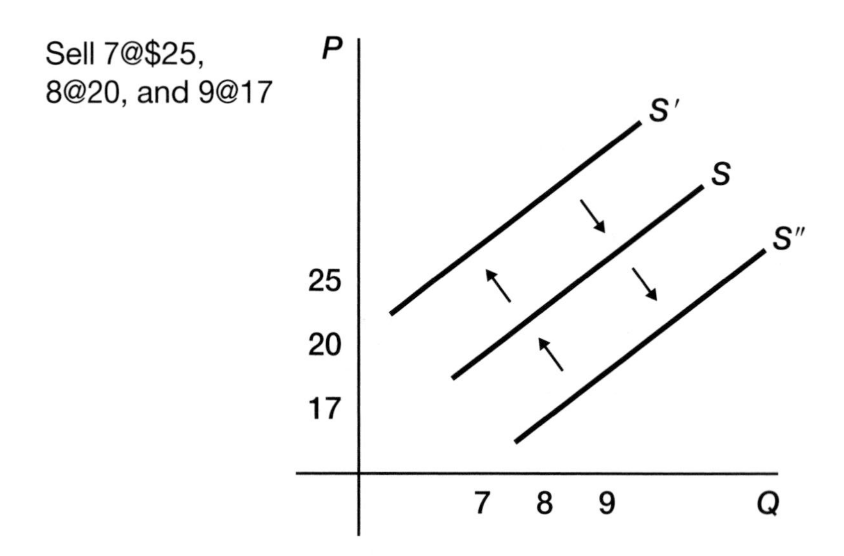

PRODUCTIVE AND ALLOCATIVE EFFICIENCY

Productive and allocative efficiency occur in the long run. Productive efficiency means the firm is producing a good in the least costly way. ATC is at its minimum. Marginal product is the same for all inputs. Allocative efficiency means marginal benefit and marginal cost are equal and the sum of consumer and producer surplus is maximized.

Entry and exit of firms help to improve resource allocation. The exiting of firms causes the firms to release resources for use by other firms. The entry of new firms causes those firms to bring resources with them to the industry.

KEY TERMS

Allocative efficiency	Marginal revenue	Productive efficiency
Average revenue	Price taker	Total revenue

Monopoly and Antitrust Policy

How do firms such as Microsoft form a monopoly? Are all monopolies legal? What is the difference between forming a monopoly and monopolizing the industry? In this chapter, we will:

- Examine the characteristics of monopoly
- Determine the profit maximizing output
- Define price discrimination
- Examine antitrust policy

A firm operating under the competitive structure of monopoly exhibits the following characteristics:

- No close substitutes
- A single seller of a good or service
- Barriers to entry (patents, government license, economies of scale)
- Price maker

DEMAND CURVE

The demand curve for a monopolist is the same as the demand curve for the industry. The monopolist is the industry. The demand curve is downward sloping and the monopolist will charge a price in the elastic region of the demand curve. As you may recall from the elasticity chapter, total revenue increases as the price increases. Does that mean the monopolist charges the highest price? No. Let's examine the price charged by a monopolist graphically and numerically.

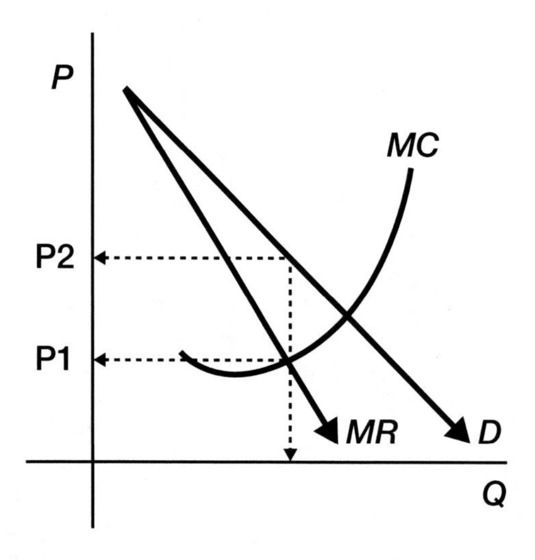

Take a look at the graph. The demand curve is downward sloping. The marginal revenue curve is set below the demand curve. Marginal cost decreases initially and then begins to increase. The MR = MC rule applies to the monopolist. To find the price charged by the monopolist, find the point where marginal revenue equals marginal cost. Once you find the point where MR = MC, go up to the demand curve at the same quantity. The monopolist would charge P2 at the quantity of 200.

Now let's examine profit, loss, and break-even graphically. To find profit, compare the price to ATC. Take a look at the three graphs. Notice the location of the price charged by the monopolist and the average total cost. If P > ATC, the monopolist is making a profit. If P = ATC, the monopolist is making a normal profit. If P < ATC, the monopolist is suffering a loss. Now let's examine profit numerically.

Q	P	TR	MR	TC	MC	ATC	TR-TC
0	800	0		350			−350
1	775	775	775	425	75	425	350
2	750	1500	725	550	125	275	1225
3	725	2175	675	675	125	225	1500
4	700	2800	625	750	75	187.50	2050
5	675	3375	575	810	60	162	2565
6	650	3900	525	1100	290	183.33	2800
7	625	4375	475	1575	475	225	3275
8	600	4800	425	2075	500	259.38	2725
9	575	5175	375	2600	525	288.88	2575

To find profit, consider the price, total revenue, marginal revenue, total cost, marginal cost, and average total cost. Here are the formulas:

- $TR = P*Q$
- $MR = \Delta TR/\Delta O$
- $MC = \Delta TC/\Delta O$
- $ATC = TC/O$

Step 1: Find where MR = MC.
Step 2: Find TR − TC.
Step 3: Is P > ATC.

At a quantity of 7, MR = MC and TR > TC. The firm earns an economic profit of $3275.

ECONOMIES OF SCALE

One of the major barriers to entry is economies of scale. Economies of scale arise when a firm's ATC decreases as output increases. Economies of scale exist for two reasons: simultaneous consumption and network effects.

Simultaneous consumption is a product's ability to satisfy a large number of consumers at the same time. For example, Apple creates one computer for every customer whereas Microsoft only produces one software program for multiple customers. Microsoft experiences simultaneous consumption.

Network effects occur because of increases in the value of a product to each user as the total number of users rises. When multiple people use Microsoft Word or Excel, they can easily share the documents with one another.

PRICE DISCRIMINATION

Price discrimination is the practice of charging some consumer a lower price than others for an identical good. Three levels of price discrimination exist:

- First Degree: Charging a different price for every sale. Think about the airlines. There are business customers and normal customers. Business customers fly for business meetings. Normal customers fly for vacations or leisure time.
- Second Degree: Charging different prices for different quantities. Sam's Club and Costco are examples of second degree price discrimination.
- Third Degree: Charging different prices for the same product in different areas of the market. Day time, night time, and weekend minutes for cell phones is an example of third degree price discrimination.

To legally charge customers different prices for the same good, the following conditions must occur:

- The firm must have a downward sloping demand curve.
- The firm must be able to identify buyers with different elasticities.
- The firm must be able to prevent the resale of the good or service.

ANTITRUST POLICY

Various laws were created to prevent monopolization and illegal price discrimination. Here is a brief list of some of the laws:

1. Sherman Act of 1890
    - Outlaws restraints of trade:
        - Collusive price fixing

    - Monopolization
    - Sherman Act was unclear regarding legal and illegal activities
2. Clayton Act
    - Amended the Sherman Act of 1890
    - The following items deemed illegal:
        - Price discrimination if it is not justifiable
        - Tying contracts: requiring buyers to purchase another of its products with the initial product
        - Acquisition of stocks of competing corporations to lessen competition
        - Prohibiting interlocking directorates: a director of one firm cannot be a board member of a competing firm
3. Federal Trade Commission Act of 1914
    - Granted the FTC power to investigate unfair competitive practices on its own initiative or at the request of the injured firms
4. Wheeler-lea Act
    - Provided additional responsibilities to the FTC; The FTC now has the responsibility of preventing deceptive acts or practices in commerce:
        - Established the FTC as an independent antitrust agency
        - Made unfair and deceptive sales practices illegal
5. Celler-Kefauver Act of 1950
    - Amended the Clayton Act
    - Prohibited firms from merging with competing firms to lessen competition
    - Types of mergers:
        - Horizontal: Two firms merging together within the same industry (Coke and Pepsi)
        - Vertical: Two firms merging together in different stages of production (Ford and a tire company)
        - Conglomerate: Two firms merging together within different industries (Pizza Hut and Sears)

Here is an overview of some landmark cases:

1. U.S. Steel Case of 1920: Through this case, it was found that not every monopoly is illegal.
2. Alcoa Case of 1945: Established that even though a firm's behavior may be legal, possession of monopoly power may be illegal (structuralist view versus behavioralist view).
    a. Structuralist View: A firm with a high market share will behave like a monopolist. If the firm is behaving as a monopoly, the firm's structure should be changed.
    b. Behavioralist View: The relationship between behavior, structure, and performance is unclear.

Monopolistic Competition and Oligopoly

In the previous chapter, we explored monopoly. Now we must examine two other competitive structures: monopolistic competition and oligopoly.

The characteristics for monopolistic competition include:

- many sellers
- differentiated products
- free entry and exit
- price maker

The monopolistically competitive firm possesses some market power because it provides differentiated products. Because of the firm's ability to set its own price, the demand curve under monopolistic competition is downward sloping. Just like a monopoly, the marginal revenue curve is set below the demand curve. Let's take a look at profit maximization in the short run and the long run.

SHORT RUN PROFIT MAXIMIZATION

The MR = MC rule applies in the short run for monopolistic competition. The firm find the best price to charge by locating the point where MR = MC. The price charged is on the demand curve. The following curve demonstrates the process.

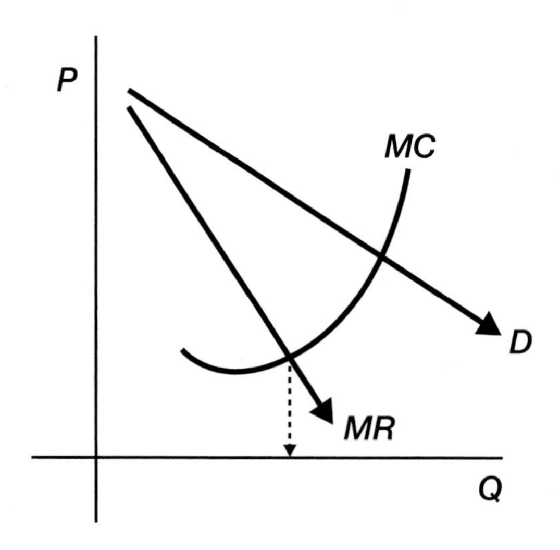

Now, we need to examine the average total cost and compare it to the price the monopolistic competitive firm charges. Suppose the price was $5.50, average total cost was $6.75, and the marginal revenue curve equals the marginal cost curve at $2.75. Would the firm generate an economic profit, suffer a loss, or break even? Since MR = MC, the firm passes the profit maximization rule. The ATC > P; therefore, the firm suffers a loss.

PROFIT MAXIMIZATION IN THE LONG RUN

Firms have the freedom to enter and exit the industry under monopolistic competition. Firms enter when profits occur and leave the industry when losses occur. Firms only earn a normal profit in the long run because of the freedom to enter and exit the industry.

EXCESS CAPACITY

Excess capacity is the gap between the minimum ATC output and the profit maximizing output. Excess capacity occurs because firms are under-allocating resources.

OLIGOPOLY

The characteristics of oligopoly include the following:

- small number of large producers
- mutual interdependence
- homogeneous or differentiated products
- barriers to entry
- strategic pricing

The characteristic that distinguishes an oligopoly from other competitive structures is mutual interdependence. An oligopolist watches the reactions of other firms. Let's take a look at an example. Suppose we have two firms selling game consoles: Microsoft XBOX and Sony PlayStation. Both firms sell the systems for $299. The demand curves are shown.

MICROSOFT XBOX

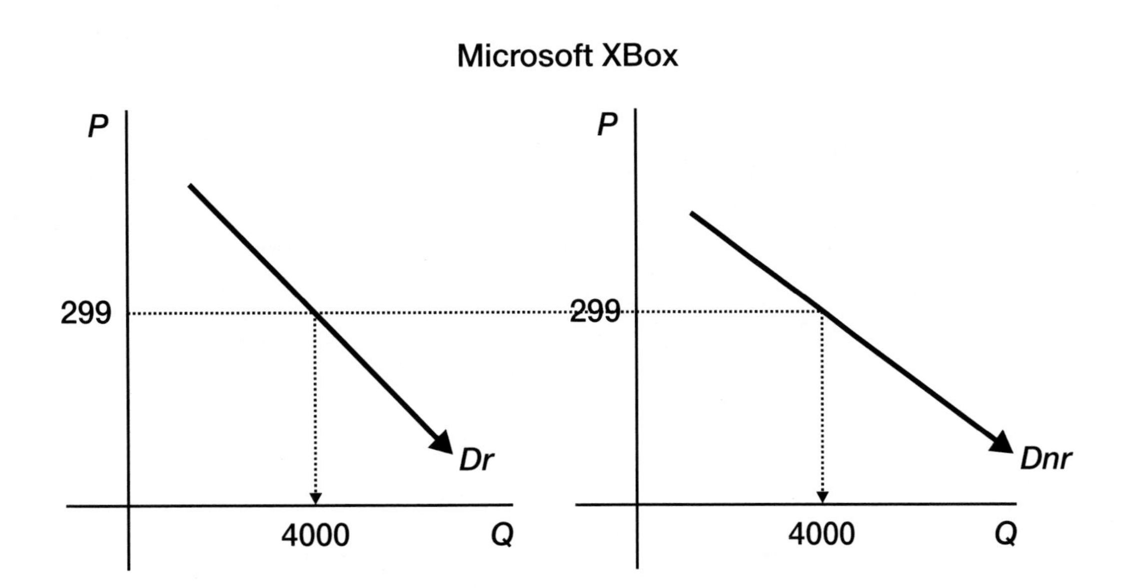

The demand curves for Xbox are shown. We must examine two demand curves. The first demand curve represents Sony responding to a change in the price. The second demand curve represents Sony not responding to a change in price. Let's see what would happen if Xbox increased the price to $450.

f XBOX increases their price to $450, will Sony increase their price as well'

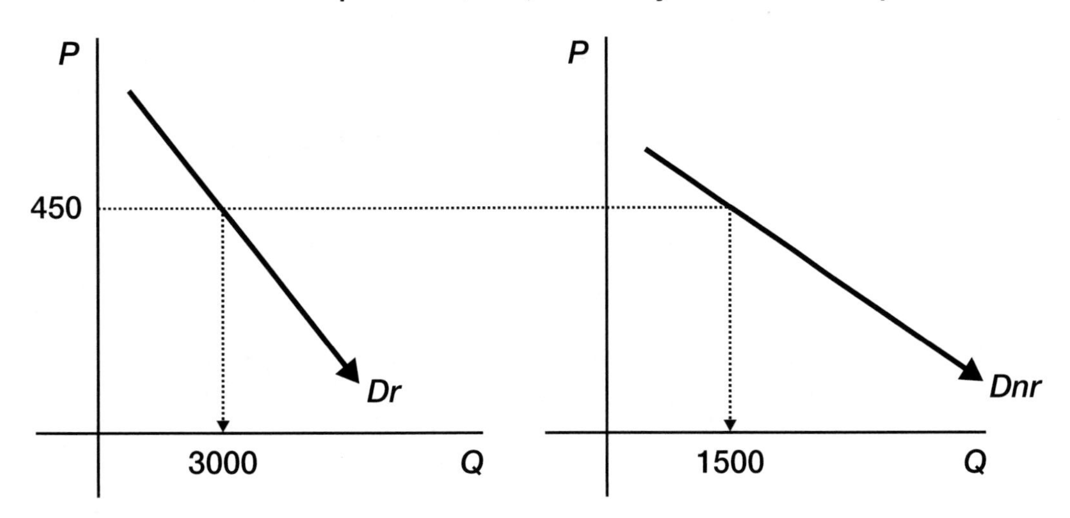

If Xbox increases it price to $450, Sony will not increase its price. Sony does not respond to an increase in the price. Xbox's demand curve is shown on the right when Sony does not respond to a change in price.

Suppose Xbox lowered the price to $199. Sony will lower its price as well. Sony follows price decreases. The demand curve for Xbox is shown on the left when Sony responds to a change in the price.

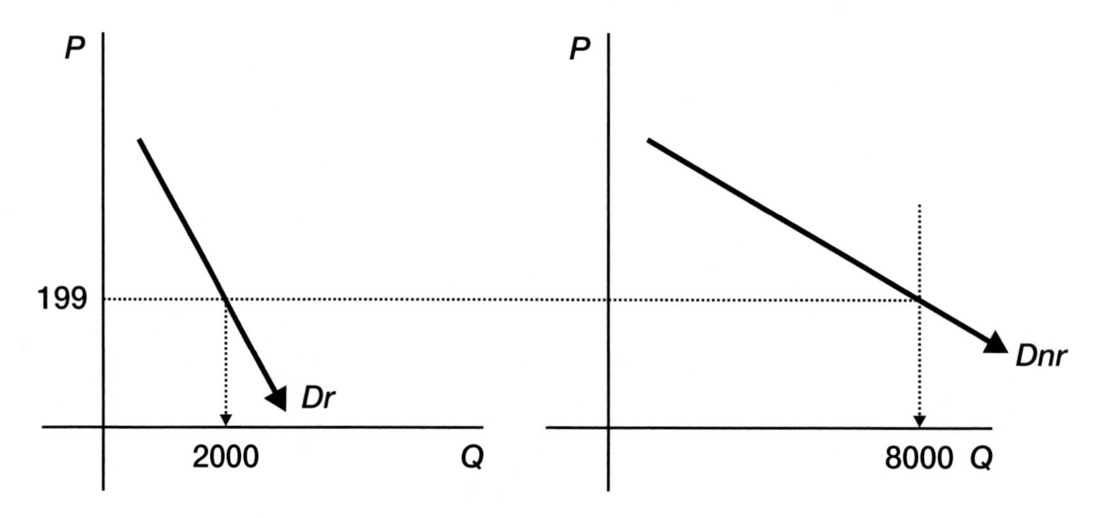

Since Sony follows price decreases and does not follow price increases, the demand curve for Xbox is kinked (combination of two demand curves).

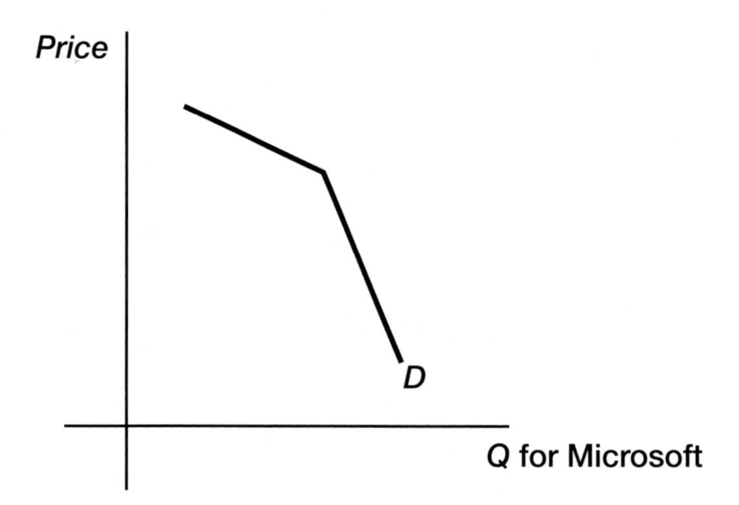

End result, Sony follows price decrease but not price increases.

BARRIERS TO ENTRY

Firms competing under the oligopoly competitive structure can exhibit economies of scale. As you may recall, economies of scale arises when a firms average total costs decrease as output increases. Another form of a barrier to entry is a collusive agreement. Have you ever noticed Walgreen's and CVS are located within blocks of each other? Why do you think this strategic placement of firms occurs? Walgreens and CVS carry the same products at relatively the same prices. The two firms can dominate the market.

GAME THEORY

One of the strategies oligopolist firms employ is known as game theory. Oligopolists examine the strategies of competitors. The strategies are shown in a payoff matrix. For example, Xbox decided to create a new game console with new and improved graphics. Xbox should consider how much of a profit the firm will generate if they advertise the game console six months before the unit is available. Sony, the firm's biggest competitor watches the strategic moves of Xbox closely. Sony will launch a system around the same time frame. Should the firms advertise?

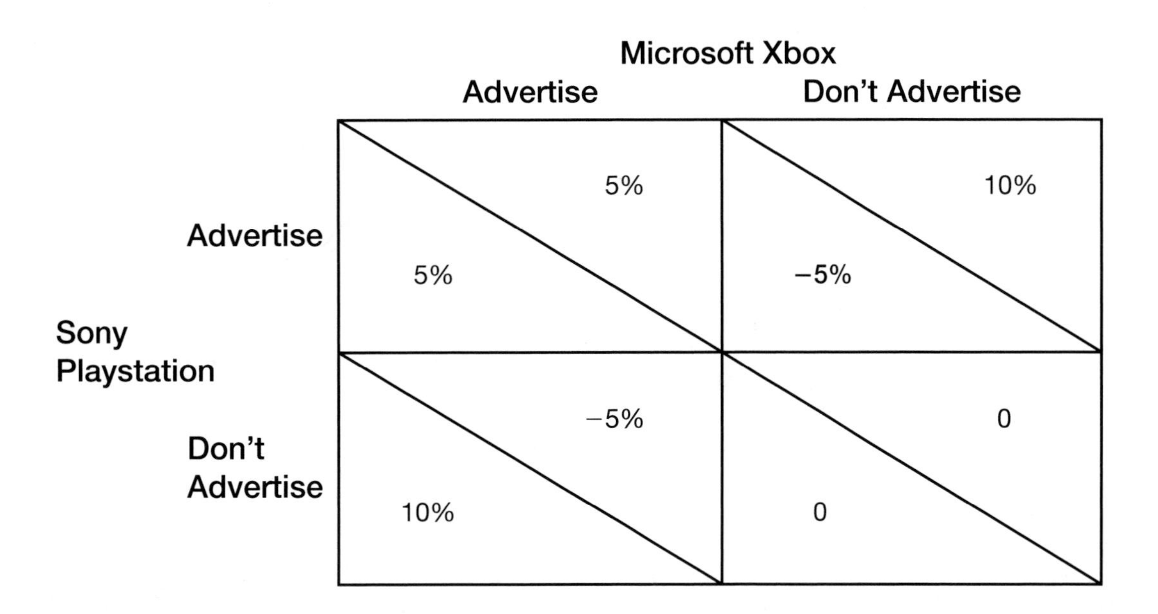

The payoff matrix shows the results of advertising or not advertising. The object is to select best outcome for both companies. If both firms advertise, they will increase the profitability by five percent. If Xbox advertises and Sony does not advertise, Xbox will generate an additional profit of 10 percent while Sony will suffer a five percent loss. If neither firm advertises, both firms will generate a normal profit. The best strategy for both firms is to advertise.

MARKET SHARE STRATEGIES

Oligopolist firms use two strategies to gain market share: advertising and product proliferation. Advertising creates brand loyalty. Advertising is a low cost method which allows consumers to see what products and services firms have available. On the negative side, advertising is used to manipulate consumers. Think about a few of the commercials you've seen in the last few days. Did the commercial entice you to purchase the good or service? Also, consider the advertising used for Black Friday. The stores advertise a lot of merchandise for relatively low prices. When you arrive at the store, you learn that only a few units of the good were available for sale.

EFFICIENCY

As you may recall, productive efficiency requires the price to equal the minimum average total cost. Allocative efficiency requires the price to equal marginal costs. Economic efficiency requires price, marginal cost, and minimum average total cost to equal. Economic efficiency does not occur for oligopolist firms.

Derived Demand

The demand for labor is derived from the demand for the goods and services that labor produces. For example, car companies demand workers to make cars because consumers demand cars. The goal of all businesses is to maximize profits. Businesses will want to hire the amount of workers that will maximize their profits. Business firms maximize profit by hiring up to the point where:

MRP (marginal revenue product) = MFC (marginal factor cost)

Firms will hire additional labor until the last unit of labor adds just as much to revenue as cost. MRP (marginal revenue product) is the workers' value to the firm. MRP = MR × MP. The MRP (marginal revenue product) is the additional revenue that each additional worker's additional output produces. The MRP (marginal revenue product) is always the same as the labor demand curve. Any demand curve shows the most buyers are willing and able to pay for a given quantity. If the second worker's additional output brings in an additional $150, the most the firm would be willing to pay for the worker's labor is $150. VMP = P × MP. The value marginal product (VMP) is the workers' value to society. The value marginal product represents the price society is willing to pay for the additional output that each additional worker produces.

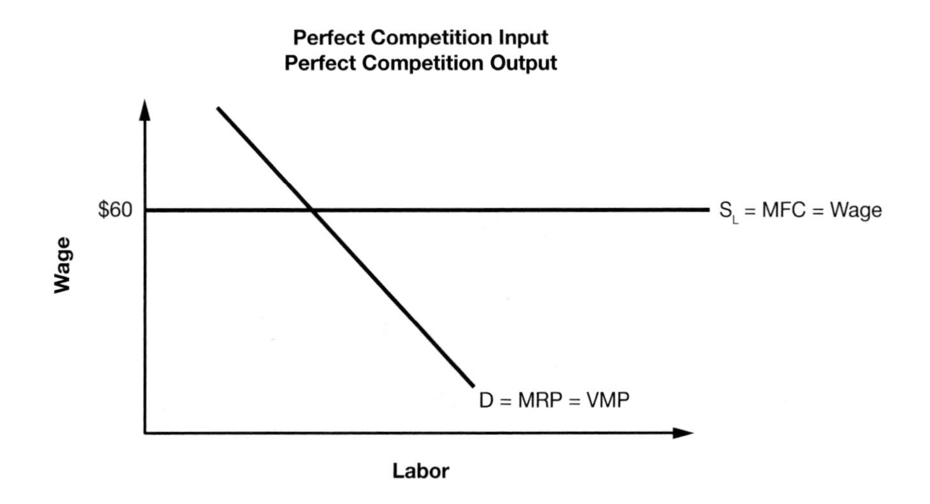

Refer to the graph above. If you have perfect competition in the input market, there is a perfectly elastic supply of labor which is equal to the MFC and the wage. This means that the businesses can hire as many workers as they want without having to offer a higher wage. Since there are many firms each firm is so small it could not affect wages based on how many workers the firm hires. If there is perfect competition in the output market, the MRP curve will be equal to the VMP curve. This is because a perfectly competitive firm will have a perfectly elastic demand curve which is also equal to price and marginal revenue.

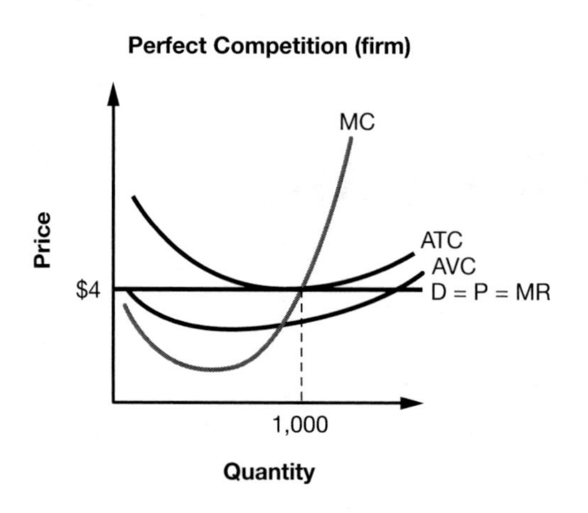

Refer to the graph above. Remember, VMP = P ∞ MP and MRP = MR ∞ MP any time price (P) is equal to marginal revenue (MR), MRP will equal VMP. Since, for a perfectly competitive firm, price (P) is always equal to marginal revenue (MR), MRP will equal VMP whenever there is perfect competition in the output market.

The following table assumes both perfect competition input and output markets.

Labor	TP_L	MP_L	Price	TR	MR	MRP	MFC = Wage
0	0	—	5	0	—	—	—
1	40	40	5	200	5	200	60
2	70	30	5	350	5	150	60
3	90	20	5	450	5	100	60
4	100	10	5	500	5	50	60

Refer to the above table. You can recognize that there is perfect competition in the output market because price is constant and equal to marginal revenue. You can recognize that there is perfect competition in the input market because MFC is constant and equal to the wage. The total product of labor TP_L is the total output that workers produce combined. For example, the TP_L of 2 workers is 70. This means that both workers' output combined is 70. The marginal product of labor MPL is the change in TPL divided by the change in labor. Since labor is always changed by 1 and anything divided by 1 is the same number, the easiest way to calculate MP_L is to take the TP_L and subtract the previous TP_L.

Labor	TP_L	MP_L
0	0	—
1	40	40(40–0)
2	70	30(70–40)
3	90	20(90–70)
4	100	10(100–90)

To calculate total revenue (TR), multiply price (P) ∞ quantity (Q). TPL is the same thing as quantity.

Labor	TP_L	MP_L	Price	TR
0	0	—	5	0 (5 ∞ 0)
1	40	40	5	200 (5 ∞ 40)
2	70	30	5	350 (5 ∞ 70)
3	90	20	5	450 (5 ∞ 90)
4	100	10	5	500 (5 ∞ 100)

To calculate marginal revenue product (MPR) multiply marginal revenue (MR) ∞ marginal product (MP).

Labor	TP_L	MP_L	Price	TR	MR	MRP
0	0	—	5	0	—	—
1	40	40	5	200	5	200(5 ∞ 40)
2	70	30	5	350	5	150 (5 ∞ 30)
3	90	20	5	450	5	100 (5 ∞ 20)
4	100	10	5	500	5	50 (5 ∞ 10)

How many workers should be hired? You will want the worker to bring in at least as much additional revenue as his or her additional cost, otherwise it would not make sense to hire the worker.

If MRP is greater than or equal to MFC the worker should be hired.

Labor	MRP	MFC = Wage
1	200	60 Hire
2	150	60 Hire
3	100	60 Hire
4	50	60 Don't Hire

This firm should hire three workers.

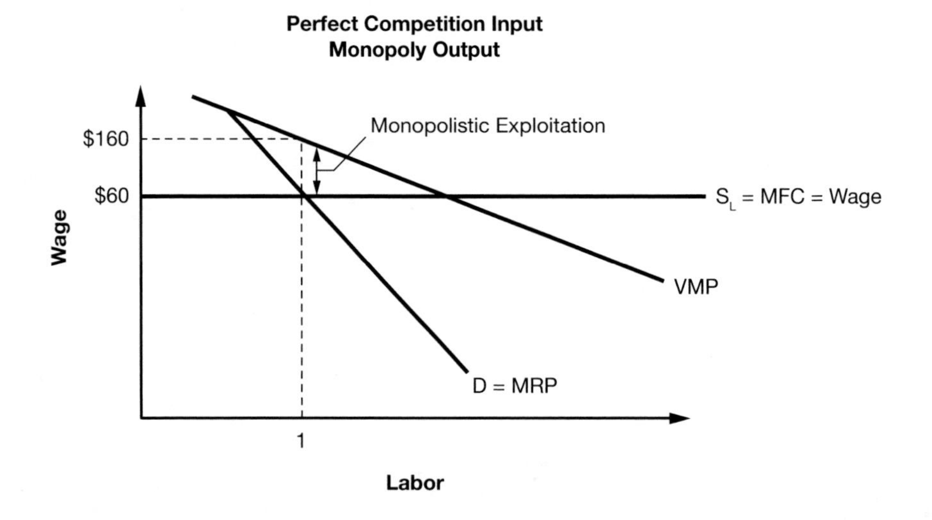

Refer to the graph above. You can recognize that there is perfect competition in the input market, because there is a perfectly elastic supply of labor which is equal to the MFC and the wage. You can recognize that there is a monopoly in the output market because VMP is above MRP. The MR curve for a monopoly in the output market will always fall below its demand curve because a monopoly will have to lower its price to sell more. For this reason whenever you have a monopoly in the output market the price it charges will always be greater than its MR. Remember VMP = P ∞ MP and MRP = MR ∞ MP any time price (P) is greater than marginal revenue (MR), MRP will be greater than VMP. The firm will always maximize profit by hiring where MRP = MFC. In this case the firm will want to hire one worker at the going wage of $60. However, if you go straight up to the VMP curve the workers' value to society is $160. Since the worker is not getting paid his or her true value to society you could say that the worker is being exploited. This is known as monopolistic exploitation because it is due to the fact that there is a monopoly in the output market.

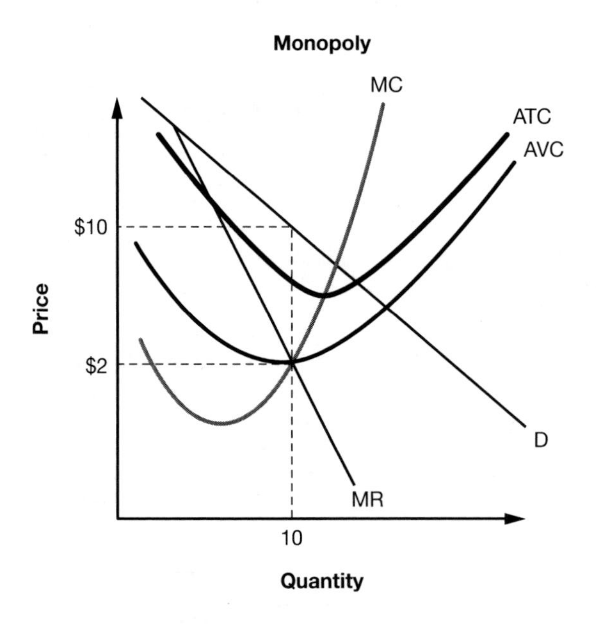

Refer to the graph above. From a quantity of 10 go up to the MR curve and notice MR is $2. From a quantity of 10 go up to the demand curve and notice the price is $10. Notice a monopoly will charge a price greater than its marginal revenue. Remember,

VMP = P ∞ MP and MRP = MR ∞ MP. The only way to have VMP above MRP is if price is greater than marginal revenue.

The following table assumes perfect competition input and monopoly in the output market.

Labor	TP_L	MP_L	Price	TR	MR	MRP	MFC = Wage
0	0	—	5	0	—	—	—
1	40	40	4	160	4	160	60
2	70	30	3	210	1.7	51	60
3	90	20	2	180	−1.5	−30	60
4	100	10	1	100	−8	−80	60

Refer to the table above. You can recognize that there is a monopoly in the output market because price is not constant. Since a monopoly is the only firm in the market, the monopoly will have to lower price to sell. You can recognize that there is perfect competition in the input market because MFC is constant and equal to the wage. The total product of labor TP_L is the total output that workers produce combined. For example, the TP_L of 2 workers is 70. This means that both workers' output combined is 70. The marginal product of labor MPL is the change in TP_L divided by the change in labor. Since labor is always changed by 1 and anything divided by 1 is the same number, the easiest way to calculate MP_L is to take the TP_L and subtract the previous TP_L.

Labor	TP_L	MP_L
0	0	—
1	40	40(40–0)
2	70	30(70–40)
3	90	20(90–70)
4	100	10(100–90)

To calculate total revenue (TR) multiply price (P) ∞ quantity (Q). TP_L is the same thing as quantity.

Labor	TP_L	MP_L	Price	TR (P ∞ Q)
0	0	—	5	0 (5 ∞ 0)
1	40	40	4	160 (4 ∞ 40)
2	70	30	3	210 (3 ∞ 70)
3	90	20	2	180 (2 ∞ 90)
4	100	10	1	100 (1 ∞ 100)

To calculate marginal revenue take the change in TR and divide it by the change in TP_L.

Labor	TP_L	MP_L	Price	TR	MR
0	0	—	5	0	—
1	40	40	5	160	4{(160 − 0)/(40 − 0)}
2	70	30	5	210	1.7{(210 − 160)/(70 − 40)}
3	90	20	5	180	−1.5{(180 − 210)/(90 − 70)}
4	100	10	5	100	−8{(100 − 180)/(100 − 90)}

To calculate marginal revenue product (MPR) multiply marginal revenue (MR) ∞ marginal product (MP).

Labor	TP_L	MP_L	Price	TR	MR	MRP (MR ∞ MP)
0	0	—	5	0	—	—
1	40	40	5	160	4	160(4 ∞ 40)
2	70	30	5	210	1.7	51(1.7 ∞ 30)
3	90	20	5	180	−1.5	−30(−1.5 ∞ 20)
4	100	10	5	100	−8	−80(−8 ∞ 10)

How many workers should be hired? You will want the worker to bring in at least as much additional revenue as his or her additional cost, otherwise it would not make sense to hire the worker.

If MRP is greater than or equal to MFC the worker should be hired.

Labor	MRP (MR × MP)	MFC = Wage
1	160 (4 ∞ 40)	60 Hire (160 > 60)
3	51 (1.7 ∞ 30)	60 Don't Hire (51 < 60)
4	−30 (−1.5 ∞ 20)	60 Don't Hire (−30 < 60)
5	−80 (−8 ∞ 10)	60 Don't Hire (−80 < 60)

The monopoly should hire 1 worker.

A monopsony is a single hirer of labor. The closest example in the real world was the "company town" where most people in a town worked at the same company. For example, you could have a coal mining town where most people would work at the coal company.

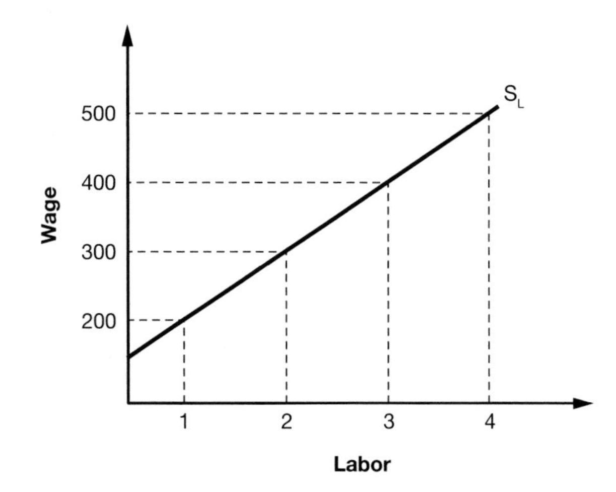

Refer to the graph above. If there is a monopsony in the input market the supply of labor (S_L) will be upward sloping. If there is only one firm hiring that firm will be large enough that they will need to offer a higher wage to attract more workers. Remember, the supply curve for anything is showing the lowest price people need to supply a given quantity. To get the first worker to work the company must offer a wage of \$200. To get the second worker to work the company must offer a wage of \$300. To get the third worker to work the company must offer a wage of \$400. To get the fourth worker to work the company must offer a wage of \$500. Whenever the supply of labor is upward sloping the marginal factor cost curve (MFC) will fall above the supply of labor. This is because of the assumption that if the firm offers a higher wage to attract more workers, they must then pay all workers the higher wage.

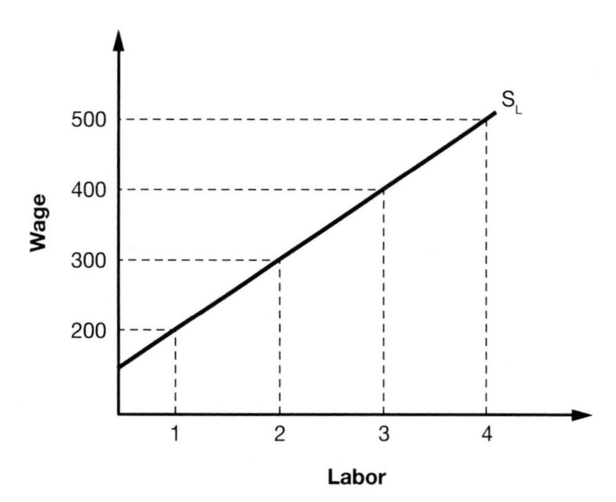

Labor	Wage	TC
1	200	200 (1 ∞ 200)
2	300	600 (2 ∞ 300)
3	400	1,200 (3 ∞ 400)
4	500	2,000 (4 ∞ 500)

Refer to the table and graph above. If the firm hires one worker at a wage of 200 the total cost of labor is 200. If the firm hires a second worker at 300, the firm must also raise the pay of the first worker to 300. The total cost of labor for both workers is 600. If the firm hires a third worker at 400, the firm must now pay all workers 400. The total cost of labor for all three workers would be 1,200. If the firm hires a fourth worker at 500, the firm must now pay all workers 500. The total cost of labor for all four workers would be 2,000.

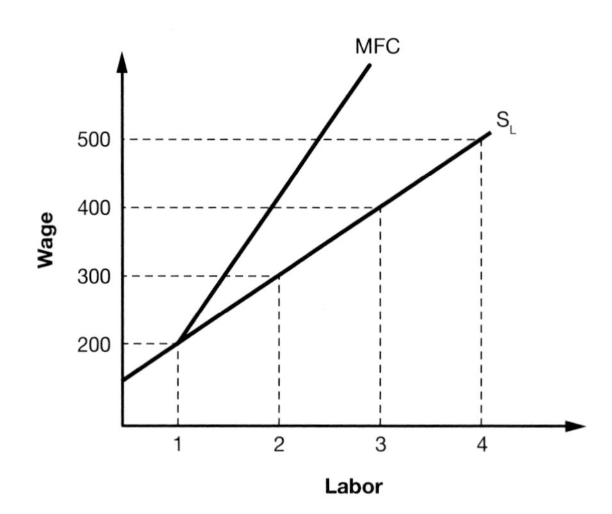

Labor	Wage	TC	MFC
1	200	200	200 (200 – 0)
2	300	600	400 (600 – 200)
3	400	1,200	600 (1,200 – 600)
4	500	2,000	800 (2,000 – 1,200)

Refer to the table and graph above. Remember, marginal means additional. To calculate marginal factor cost (MFC) just subtract the previous total cost of labor. If you have zero workers the labor cost is obviously zero. The first worker adds an additional 200 to the total cost of labor. So the marginal factor cost of the first worker is 200. To calculate the marginal factor cost (MFC) of the second, subtract the total labor cost of one worker from the total labor cost of two workers. To calculate the marginal factor cost (MFC) of the third worker, subtract the total labor cost of two workers from the total labor cost of three workers. To calculate the marginal factor cost (MFC) of the fourth, subtract the total labor cost of three workers from the total labor cost of four workers. So, you can see, whenever there is a monopsony in the input market the marginal factor cost curve (MFC) will be above the supply of labor curve (S_L).

Refer to the graph on the next page. You can recognize there is a monopsony in the input market because supply of labor is upward sloping and the marginal factor cost falls above the supply of labor. You can recognize there is perfect competition in the output market, the MRP curve will be equal to the VMP curve. All firms will maximize profit by hiring where MRP = MFC. This firm will hire two workers. To find the wage the firm will go to the supply of labor curve and pay the lowest wage workers are willing and able to work for. Each of the two workers will receive a wage of \$60. However, the workers' true value to society comes from the value marginal product curve (VMP). The

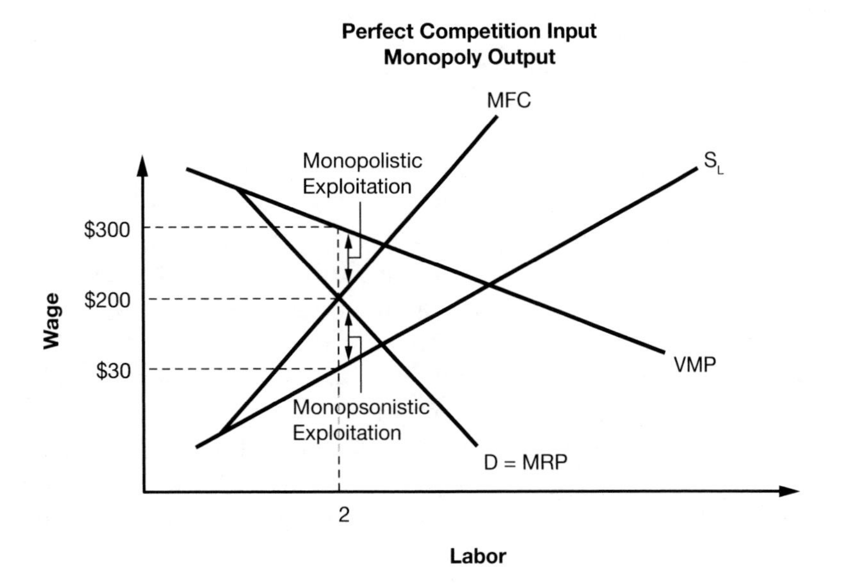

workers' value to society is $100. This is the price society is willing to pay for the additional output of each additional worker. Since the workers are not paid their true value to society you could say they are being exploited. This is known as monopsonistic exploitation because it is due to a monopsony.

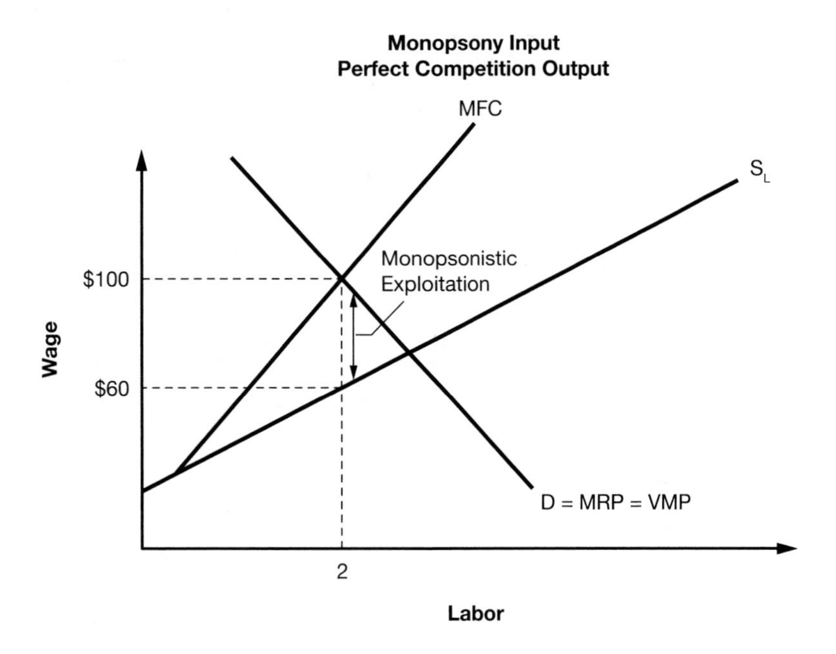

Refer to the graph above. You can recognize there is a monopsony in the input market because supply of labor is upward sloping and the marginal factor cost falls above the supply of labor. You can recognize that there is a monopoly in the output market because VMP is above MRP. All firms maximize profit by hiring where MRP = MFC. This firm will hire two workers and pay them each $30 per hour. However, the workers' true value to society is $300 per hour (from VMP). Since the workers are getting paid less than their true value to society some could say they are being exploited. The distance between VMP and MRP is known as the monopolistic exploitation because it is due to the fact that there is a monopoly. The distance between the supply of labor and MFC is known as the monopsonistic exploitation because it is due to the fact that there is a monopsony. I would argue there is a limit to worker exploitation. In the long run, with a free market economy, workers tend to make close to their marginal revenue product (MRP). The second worker's marginal revenue product is $200 (from MRP). If the firm hires this worker at $30 obviously the firm will make a lot of money off of the worker's labor. There are very few pure monopolies with only one firm in the market, and even if there is a pure monopoly, there are other firms that use labor. For example, if a construction worker makes $30 an hour working for a power company, even though he generates $200 in revenue per hour for the company, other firms outside of electric power generation would offer him more and still make money. So, in the long run, each worker will make close to his or her marginal revenue product. Also keep in mind, if a business gets more revenue than their worker is paid that is known as profit which is usually invested in new capital. Over time, the investment in new capital will raise the worker's MRP allowing the business to pay higher wages and lower the price of their goods. This is why our standard of living raises over time. If workers were paid their full value, businesses would not be able to invest in new capital and wages and our standard of living would stay the same!

UNIONS

Initially unions in our country were viewed as anticompetitive. As unions became more acceptable they tried to assert more control over labor contracts. The most extreme case of union control was the closed shop, which made union membership a prerequisite for employment. The closed shop was outlawed by the Taft-Hartley Act of 1947. Since then unions have been declining in this country. Today unions are mostly for government workers.

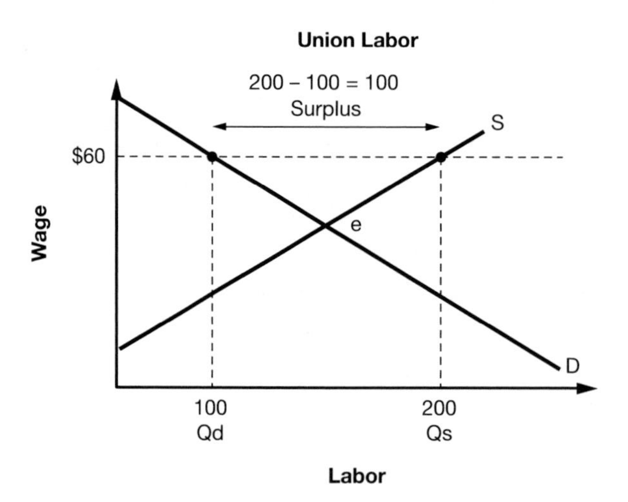

Refer to the graph above. If unions were to demand a wage of $60, which is above equilibrium, the result would be a surplus of labor. At the wage of $60 per hour not everyone who wants a job can find one. Who gets the job is usually based on seniority. Where do the people who can't get a union job go? They have to go in to the market for nonunion labor, i.e., McDonald's.

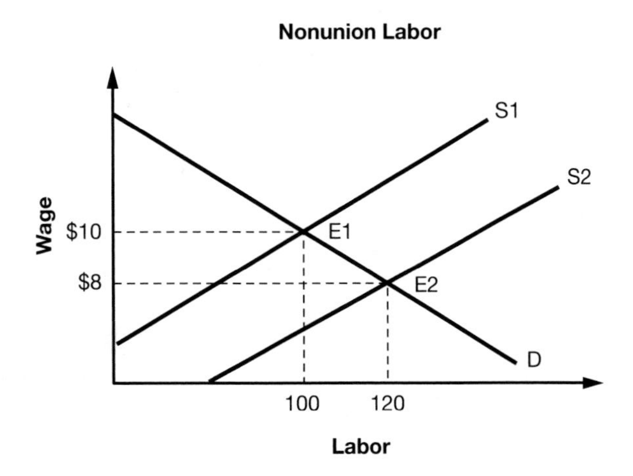

Refer to the graph above. Since the people who cannot get a union job must look for work in the nonunion labor market, the supply of nonunion labor will shift to the right. The result is a lower wage for people working at McDonald's; their wage will fall from $10 per hour (at E1) to $8 per hour (at E2). So, notice the union workers make themselves better off at the expense of nonunion labor and consumers of union produced goods. Unions have also tried to boost wages by increasing the demand for union labor or restricting the supply of labor. If a union can either increase the demand for its labor or decrease the supply of labor, the union can increase wages without having a surplus of labor.

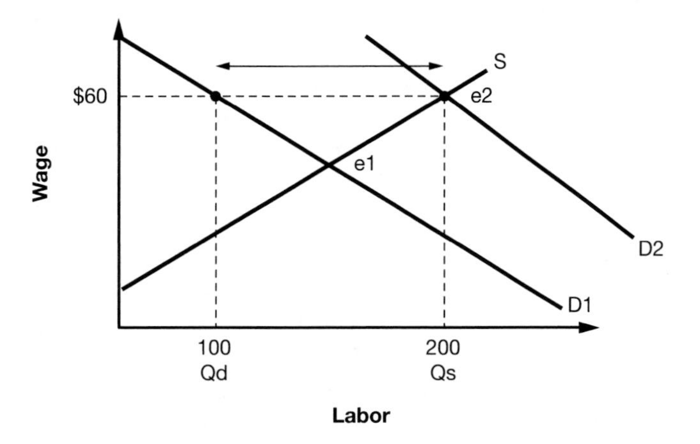

Refer to the graph above. Unions have tried to stimulate the demand for their labor by using political clout to obtain building codes that are labor intensive. The most extreme case is "feather bedding" which made employers use union workers for jobs that no longer existed. For example, after coal power trains were replaced by diesel trains because of unions there still had to be a "coalman" working on the train with no coal! This is obviously inefficient. Feather bedding was made illegal in 1947 by the Taft-Hartley Act. However, even today unions require more workers than necessary to do a job. When I drive through road construction sites I still see someone whose job is to hold up a stop sign. This inefficiency adds to the cost of production and raises prices for consumers. Also unions have tried to stimulate the demand for their labor by lobbying for limits on imported goods. If consumers cannot buy cheap stuff from China, they have to buy more expensive stuff made by union labor in America. Again, when unions try to increase the demand for their labor it raises prices for consumers. So, notice how unions make themselves better off at the expense of consumers.

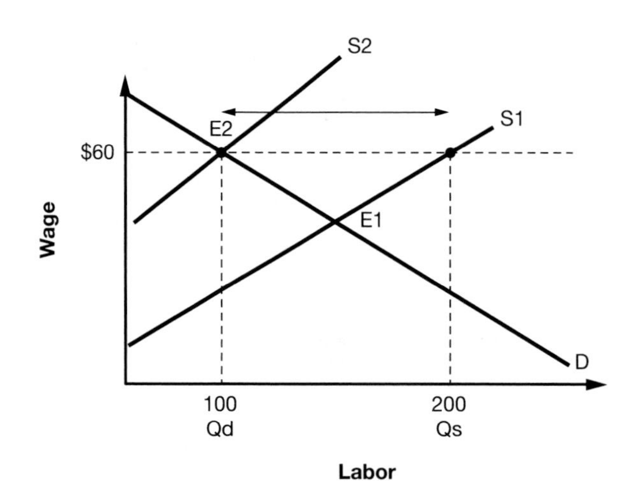

Refer to the graph above. The union movement has restricted the supply of labor by supporting policies such as child labor laws, restrictive immigration policies, compulsory retirement, and shorter work weeks. Some of these policies, such as child labor laws and shorter work weeks, may be popular. It is true that at one point in our nation's history we did have nine-year-olds working in factories. Although unions lobbied for legislation that helped bring about a change, the real reason we no longer have nine-year-olds working in factories is we are now rich enough as a country to afford to have them in school. This was made possible not by unions but by capitalists. The business owners took their profits and invested them in new capital which increased the worker's marginal revenue product (MRP) and allowed the business owners to pay them more. This would have happened sooner without union interference and inefficiency. Shorter work weeks and early retirement may sound nice for workers, however it takes away their choice. Now if wage earners want to work more than 40 hours a week, in many cases, they must take on a second job. Businesses are reluctant to pay overtime. Also keep in mind without union interference the people most likely to get a job and get promoted would most probably be the workers willing to work extra hours.

Mandatory retirement may give an opportunity to younger workers, however older workers who would like to continue working in their "golden years" will have a harder time doing so. Keep in mind that the older workers are usually the most productive since they have the most skill. So, mandatory retirement also leads to a loss of efficiency. Restrictive immigration policies may raise the wages of domestic workers, especially union workers since they lobbied to protect their jobs; however, it also raises the cost of production. This means higher prices for consumers and a loss of efficiency. Union workers do not need to be as productive if they don't have as many people that could take their job.

Name ______________________ Date ______________

Chapter 9

QUESTIONS

Labor	TP	MP	Price	TR	MR	MRP
0	0	$2		—	—	—
1	16		$2			
2	30		$2			
3	42		$2			
4	52		$2			
5	60		$2			
6	64		$2			

1. Fill in the table.
2. What type of output market exists? Explain how you know.

3. How many workers will the firm hire if the going wage rate is $25?

4. How many workers will the firm hire if the going wage rate is $18?

Labor	TP	MP	Price	TR	MR	MRP
0	0	—	$7		—	—
1	16		$6			
2	30		$5			
3	42		$4			
4	52		$3			
5	60		$2			
6	64		$1			

1. Fill in the table.
2. What type of output market exists? Explain how you know.

3. How many workers will the firm hire if the going wage rate is $30?

CHAPTER TEN

Determining Wages

> We might think of dollars as being "certificates of performance." The better I serve my fellow man and the higher the value he places on that service, the more certificates of performance he gives me. The more certificates I earn, the greater my claim on the goods my fellow man produces. That's the morality of the market.
>
> WALTER WILLIAMS

HOW MUCH IS ENOUGH?

In 2011 Carl Crawford was paid $20 million to play left field for the Boston Red Sox. This was $13 million *less* than Alex Rodriquez was paid by the New York Yankees that year. Alex Rodriquez earned $27 million *less* than boxer Floyd Mayweather Jr. that year.

Photo courtesy Jack Chambless

Former California governor Arnold Schwarzenegger was once paid $30 million to make one movie *(Terminator 3)*. Former Disney CEO, Michael Eisner, once received over $500 million, in one year, for his services. All the while, police officers, firefighters, nurses, public school teachers—and just about all the rest of us—went to work knowing that we might not earn in our lifetime what an athlete or actor might make in one year. How does this happen? Why do people who seem to have jobs that do not add much to the social fabric of society make so much, when so many people with dangerous jobs, or jobs critical to education, make so much less?

THE DEMAND FOR LABOR

In any labor market, the demand for labor is a *derived demand.* This means the demand for a worker comes from the demand for the good or service the worker produces. For example, over the next few decades, the number of elderly people in America is going to increase dramatically as the baby-boomers age and medical breakthroughs continue to prolong our lives. Surely the elderly are going to want to be active and fit as they age. This will translate into a large increase in the demand for personal training services geared toward seniors.[1] As can be seen in Figures 10.1 and 10.2, the increase in the demand for personal training services will lead to an increase in the demand for personal trainers. In each market, the result will be higher prices and an increase in quantity supplied.

CONCEPT CHECK

Who has a greater derived demand—Oprah Winfrey or your economics professor? Why?

THE LABOR SUPPLY

The labor supply is the relationship between the prevailing wage rate in an industry and the quantity of labor hours offered in that industry. The number of people who are willing and able to do a particular job at various wage rates determines the labor supply curve. The willing part is easy. Many of you might be willing to be the starting goalie for the Chicago Blackhawks or play the lead opposite Mark Wahlberg. The hard part is satisfying the *able* part of the equation. As we will see, major differences in wages and salaries in America stem largely from widely divergent labor supply curves, rather than large differences in the demand for labor.

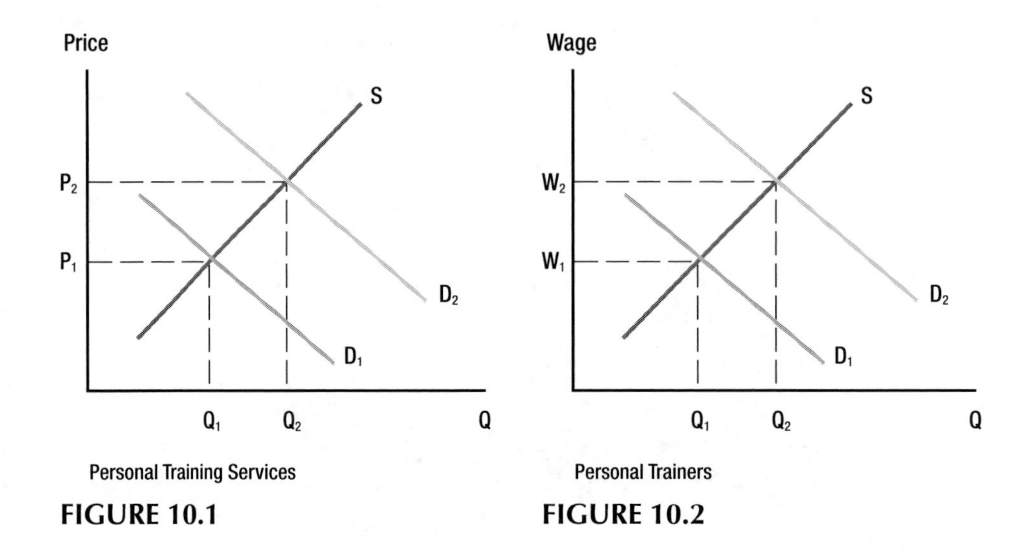

FIGURE 10.1

FIGURE 10.2

What would you do if, while you were reading this section of the book, your boss called you and offered you $200 per hour to come in to work today? Would you turn down the money in order to keep reading, or would you run every stoplight as you drive like Dale Earnhardt Jr. to get to work? For some of you, it is pretty straightforward: The more money you could make, the more hours you would be willing to work (Figure 10.3).

THE SUBSTITUTION EFFECT

John Allen is a very busy man. As an investment banker and Internet entrepreneur he routinely puts in 90 hours in a single workweek. Why does he do this? Because he is what an economist calls a "substitution effect" person.

Mr. Allen earned his degree in economics from the University of Virginia in 1995. After leaving Virginia where he received "high distinction" from the distinguished majors program, he went to work for Stern Stewart & Co.—a company that specializes in value-based management. By the time he was 28, he was a vice-president. Mr. Allen

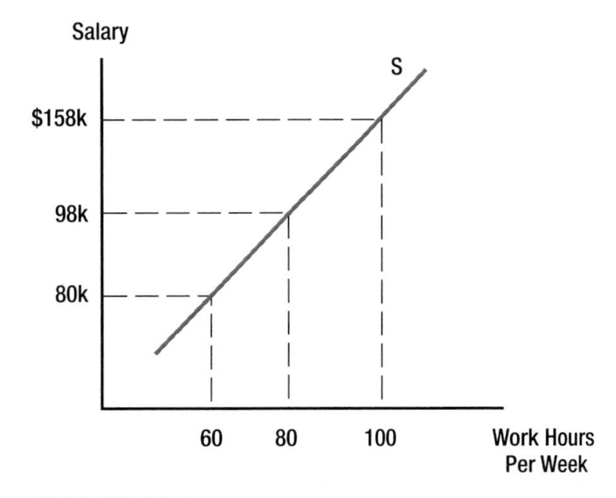

FIGURE 10.3

Photo courtesy Jack Chambless

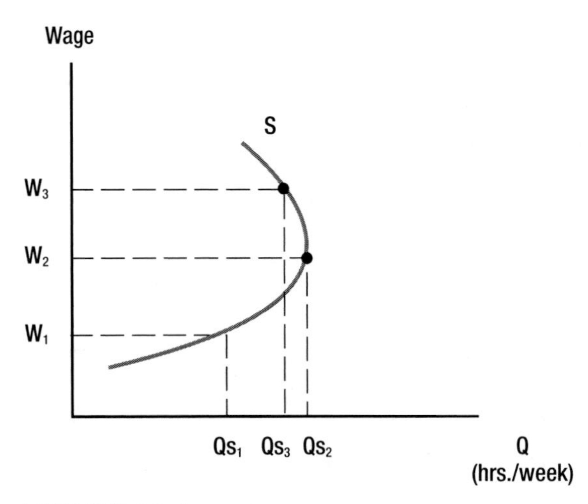

FIGURE 10.4

quickly ascended the corporate ladder and left Stern Stewart's New York office in 1999 to open a similar office in Century City, California.

Today he earns a six-figure salary as a financial executive in Los Angeles, and he does so at the expense of leisure time. Why does he work so hard? "Because I am willing to sacrifice leisure now, in order to gain leisure in the future, and the money to enjoy leisure in the future."

Mr. Allen is a classic example of the tendency of some workers to work a lot of hours, at the expense of relaxation. This substituting of work for leisure reflects their belief that, as their pay rate increases they cannot afford to take time off, because the opportunity cost of each hour of leisure is too great. In essence, leisure becomes too expensive to consume as the price of it—measured in lost income—increases. As a result, Mr. Allen faces an upward sloping supply curve like the one presented in Figure 10.3.

THE INCOME EFFECT

On the other hand, many of you may know people—or may be one of the people—with a *backward-bending* labor supply curve. This curve (as depicted in Figure 10.4) indicates a willingness to forgo higher levels of income, and actually reduce work hours, as income increases. This means that, as income rises, the individual can more easily afford to take time off. In essence, these people choose to purchase more leisure time without being concerned about working less. They feel they have earned enough money, in advance of the cut back in work hours, so leisure is a more desirable pursuit.

Which type of person are you? Before you answer, consider this. The type of labor supply curve that you are inclined to have says a great deal about the type of person you might consider marrying. Mismatching of "income-effect" and "substitution-effect" people has been proven to be a recipe for divorce. If you want to work 103 hours per week and your spouse wants you home, or vice versa, imagine the acrimony this can create. Perhaps before you consider asking or answering "The Question," you should sit down and find out what philosophy you and your loved one have with respect to work hours and money. You may find out that you are better off avoiding marriage—to that person—and the greater probability of disastrous consequences.

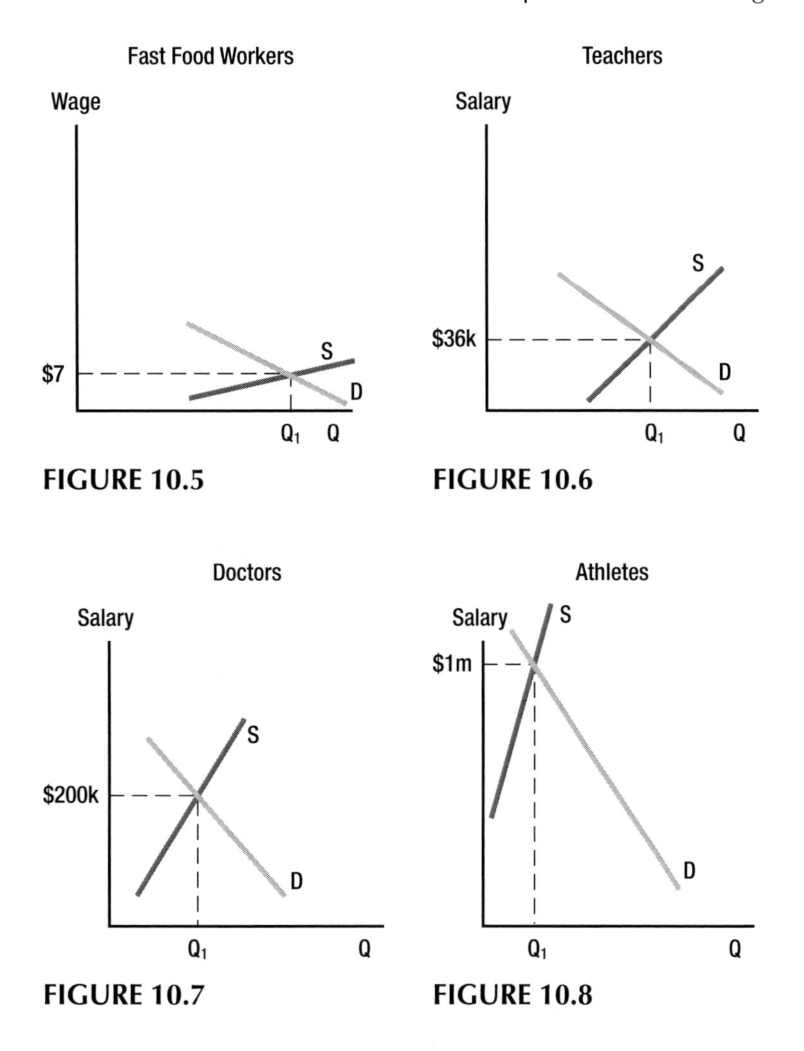

FIGURE 10.5

FIGURE 10.6

FIGURE 10.7

FIGURE 10.8

UNDERSTANDING EARNINGS DIFFERENCES

Figures 10.5–10.8 illustrate four distinct labor markets—the market for fast-food workers, elementary school teachers, doctors, and professional athletes.

As you can see in each diagram, the derived demand for labor is quite large. This is empirically true for each market. Americans spend more money on fast food, education, health care, and professional sporting events than any nation on Earth. This creates a constantly growing demand for all of these employees. With such a large demand for each, why are salaries that are paid to each type of worker so different? The answer lies with the overall supply of labor in each market.

There are currently approximately 165 million people in America's labor force. Of that number, 165 million have the ability to work as a food preparer at Taco Bell or Burger King. Because of the nature of the job, those relatively unskilled positions can be easily filled by almost anyone looking for gainful employment. This means that the overall supply of fast-food workers is extremely large. When you combine a relatively large demand for labor with an enormous supply of labor, the result is downward pressure on wages.

The supply of teachers is smaller than the supply of fast-food workers. Elementary school teachers have to spend at least four years of their lives learning how to educate America's youth. This requirement of higher education means that fewer people are willing and able to become teachers. With a smaller supply and a relatively large demand, teachers can always expect to earn more than a fast-food employee.

With respect to the labor market for doctors, the weeding-out process is even more intense. Because of the extremely long commitment to medical school, excruciatingly difficult coursework, long hours, and stressful working conditions, the supply of doctors is much smaller than the supply of teachers. It also helps that the American Medical Association has helped facilitate rules of medical practice that reduce competition for physicians' services. Given a very large demand for doctors and a very small supply of people who can meet the demand, salaries tend to stretch well into six-figures. For specialized fields like neurology and vascular surgery, the compensation can easily reach over $1 million per year.

CONCEPT CHECK

Laborers in Costa Rica earn about $2,800 per year to make baseballs for Major League Baseball.[2] Major league baseball players earn, on average, over $3.3 million per year. On two graphs, illustrate why there is such a large difference in earnings. Are these differences fair? Why, or Why not?

Speaking of millions per year, the gentlemen in the photo below represent a labor market that for many Americans defies all common sense and rationality. Of course, this is referring to the labor market for professional athletes.

NBA players earned an average of $3.4 million in 2010–2011. Professional baseball and hockey players earn an average over $2 million per year. NFL players earned a median salary of over $750,000 in 2010. During Michael Jordan's last year with the Chicago Bulls, he received *$36 million* for his services. If we attempt to get past the emotional reaction to numbers like these, we can easily understand—and perhaps even accept—the reasoning behind such huge levels of compensation. After all, it is *our fault* athletes make the money they do.

When people plunk down their hard-earned money to be entertained by the skills of professional athletes, they expect—as the paying customer—to see the highest quality product available.

That means those of us who attend professional sports events expect, and demand, to see the highest-quality athlete available. No one wants to see Sidney Crosby's gardener playing hockey for the Pittsburgh Penguins or Josh Hamilton's accountant swinging for the fences in Texas.

People pay money to see the best athletes in the world. The problem, if we wish to call it a problem, is that that the overall supply of people who can perform like Kobe

Photo courtesy Jack Chambless

Bryant or Peyton Manning is so limited (the able part of willing and able), that the supply of world-class athletes is extraordinarily small.

> People don't know how hard it is to play this game. It's like when Michael Jordan came over to play baseball. I heard guys in this clubhouse say "Yeah, Michael Jordan, he's not much. I could have guarded him in basketball." Michael Jordan! Nobody in the NBA could guard him! And you could? Why hasn't the NBA snapped you up? People are unrealistic.[3]

When we think about this situation analytically, we can see that—with only a small fraction of the world's population capable of satisfying the sports consumer, and a voracious appetite for pro sports in America—salaries naturally rise to the levels they do. In essence, it is not the athlete's fault for earning so much money. They simply charge what the market will bear.

Look at what soccer players in Europe earn compared to the U.S. In America, where soccer is not as popular on the professional level, the derived demand for star soccer players is so low that they make far less here than in Great Britain or Brazil. It is also ironic to point out that athletes are cheaper, for many of you, than teachers! If you never go to a game, never buy a jersey, or do not live in a city that is building stadiums with your tax dollars, it costs you nothing when an athlete earns a big salary. However, you do have to pay your taxes, and your taxes pay for teacher salaries.

THE ECONOMICS OF LABOR UNIONS

In the nineteenth century, workers in America faced a difficult situation when it came to negotiating the terms of labor with business firms. During this time, if a worker wanted more money or better working conditions, the worker had to bargain individually with his or her employer. This put the employee at a tremendous disadvantage, because if the company did not want to pay what the person was asking, the company could say no without fearing repercussions from the disgruntled employee. Things began to change in the late 1800s and the early 1900s as more and more people began to join labor unions.

A union is a worker association that bargains with employers over wages and working conditions.

Today, there are many different types of unions that negotiate wages on behalf of teachers, firemen, steel and auto workers, airline pilots, and electrical workers, to name just a few.

The major objective of each union is to use the collective bargaining process to increase wages and improve working conditions for union members.

Collective bargaining is the process by which unions and firms agree on the terms of employment.

In America, there are two types of unions—the *craft union* and the *industrial union.* A craft union is a group of workers who have a similar range of skills but who work for firms in many different industries and regions. Examples include the carpenters' union and the International Brotherhood of Electrical Workers that represents electrical workers. An industrial union is a group of

CONCEPT CHECK

During the 1920s, oppressive Jim Crow laws led to many black residents moving out of the state of Florida.[4] This movement led to a labor shortage in Florida during that time period. Illustrate and explain why.

Shutterstock © digitalrefl ections, 2011.

workers who have a variety of skills and job types but who work for the same firm or industry.

The United Auto Workers and the Steelworkers Union are examples of industrial unions. In 1886 the American Federation of Labor was formed to organize craft unions. In 1938, the Congress of Industrial Organizations was formed to organize industrial unions. Today the AFL-CIO represents millions of workers around the country, although union participation has fallen from a high of 35% of the nonagricultural work force to about 12% today.[5]

HOW UNIONS IMPACT WAGES AND WORK HOURS

Historically, the goal of labor unions has been to restrict the supply of labor and drive up wages and benefits for union members. This is accomplished in three key ways. The first method is for the labor union to restrict the number of people who can join to begin with. With fairly rigorous apprenticeship and training programs and a selective mindset, unions have been successful in controlling the total number of workers that they offer to management in a collective bargaining setting. The second method is to successfully organize labor to become part of the union.

For example, the Farm Labor Organizing Committee once attempted to unionize the farm workers in North Carolina.[6] The more workers a union can get to join, the more bargaining power the union will have in contract negotiations. Of course, the final—and most publicized—way unions attempt to impact wages and working conditions is by threatening a strike if desirable labor terms are not met.

A strike is the organized withdrawal of labor from a firm by a union.

In 2001, the writers and actors in Hollywood—through the Screen Actors Guild—threatened to go on strike if union members did not receive higher residual payments from commercials and television programs that are rerun. The writers and actors argued

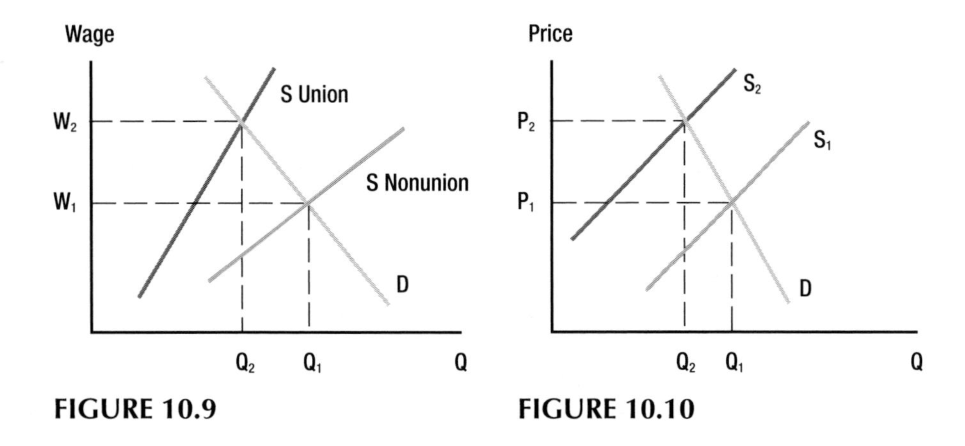

FIGURE 10.9

FIGURE 10.10

that the studios were able to make money each time an episode of *Seinfeld* or a shampoo commercial aired, but that the actors and writers were being paid far too little money from these rebroadcasts.

More recently, labor unions have taken up the fight against the proliferation of Wal-Mart stores, in an attempt to force Wal-Mart to hire more union labor[7] while simultaneously pushing to get more union labor involved in reality television shows.[8]

What is the impact of restrictions on union entry, union organizing efforts, and strikes? Figures 10.9 and 10.10 will help provide an answer to this question. In Figure 10.9, we see that, by restricting the supply of labor, unions are able to increase the earnings of their members. However, this practice also means that the quantity of labor hours demanded by the employer will fall—leading to fewer total jobs and work hours.

At the same time, we see in Figure 10.10 that unions cause the input costs of production to increase as a result of higher wages and benefits. For example, the average autoworker in Detroit, working as a member of the UAW, earns over $70 per hour in wages and benefits. This pay structure is one reason why car prices are higher than would be the case if nonunion workers built the cars. In Tennessee and Kentucky, where many nonunion members build Japanese cars, the prices of these cars have been kept down by much lower hourly wages.[9]

ARE UNIONS GOOD OR BAD FOR THE ECONOMY?

Studies show that union members tend to have a higher marginal product than nonunion members do.[10] With higher productivity come lower costs of production. However, unions also help create a reduction in employment opportunities and higher prices for goods and services that union members produce.

The real question for labor economists is whether the productivity differences between union and nonunion labor equals the wage differences. If productivity is 10–25% higher on average but wages are 30% higher—as the research suggests that it is—then nonunion labor makes more sense for employers. Employers that hire union labor face higher long-run costs, lower profits, and the reality of charging uncompetitive prices.[11] The Mackinac Center for Public Policy found that from 1970 to 2000, states with right-to-work laws added 1.43 million manufacturing jobs while heavily unionized states like Michigan, lost 2.18 million jobs due in large part to the widening gap between pay and productivity among union workers.[12]

Recently, President Obama pushed for a new law that would do away with secret ballots used by workers to vote on whether they want a union or not. The regulation was designed to put pressure on more workers to select the union option. Studies show that if the level of unionization in America in this decade reached the same level of the 1970s, employment would fall by 4.5 million and the GDP would be reduced by $500 billion.[13] One study in America even found that union-management problems at Firestone played a role in low productivity and the production of defective tires responsible for more highway deaths.[14]

Finally, the public sector union uprising that took place in Wisconsin in 2011, illustrates some of the economic dilemmas that occur from union labor. In Wisconsin and many other states around the U.S., the rising cost of public sector union pensions has left many states on the brink of financial insolvency. Thus, when Wisconsin's governor tried to rein in union power in this state, the unionized teachers, firefighters, and police officers naturally protested and helped draw attention to the high cost of allowing collective bargaining to take place in many sectors of our economy.

THE ISSUE OF WORTH

Whenever the issue of pay and worth comes up, it can spark a great deal of controversy. At the college where I work, I spent more than two years on a committee that was in charge of coming up with a new salary model for professors. At one point the committee recommended higher salaries for professors who taught in areas where there was a shortage of qualified instructors. One of my colleagues in the science department fired off a memo that stated in part:

The precedent has been established to offer additional compensation to professors in disciplines that are in demand in the marketplace. Does this mean that humanities professors are WORTHLESS?

Obviously, this professor either never took a microeconomics class or has simply forgotten her economics altogether. Of course, not all humanities professors are worthless. Many do wonderful things in the classroom.

How would you know if you were being paid what you are worth? Should the calculation be based on the earnings of your co-workers? Should it be based on how hard you work compared to others? Labor economists have devised a methodology for determining value. The methodology involves calculating the marginal revenue product of labor.

The marginal revenue product of labor (MRPL) is the extra revenue earned from each additional worker.

In the previous chapter, we learned that the marginal product of labor is the change in the total product of labor that takes place from the addition of one more worker. The MRPL is simply the marginal product of labor, multiplied by the price of what the employer can charge for the output the worker produces.

SUGGESTED CLASSROOM DEBATE

Increasingly, colleges and universities all over America are trying to measure the economic value of professors.[15] Read the article footnoted here then engage in a debate over how best to measure the value of a professor.

Chuck owns a salmon farm in Washington. He can sell each salmon for $11. Chuck wants to know how much each worker he adds to his farm is worth. The table below will help him find out.

As you can see, the value of each worker depends on individual productivity and the price of the product that the worker helps to sell. This means that we look only at the revenue a worker is directly responsible for creating for the employer in determining that worker's economic value. This may seem caustic, but to the extent that economic models cannot measure the quality of a person's character or the value of his or her smile, we must rely on measurable components of worth.

CONCEPT CHECK

A recent study found that America's 5.4 million stay-at-home parents would earn $131,471 in annual salary, including overtime pay, if they were doing the same work for an employer that they do at home.[16] Does this figure make sense? Why, or why not? Another study found that NFL quarterbacks that are good-looking make more money, ceteris paribus than more homely quarterbacks.[17] Does this make sense? Why, or why not?

THE LINK BETWEEN PAY AND WORTH

Now that we have a firm understanding of the supply and demand conditions that create differences in pay, as well as an idea of how we measure worth, we turn to the issue of how the level of competition on the demand and supply side of the labor market impacts wages and salaries.

To the extent that workers find themselves operating in markets with disparately competitive conditions, the answer to the question of how pay compares to the MRPL can be uncovered. At any time, a worker can find himself or herself in one of four economic environments. They are:

- A perfectly competitive labor market with respect to supply and demand.
- A perfectly competitive supply side of the labor market and an imperfectly competitive demand condition.
- An imperfectly competitive labor market with respect to supply and demand.
- A perfectly competitive demand side of the labor market and an imperfectly competitive supply condition.

Quantity (L) (Workers)	Total Product of Labor TPL (Salmon Caught per Hour)		Marginal Product of Labor MP_L = _TP/_L (Salmon Caught per Worker)	Marginal Revenue Product of Labor $MRP_L = P_X MPL$
0	0	>		
1	5	>	5	$55
2	9	>	4	$44
3	12	>	3	$33
4	14	>	2	$22
5	15	>	1	$11

THE PERFECTLY COMPETITIVE LABOR MARKET

If you are like thousands of other college students in the United States, you have decided to major in accounting for your degree plan. Of course, you already know that this is a particularly difficult subject, and naturally you expect to be appropriately rewarded for your services in this labor market. There is good news and bad news.

The good news is that there is a very competitive demand condition in this market. In other words, there are a very large number of firms in the U.S. who employ accountants now and will do so in the future. With the tax laws becoming infinitely more complex almost every year, you should feel comfortable knowing that there should be a strong demand for quite some time—especially in the wake of the Enron scandal where auditors have become more important then ever.

The bad news is that you cannot swing a dead cat without hitting someone who either is an accountant or is aspiring to be one. They are all over the place—meaning a very competitive supply side of your market. What will this mean to you in terms of pay versus worth?

Suppose that, upon receiving your degree, you find out that the average salary of a first-year accountant at any given corporation is $39,000. You decide that your hard work and dedication to your field is worth at least $53,000 per year. On your first interview, you inform the human resources manager that you do not really regard $39,000 as the salary commensurate with your skills and that you will require the higher figure to work for them.

Three seconds later, when your interview is over, you will find out the hard way that if the market for accountants is very competitive on each side of the market, you will not be able to get more than the market clearing wage rate. You should take comfort in knowing that the firm will not offer you $24,000 per year either. If a company in this market offers less than the MRPL, you can simply seek employment with any of their competitors for a salary that is equal to $39,000. In a nutshell, *you will be paid what you are worth* due to the mutual *lack of market power* you and prospective employers possess.

A common question at this point in the proceedings is "How do companies make profit if they pay their workers a salary equal to the workers' MRPL?" This is a very good question and one that is easy to answer. If we consider all of the factors that go into the production process—labor, fuel, materials, insurance, and so forth, any given company can expect to pay the market equilibrium price for the inputs of production.

What they do next is *mark up the final price* of the good or service to a level that will help them make profit. Of course, the amount of mark-up depends on several factors like the amount of competition in the product market, location, the ability to keep out new competitors, and luck. The bottom line is that wages are but one part of the cost of doing business, and you must come up with competitive wages and salaries to attract workers.

YOU WILL BE UNDERPAID IF . . .

Several years ago, the German automaker Daimler-Benz built a factory in Vance, Alabama, where the M-class Mercedes is built.[19] Vance, Alabama? What could this com-

SUGGESTED CLASSROOM DEBATE

The average CEO's salary in the U.S. is 475 times greater than the average worker's salary. In Japan it is 11 times greater; in France 15 times; in Canada 20 times.[18] Why are the differences so large? Is this good, or bad for our economy? Why?

pany possibly be thinking building a plant nowhere near Germany or Detroit—where many cars are made? Perhaps the carmaker knows something about a concept that has helped many small towns gain large employers. It is the concept that has driven the labor market for many unskilled and skilled workers alike all over the world. It is even used by professional sports organizations and the NCAA.[20] It is known by economists as the use of *monopsony* power.

As the following analysis (from the July 5, 1994, edition of *The Wall Street Journal*) clearly illustrates, when a monopsony exists and there is a very competitive labor supply to draw from, workers will be paid less than their MRPL. It does not matter how much the employee of the monopsonist earns. Workers can be underpaid even when they earn millions of dollars per year. One study found the existence of monopsony in the market

Poor Underpaid Millionaires

By JACK A. CHAMBLESS

When I was a youngster, I passed many scorching summer days in the air-conditioned confines of my home watching NBC's baseball Game of the Week with my father. Inevitably, at some point during every game we watched, someone would commit a fielding error and my father would cry out, "There is no way in the world that player is worth the hundreds of thousands of dollars he's being paid." After hearing him repeat this assertion year after year, I began to wonder: If the players are not worth the money, why do the owners pay such exorbitant salaries? Are they fiscal illiterates incapable of rational decision making?

As it turns out, the owners are pretty smart. They squeeze more revenues out of ballplayers than they pay out in salaries. And they keep players locked into a form of indentured servitude where the vast majority don't have any control over their future. That's a big reason why ballplayers are likely to walk out sometime this month for the first time since 1985. This prospect may be painful to fans transfixed by Ken Griffey Jr.'s quest for the season home run record of 61 (set in 1961 by Roger Maris), but the players would be justified in striking. Simply put, the bulk of them are underpaid.

I have created a computer model that calculates an individual player's impact on the bottom line. This multiple regression model calculates the impact on total team revenues of such variables as population, unemployment rate, attendance at games, even team colors. According to my model, the most important impact on the bottom line is the number of wins. Every game that a major league team wins increases its revenues by $349,000. It's also possible to determine each player's contribution to a win based on his offensive and defensive statistics; for example, the model has found that every run scored by a player creates .043 wins.

Based on this model, I've found that a few major league players are grossly overpaid. For example, outfielder Darryl Strawberry, who played for the Los Angeles Dodgers last season, earned $3.8 million but produced only $772,088 at the box office. But most players earn less than they should—even the San Francisco Giants' highly paid outfielder Barry Bonds. Mr. Bonds received $4.2 million last season. Yet his play—including 129 runs scored and 29 stolen bases—contributed $9,831,360 to the Giants' bottom line. This is no fluke. My model finds that, on average, professional ballplayers receive only 30% of the revenues they create.

And the ill-treatment of players doesn't stop there. Consider that every year, hundreds of young men ranging in age from 18 to 22 are "drafted" (note the martial term) by the 28 major league baseball teams, most of whom are sent down to the minor leagues. Once a player signs a contract to play professionally, he becomes the exclusive property of the team for seven years, with no right to renegotiate his salary or shop around for other employers. If the player quits, he cannot play for pay in the U.S., unless his team agrees to give him his unconditional release. However, at any time, the owner can fire him.

Ask yourself for a moment: "If, in my chosen profession, I could only work for one company for seven years with no opportunity to negotiate my salary or threaten to leave, would the company pay me what I'm worth?" The answer is pretty obvious.

This phenomenon is known as the use of monopsony power. A monopsonist is the single buyer of some resource. Underpaying workers as a function of monopsony power is very common in small cities where one company is the major employer. The company will pay its workers a wage that is higher than that paid by the local bowling alley or supermarket, but far less than it would pay if the workers could be bid away by a competitor.

Monopsony power over the players extends to both the minor and major leagues. As a major leaguer, a player cannot change teams or renegotiate his pay for three seasons. This means a player could have already put 10 years of his life into one team before being allowed to attempt to recover part of his lost earnings. After three years of service, the player can file for binding arbitration, which means he stays tied to his team but can now have a third party determine his salary once his contract expires. Since the arbitrators cannot "split the difference" between the amount sought by the player and what the owner offers, sometimes the player still isn't guaranteed a salary commensurate with his worth.

If the player is fortunate enough to survive the potential 13 seasons of servitude, only then can he become what each of us is, a free agent. He can sell his services to the team that pays him the salary he desires, located in the city he chooses to live in. This seems to be the type of player my dad used to refer to in his antimillionaire tirades. But as we have seen, even many of these players, like Mr. Bonds, are underpaid.

It is perhaps ironic that the players most likely will strike soon after the nation celebrates Independence Day. I wonder if my father will believe me when I tell him the players are fighting for their own independence from a tyrannical system.

Mr. Chambless is an economics professor at Valencia Community College, Orlando, Fla., and a sports agent who represents minor league baseball players.

for senior college professors.[21] Monopsony power has also appeared in markets ranging from truck driving,[22] call-center workers,[23] and teaching assistants at major universities.[24]

THE BILATERAL MONOPOLY

A relatively rare labor market outcome is a situation where one buyer (a monopsonist) and one seller (a monopolist) of labor services interact with one another. This is known as a bilateral monopoly.

A bilateral monopoly occurs where a very strong labor union faces a situation where one major employer is pretty much the union's only option. This is precisely the condition that exists in professional sports. The players in each of the four major sports belong to a union that bargains with the owners of their respective sports franchises over terms such as minimum pay, pensions, conditions for termination, drug testing, and other aspects of the job. Of course, as we saw in the preceding analysis, an athlete is severely underpaid early in his (or her) career, due to the inability to shop his services around. However, the collective bargaining agreements that have been negotiated in football, baseball, basketball, and hockey have provisions allowing for players to become "free agents" after a specified period. There once was a time when this was not the case.

Early in the history of professional sports, the owners of the teams in each league realized that there was a growing demand for entertainment in America—especially the type of entertainment created by athletes. The problem the owners faced is that, with such a small pool of people who could compete at the level that was demanded, players would have the ability to shop their services around to the highest bidder. In major league baseball this is precisely what happened as players routinely "jumped ship" for more lucrative offers, made by other teams. It was this problem that led the owners to institute what was known as a reserve clause.[25]

The reserve system gave a team the exclusive rights to a player while he was under contract with the team and for the next contract year, effectively binding the player to a team for life. From the owner's perspective, this protected the team from interference by richer teams and enabled the team to recoup its investment in the player.[26] By being able to keep players like Lou Gehrig locked up for their entire career, it also helped teams like the New York Yankees win multiple championships in a row.

However, this system effectively made the players indentured servants with no prospects to ever leave a team unless they were summarily fired by the organization that employed them. Of course, the players eventually sued the owners, claiming that this system violated the 1890 Sherman Antitrust Act, which makes artificial restrictions on the movement of resources illegal. However, in a landmark decision, the U.S. Supreme Court ruled that "giving exhibitions of baseball, which are purely state affairs" makes baseball exempt from the federal antitrust laws.[27] This ruling, which has never been overturned, gave the owners of major league baseball teams a free hand to dictate the terms of employment for players with impunity. Or so it seemed.

By the 1970s the players had had enough, and they enlisted the assistance of Marvin Miller, an attorney and expert in labor economics. Mr. Miller helped the players create a union that would eventually wrestle away the power of the owners to dictate salaries. In 1976 the players successfully fought for the right to become free agents after they had fulfilled a certain number of years with one organization. Today that number is six years. For the first six years of employment, a baseball player cannot leave his team.

After three years, he can file for binding arbitration and let an independent arbitrator decide what his compensation will be. After six years, the player is free to shop his services around to the highest bidder.

Should the "reserve clause" be reinstated?

You might wonder why the players would not fight for total free agency and the abolishment of any reserve system. The reason is fairly simple. The owners have convinced the players that if a system of total free agency existed, the richest or most successful teams—or the teams in the nicest climates—would be able to raid the rank-and-file members of the best talent.

This monopolization of the available talent would mean that only a few teams would ever be competitive. Over time, the owners argue, the demand for professional sporting events would fall as fans grew tired of the same group of teams dominating the league each year. If demand fell, eventually some teams would go bankrupt and the entire league would be in jeopardy. Imagine, for example, what would have happened if Sam Bradford—the quarterback for the Oklahoma Sooners and former Heisman Trophy winner—would have been able to stand on a stage and let all 32 NFL teams bid on his services (like many economists want[28]) rather than the NFL allowing only the St. Louis Rams the option of his services. Mr. Bradford received tens of millions of dollars from the Rams. An auction would have pushed his compensation closer to $100 million.

Therefore, the owners have been able to convince the players that—in order to ensure the solvency of their leagues—they must be able to control player movement for a certain period of time. With many players now making decisions on where to live based on non-monetary factors—like proximity to family, the playing surface a team uses, climate, and so forth, this argument is a bit questionable.

The current bilateral monopoly situation in sports has created a mutual interdependence between owners and players, where over a player's career he will receive payments close to his MRPL. Owners cannot underpay players forever, and the players cannot hold out for money in excess of their value.

Critics of this system believe that player movement has ruined sports because fans can no longer follow a player throughout his entire career with one team. It is also interesting to note that, on more than one occasion the owners of major league baseball franchises—and other sports—have told city leaders that a new, taxpayer financed, stadium would have to be built in order to keep the team profitable in today's economic climate. The owners have testified before Congress that baseball is a very unprofitable business to be in, all while refusing to open up the financial records of each team to public scrutiny.

The reality is that professional sports is an incredibly lucrative business to be in. When baseball commissioner Bud Selig told Congress that the owners lost $519 million in 2001, he did not address the fact that the Boston Red Sox had recently sold for $700 million and that in all the major sports, the annual appreciation of franchise values makes owning a team an incredible investment.[29]

The owners are also reluctant to tell the public that much of their day-to-day operations are tax write-offs, including private jet flights and player salaries! That's right. When a baseball player signs a contract for $100 million, the owner of the team is allowed to depreciate much of the value of the contract over time, just as if the player were a bulldozer or computer. The tax laws end up shielding the owners from the full financial burden of owning the team. When you combine this fact with the free stadiums many of them play in, you might find yourself in agreement with former Minnesota governor Jesse Ventura, who also testified before Congress on baseball economics and had this to say:

> Baseball wants us to build a park [for the Minnesota Twins] at public expense. Then they'll come back in five or eight years and say, "This isn't good enough either." If we build a library with public funds, we don't charge people to get in. If the public builds a stadium, the owner charges the public to get into their own stadium.
>
> The owners are not losing the money that they claim. If they were, they wouldn't be paying the salaries they are paying. It's asinine. These people did not get the wealth they have by being stupid.

The Twins got their new stadium in 2010.

It is worth addressing that at the time this chapter was being written, the National Football League was on the verge of a major work stoppage. In March 2011 the collective bargaining agreement between the players and owners expired. The owners wanted the new agreement to lower the percentage of total revenue the players receive and a new 18-game regular season schedule. The players wanted to keep the 16 game-season and their 59% revenue share. Millions of NFL fans waited anxiously for an agreement to take place because this bilateral monopoly does not afford us the opportunity to simply switch over to another high-quality football league to entertain us.

CAN A PERSON EVER BE OVERPAID?

If you have ever worked with a person with the work ethic of a slug, you would adamantly say yes, it is possible for someone to be paid more than their MRPL. However, this question is not meant to elicit examples of people not pulling their weight. Instead, economists want to know if an employer would ever face a labor market condition where a worker would be intentionally paid more than he or she is worth.

> It's like we're living in another galaxy. It seems so unreal that we would make this much.
>
> TOM CRUISE

By now you should have a pretty firm footing to help you explain how Mr. Cruise can get a $25 million paycheck for movies like *War of the Worlds.* With a huge demand for his services and only one Tom Cruise on the planet, the laws of supply and demand keep Mr. Cruise relatively happy. If Mr. Cruise were just some "regular" actor with little star appeal, he would make far less. None of us would turn down $25 million to do what we do for a living, so we can't even blame him when studio executives drop boatloads of cash in his lap.

What is a bit curious is the possibility that Mr. Cruise could be overpaid from time to time. It has nothing to do with the fact that some of his films fare poorly at the box office. It has to do with the fact that Mr. Cruise has a monopoly over his name, his looks, and his ability. However, there is not a monopsony situation that faces him when he seeks employment. There is far more than one studio competing for his services. When you have a labor market that is very competitive on the demand side of the equation, coupled with only one seller of some labor service, where does the prospective employee opt to work if they all offer a salary equal to his or her MRPL?

If Mr. Cruise is actually worth only $19 million per film—based on the revenue he specifically creates—why would any studio offer $25 million? It is because, in the bidding for his services, if all studios offer $19 million, no one studio has an advantage over the other. Someone is going to have to increase the offer in order to procure his talent for the next project. This means the studio is already $6 million in the hole before one ticket is purchased. How can this be overcome? All the executives have to do is make sure that Mr. Cruise works with a lot of underpaid actors and actresses!

You must understand that in Hollywood there is a dichotomized labor market. Stars have all of the market power. Struggling no-name performers have none. They face a monopsonistic situation. If a studio offers a young actress $50,000 to be in a film that also features Tom Cruise, would she turn it down? She may very well be worth $500,000 to this film, but for the chance to add a fi lm with a star of Cruise's magnitude to her resum;aae, she is not going to hold out for more money.[30]

ANOTHER WAY OF LOOKING AT IT

A final way to determine if you overpaid, underpaid, or paid what you are worth, is to simply examine whether the market is in equilibrium or not. If there is a surplus of labor, it is an indication that wages will have to fall to restore equilibrium and that current employees in that market are paid more than their MRPL.[31] If there is a shortage of labor, it is an indication that wages or salaries will have to increase to reach equilibrium and workers are currently paid less than their MRPL. Such has been the recent case for nurses and airline mechanics.[32] If an equilibrium condition exists (indicated by stable wages or salaries), workers are being paid equal to—or very close to—their MRPL.

OTHER PAY ISSUES

OK, so we have seen that the perception that athletes and actors are overpaid is not necessarily so. However, we have not addressed the issue of whether people who make a lot in the labor market would actually keep working even if their pay were cut—even dramatically cut. This question is part of the economics of labor markets that examines *reservation wages.*

A reservation wage is the lowest wage an individual would be willing to work for in any given market before he or she would opt out of that market.

SUGGESTED CLASSROOM DEBATE

The President of the United States receives a salary of $400,000 per year. Would it be good for the country if the salary was $40 million per year? Why, or why not?

People like the Tampa Bay Buccaneers' Mike Alstott—a former running back—have found that it is often better to take a pay cut than to lose their job and be forced out of the league or to a new team in a city that represents their second-best choice. Mr. Alstott agreed to pass up a $2 million bonus he was set to receive in April of 2002. He passed up the bonus when he was informed that it was either that choice or be cut from the team. To Alstott, the decision was not as tough as one might think. "When you build something with the teammates you have, the core teammates, you don't want to leave. . . . It's tough to leave. I know it's a business; there's a business side to football and sometimes there's change. But for me to stay here . . . it is an honor."

EFFICIENCY WAGES

Suppose your boss approached you today and said, "I fully realize that the market equilibrium wage rate for your particular job is $10 per hour, but I would like to pay you $11.32 per hour and offer you a free membership to the local health club of your choice." After you emerged from your coma, what would you think about such an offer? After all, if we recall the lessons of Adam Smith, why should your boss pay you more than the market requires? Because maybe he or she did think about Adam Smith and reached the conclusion that paying you an "efficiency wage" would make you *more efficient.*

Efficiency wages are above-market wages designed to increase productivity, reduce employee-monitoring costs, and reduce shirking by employees.

The efficiency wage theory is fairly new to the labor economics literature, although there is a lot of research on this issue.[33] The research finds that employers offer up efficiency wages largely to improve workers' morale in order to reduce absenteeism and labor turnover. It is also done in order to improve the quality of recruitment when quality cannot be directly observed, improve work effort, improve the perception of "fairness" in the labor market, and reduce the costs of monitoring worker effort.

The idea is that, if your employer pays you more than you know the market would suggest, you will be grateful, improving your morale and therefore your productivity. All of this should lead to lower costs of production for your employer, as turnover rates fall and effort rises. The costs of checking up on people should fall as well, since workers getting paid more will not want to lose their jobs.

Why don't all firms pay efficiency wages? From the employee's perspective it seems to make perfect sense—pay me more and I will give you more.

However, the real question is: *How much more* will you give? What if your pay increased by 22% but your productivity increased by 4%? This would

CONCEPT CHECK

What is your reservation wage at your current job?

Photo courtesy Jack Chambless

translate into higher average variable costs of production for your employer and potential economic losses and even bankruptcy if worker productivity did not increase much across the board.

There is the very real possibility that, for many workers, productivity could fall even after the pay hike. After all, if a person sees an increase in pay for no obvious reasons, but rather the hope that productivity will rise, what incentive does the worker have to work harder? In fact, some might be absent more often or shirk their responsibilities with greater frequency since they are making more money without being first required to improve productivity. There is a reason why, in most labor markets, higher productivity precedes higher pay. Efficiency wages constitutes a risky venture that requires a lot of trust—a trust that may or may not be well founded.

CONCEPT CHECK

When George Vanderbilt set out to construct and maintain the Biltmore House in Asheville, North Carolina, he paid his construction workers and servants a wage that was far greater than the local labor market dictated. Was this a rational strategy?

THE "LIVING WAGE" MOVEMENT

What do Ben Affleck, Jesse Jackson, and the musical group *Rage Against the Machine* have in common? If you say, "They are all rich!" then you are right. If you said, "They all care about janitors at Harvard!" you are right again. If you said, "They need a refresher course on supply and demand!" then you are a genius.

Over the past several years, a movement has spread across America that calls for government to impose city-by-city "living wages" on America's businesses.[34]

> A living wage is a wage that would be sufficient for an individual to be able to afford food, clothing, and shelter in the city in which the individual resides.

This sounds like a great idea, and certainly no economist wants to see people earning pennies per hour before they return "home" to their box under the bridge and their roasted rat dinner. The question for you, the student, is how many labor markets like this are out there, at least in the United States? What market exists where people earn so little money that they are homeless, malnourished, and barely clothed at the end of the day? If you remember the material on reservation wages, you will be able to see the first of many economic flaws in the logic of the living wage movement.

If being on welfare—or even being homeless and panhandling for money—pays more per hour than work, the rational person lacking in skills, education, and training will opt for the more lucrative alternative of avoiding work. How could any business find enough people to carry out day-to-day operations if the business offered $.08 per hour? Very few (no one?) would work for that.

According to Affleck, Reverend Jackson, and others, Harvard University was exploiting the custodial staff by paying less than $10.25 per hour to keep the buildings clean. Reverend Jackson and others recently called upon Harvard to do the "decent" thing and increase the pay rate to a level where custodial staff could earn a dignifying wage that would allow them to have the basic necessities of life.

Maybe Jesse and Ben never took an economics class, but perhaps they should. According to labor economists at the Employment Policies Institute, an artificial increase in the wage rate for the most unskilled Americans would have two harmful effects on those very people Ben and Jesse want to help. First, much like the minimum wage, a forced creation of a living wage would push wages to a level where many janitors would find themselves unemployed and many Harvard kids would find dirtier bathrooms. The second problem is that employers, facing higher wages, would opt to look for people with higher skills to fill those jobs.

Let's say someone in Cambridge is making $9.22 per hour working at a local copier business while the custodians are earning $8.04 per hour. If the living wage is pushed to $10.25, employers are going to want to get more productivity for the extra pay. The person at the copier shop might be responsible not only for fixing copiers but also cleaning the store at night. Harvard might opt to hire someone who can serve the functions not only of a custodian but could also help professors teaching at night who have found the copiers jammed. The result? The custodians who were earning $8.04 per hour would now earn $0 per hour as a result of the misguided efforts of busybody actors and politicians.

Maybe Ben, Jesse, and the rest of this wealthy crowd could help their cause by donating half their annual pay to Harvard custodians. That would push the wage rate to *well above* $10.25 per hour.

NONPECUNIARY WAGES AND COMPENSATING WAGE DIFFERENTIALS

For most of us, money is not the only thing that influences our career choices. For some people flexible scheduling or on-site day care might be important. There is also the concern of how dangerous or distasteful certain work requirements might be. All of these are examples of nonpecuniary wages.

> Nonpecuniary wages are the non-monetary benefits or costs of any particular job that must be added to or subtracted from money wages to obtain total compensation per hour of work.

When nonpecuniary wages exist, it has been observed that some compensating wage differential will also be present.

> Compensating wage differential is a difference in money wages necessary to make total compensation for similar jobs equal when nonpecuniary wages are not equal to zero.

PARK RANGERS AND FIREFIGHTERS—WHO IS BETTER OFF?

If you are ever traveling through southern Montana, you would be well advised to stop at the Little Bighorn National Monument to watch Kurt Brockmann work.

Mr. Brockmann, a native of New Mexico, is a ranger with the National Park Service whose job it is to provide a description of the events that led up to General George Custer's demise at the hand of the Sioux and Northern Cheyenne Indians on June 25, 1876.

Mr. Brockmann provides one of the most entertaining and intellectually stimulating historical accounts of this event that a person could ever hope to hear. As a graduate of the University of New Mexico with a degree in history, Mr. Brockmann could easily earn thousands of dollars a year more than the $9.33–$10.95 per hour that seasonal rangers received when I spoke with him. Why doesn't he bolt for greener pastures? "Because I love the job and money cannot buy the things that are truly important in life," was his response to this question.

This is a classic sentiment of someone who places a great deal of non-monetary value on a job. The sheer joy of doing his job so well, being outdoors, meeting new people, and being a part of history each and every day, carry significant positive nonpecuniary wages. The problem is that the National Park Service is fully aware that park rangers have these psychological benefits stemming from their jobs with the NPS.

Therefore, the NPS does not need to pay Mr. Brockmann a salary that is commensurate with the money he could command in the private sector. The NPS knows that less can be offered, and there will still be plenty of people willing to work at the Little Bighorn National Monument. When positive nonpecuniary wages exist, a negative compensating wage differential will be present in order to make the total compensation of a job equal to that of others where nonpecuniary wages are not present. In essence, Kurt Brockmann is paying for the *psychological benefits* he receives in the form of reduced monetary compensation.[35]

What if nonpecuniary wages are negative?

After September 11th we heard countless stories of incredible heroism displayed by firefighters in New York City. For months that followed the collapse of the World Trade Center, people argued that firefighters and police officers—the "real heroes" of America—deserve more recognition and more money.

How much more? Firefighters in some markets make a great deal of money. The men and women who put out oil-well fires after the Persian Gulf War were paid a lot. Firefighters who work on oil rigs earn a great deal of money, too.

One reason some firefighters make more money than others do, is the severe negative nonpecuniary wages that they deal with on many days. Sure, there might be many days where there's not much more to do than train, wash the fire trucks, and exercise. But when the call comes to go into a place just hit by two fuel-filled jet airplanes, and then climb as many as 110 stories to save people, the stress of this job can be overwhelming.

Because of the enormously high odds of dying in the line of duty, firefighters in places like New York earn more money on average than firefighters in smaller towns that have few buildings, no skyscrapers, and virtually no chance of being bombed by terrorists. In New York, therefore, a positive compensating wage differential is paid to firefighters to help offset the negative nonpecuniary wages. If positive compensating wage differentials were not paid, there would not only be a shortage of firefighters but a lot more buildings burning to the ground in New York City.

CONCEPT CHECK

According to economists who study labor markets, working in a toll booth, as a coal miner, or cowboy puts you in some of the worst jobs in America.[36] Why might this be the case? In which of these three occupations would you argue that economists might have missed some of the nonpecuniary wages that might make the job one of the better ones a person could have?

ENDNOTES

[1]Personal training is not the only area where senior citizens are expected to be demanding more. See "Marketing Surprise: Older Consumers Buy Stuff, Too" by Kelly Greene, *The Wall Street Journal,* April 6, 2004.

[2]See "Low-Wage Costa Ricans Make Baseballs for Millionaires" by Tim Weiner, *The New York Times,* January 25, 2004.

[3]Interview with Cal Ripken Jr., former third baseman for the Baltimore Orioles, *Sports Illustrated,* April 24, 2000.

[4]Source: Florida Center of Political History and Governance, Tallahassee, Florida.

[5]Source: Bureau of Labor Statistics http://www.bls.gov/news.release/union2.nr0.htm.

[6]See "Farm Union Takes Aim at a Big Pickle Maker" by Somini Sengupta, *The New York Times,* October 26, 2000.

[7]See "The War on Wal-Mart" by Steven Malanga, *The Wall Street Journal,* April 7, 2004, page A18.

[8]See "Unions Aim to Share in the Success of Reality TV" by Jim Rendon, *The New York Times,* January 25, 2004.

[9]See "Auto Workers of the World Unite . . ." by John B. Schnapp, *The Wall Street Journal,* January 25, 2006.

[10]Source: *The Economist,* February 22, 2007.

[11]See "Weak Unions Create a Strong Economy" by Bradley R. Schiller, *The Wall Street Journal,* February 19, 2002.

[12]See "It Takes a Recession," *The Wall Street Journal,* June 16–17, 2007.

[13]See "The Right Way to Raise Wages" by Lee E. O' Hanian, *The Wall Street Journal,* July 8, 2010.

[14]See "The Hidden Cost of Labor Strife" by David Wessel, *The Wall Street Journal,* January 10, 2002; and "Labor Disputes Can be Deadly for Consumers," *The New York Times Magazine,* December 14, 2003.

[15]See "Putting a Price on Professors" by Stephanie Simon and Stephanie Banchero, *The Wall Street Journal,* October 23–24, 2010, p. C1.

[16]See "Stay-at-Home Salary: $131,471" by Pamela Yip, *The Orlando Sentinel* (from *The Dallas Morning News*), Febuary 5, 2006.

[17]See "Do Pretty-Boy Quarterbacks Make More Money?" by David J. Berri, *The New York Times,* September 14, 2008.

[18]See "Are CEOs Worth Their Weight in Gold?" *The Wall Street Journal,* January 21–22, 2006, p. A7.

[19]See "Alabama's Mercedes deal led to jobs, ill will" by Christopher Boyd, *The Orlando Sentinel,* October 19, 2003, p. A16.

[20]Many economists who study sports argue that the NCAA uses its power to restrict the earnings of college athletes. This is one reason why some athletes seek to leave college early for the riches of professional sports. See "Free at Last" by Sam Walker, *The Wall Street Journal,* February 13, 2004, p. W6.

[21]See "Seniority and Monopsony in the Academic Labor Market" by Michael R. Ransom, *The American Economic Review,* March 1993.

[22]See "Truckers From Down Under Find Themselves in Legal Limbo" by Carlos Tejada, *The Wall Street Journal,* April 11, 2000.

[23]See "City-Slicker CEO Finds Fun, Profit Home on the Range in North Dakota" by Susan Carey, *The Wall Street Journal,* April 10, 2000.

[24]See "Degrees of Academia" by Christina Nifong, *The Raleigh News & Observer,* September 22, 1999.

[25]See "Title VII and the Reserve Clause: A Statistical Analysis of Salary Discrimination in Major League Baseball" by Jack F. Williams and Jack A. Chambless, *The University of Miami Law Review,* Volume 52, Number 2, January 1998.

[26]See "Labor Relations in Professional Sports: Lessons in Collective Bargaining" by Robert A. McCormick, *Employee Relations Law Journal* 14, 501, 502 (1989).

[27]See *Federal Baseball Club of Baltimore v. National League of Professional Baseball Clubs,* 259 U.S. 200 (1922).

[28]See "Why the NFL Draft Drives Economists Crazy" by Reed Albergotti, *The Wall Street Journal,* April 22, 2010, p. D8.

[29]See "Artful Dodging" by Peter Keating, *ESPN Magazine,* January 7, 2002, p. 93.

[30]For more on compensation issues in Hollywood, see "The new age of greed" by Josh Rottenberg, *Entertainment Weekly,* April 22, 2005.

[31]See "Getting a Job in the Valley is Easy, if You're Perfect" by Matt Richtel and Laurie J. Flynn, *The New York Times,* November 19, 2003, p. C1.

[32]See "Airlines Find Good Mechanics in Short Supply" by Susan Carey, *The Wall Street Journal,* May 10, 2001.

[33]For some of this research, see www.bath.ac.uk/;slhssdac/macro-2001-2/macro-2001-2-week5-efficiency-wages.htm and greywww.kub.nl:2080/greyfiles/center/1995/doc/31.pdf.

[34]See "Effort mounts for 'living wage'" by Jason Garcia, *The Orlando Sentinel,* April 11, 2005.

[35]These benefits can also take the form of job security, health care benefits, family leave, and more. Studies show that nonmonetary benefits are increasingly important to U.S. workers. See "The Wages of Prosperity" by Stephen Moore, *The Wall Street Journal,* August 29, 2005, p. A9.

[36]See "Working in a Toll Booth is All Change, and None" by Jared Sandberg, *The Wall Street Journal,* April 9, 2003; "Despite dangers, miners keep going underground" by Jay Reeves, *The Orlando Sentinel,* January 8, 2006; and "Cowboy as a Career?" by Perri Capell, *The Wall Street Journal,* June 14, 2005.

Name ________________________________ Date ________________

CHAPTER REVIEW

1. Why do underwater welders make more money than people who feed gorillas at a zoo? Use two graphs to assist your answer.

2. What is the marginal revenue product of labor? How could an economist use this concept to evaluate the worth of a hairdresser? Could it be used to evaluate the worth of a preacher at a church? Why, or why not?

3. When Lou Gehrig played baseball for the New York Yankees, he was underpaid every year of his career. Why?

4. What is good and bad (economically speaking) about labor unions?

5. Where do nonpecuniary wages enter into the earnings of lifeguards, nature photographers, and military snipers?

The Market of Public Goods

OBJECTIVES

- Explain the difference between public and private goods.
- Define the method for determining an optimal public good.
- Learn the meaning of "externalities" and understand their implications for markets.
- Understand the concept of "Coase Theorem."
- Explain the meaning of "market failure."

■ ■ ■

Recently, the financial industry saw its worst crisis in many decades. The financial industry was operating in a competitive market where it did a good job in allocating scarce resources efficiently. However, some markets may have been at a disadvantage, courtesy of deregulation, which caused distortions in the financial markets that eventually led to the current economic crisis. Today, the government plays a major role in making sure that the financial industry returns to its normal efficiencies. When private markets fail, there is an economic role for the public sector. In this chapter, we will examine that role as it relates to public goods, and also its effects, such as externalities. We will also see the negative effects of too much government, fear of which can hinder the role of government in its economic recovery efforts.

PRIVATE VERSUS PUBLIC GOODS

Most goods produced and sold in competitive markets are considered to be private goods. Private goods include all goods offered and sold in the malls and stores near you, including cars, clothing, TVs, shoes, food, and so on. Private goods are defined as goods that have two characteristics: rivalry and excludability. Rivalry means that one person purchasing and consuming a given commodity precludes another person from buying and consuming that same commodity. For example, if Steve buys a whole pizza, then it will not be available for purchase and consumption by John. Excludability means that sellers can keep people who do not pay for a commodity from benefiting from it. Thus, only people who can afford to pay for a certain product can obtain that commodity.

Public goods, on the other hand, are commodities that are non-rival and non-excludable. Non-rivalry means that one person's consumption of a good does not preclude consumption of the good by others. Everyone can simultaneously obtain the benefit from public goods such as roads, bridges, street lighting, and national parks. Non-excludability means that there is no effective way of excluding individuals from the benefit of the good once it becomes available. One problem with public goods is the creation of a "free-rider" problem. Once the product is available as a public good, nobody can be excluded from enjoying the product, even people who could not otherwise afford it. Thus, people have no incentive to pay for these products since they are available and are free.

Free-ridership is a big issue, especially in terms of health care. There are proponents for offering a universal health care policy. Basically this means that the government would be responsible for providing health care services to everyone in the country. This would make health care a public good: a non-rival good because one person's consumption of health care services would not preclude the consumption of health care services by another person; and non-excludable because health care services could not denied to anyone. The problem with providing health care services as a public good is the free-ridership problem. Not everyone can pay the fees demanded by health care services, so the government could only finance these services through expanded taxation policies.

OPTIMAL PUBLIC GOOD

In the case of public goods, consumers need not reveal the true demand in the marketplace. But the question that the government sector is faced with is the issue of how much quantity of a public good is needed in order to avoid any surplus or shortage. The government has to estimate the demand for a public good through primary data (i.e., public surveys or questionnaires). The criterion for the optimal demand for public good is to compare the marginal benefit of an incremental unit of commodity against the marginal cost incurred in providing it. Thus, the criterion can be summarized as follows:

Marginal Benefit = Marginal Cost

Another way of interpreting this criterion is the **cost-benefit analysis.** A cost-benefit analysis is simply a comparison of marginal costs and marginal benefits of a given proposed project, in this case by the government.

A good example of this analysis can be applied to the recent fiscal stimulus package implemented by the Obama administration. The purpose of this fiscal stimulus package is to revive the economy through infrastructure and public works. Because the economy's resources are limited, any decision to use more resources in the public sector means fewer resources for the private sector. For a government project to be optimal, we compare the marginal benefit and the marginal cost of providing that project. Cost-benefit analysis can indicate more than whether a public project is worth doing. It can also help the government decide on the extent to which a project should be pursued, in other words, how big or small the project should be.

EXTERNALITIES

In a competitive market, we assume that the benefits and costs of a commodity are fully reflected in the market. There are some markets, however, where the benefits or costs may be implicit to the buyer or the seller. The costs and/or the benefits of a good that are passed on to a third party in a given market are called **externalities.** An externality is an external benefit or cost that accrues to a party that is not directly related to the buyer or seller in a market transaction.

NEGATIVE EXTERNALITIES

Negative externalities are costs inflicted on a third party without compensation. The most common example of a negative externality is pollution. When a manufacturing firm dumps its waste in a lake or an oil company pollutes the air with smoke, people who live in and around the area suffer negative externalities. Community residents who live around the lake or around the factory may suffer health problems related to the externality, but the company that polluted the lake or air does not compensate the residents of the area. Therefore, the cost of health care services due to the environmental pollution is borne by the community residents.

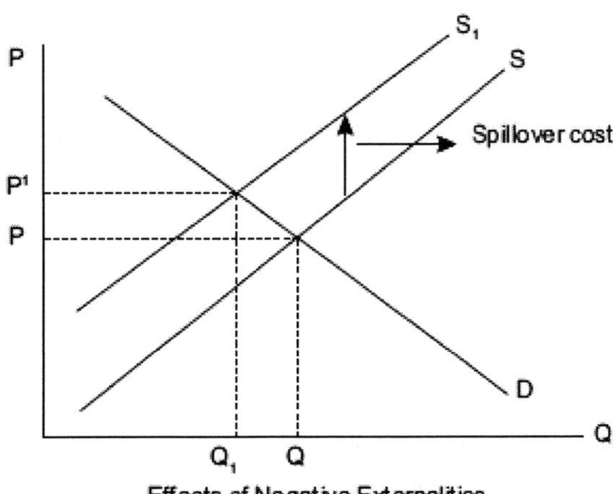

Effects of Negative Externalities

The figure above illustrates the implications of negative externalities. When a producer shifts some of its spillover cost onto the resident community, the marginal cost is lower. This is showed by the supply curve S. However, this supply curve does not reflect all of the cost incurred in the production. Factoring the effects of the spillover costs or negative externalities, the supply curve should be at S_1. Thus, the optimal output should be at Q_1.

POSITIVE EXTERNALITIES

Spillover effects can also be positive in nature. The production or consumption of a commodity may have positive spillover, or external benefits, on a third party not involved in the given market transaction. Education is a classic example of a **positive externality.** Education benefits individual people. Higher education means that people are better informed and can allocate resources more efficiently. Better-educated people can also mean higher income for the community. Furthermore, education reduces other social costs such as crime, regulations, and welfare programs.

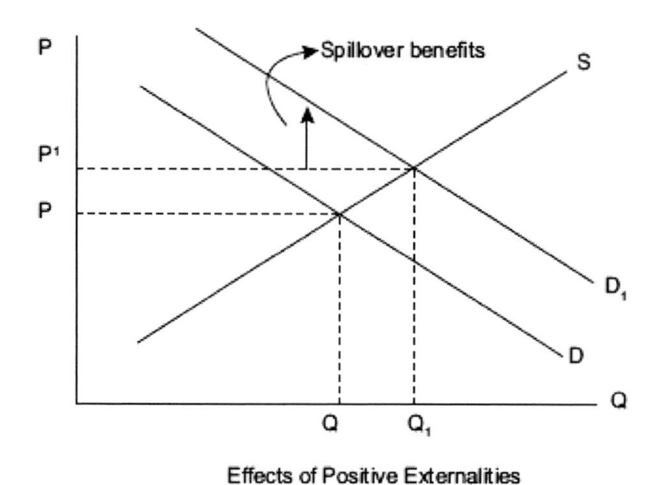

Effects of Positive Externalities

The figure on next page shows the effects of positive externalities on resource allocation. When positive externalities occur, the demand curve lies to the left of the optimal demand curve. The initial demand, D, does not include the spillover benefits or positive externalities. With positive externalities, the full-benefits demand curve is D_1. With education, the positive externalities increase the full-benefits demand to a higher level. More educated people means that people are well informed about the market and have a higher income. Therefore, the demand increases to D_1.

COASE THEOREM

Economists have suggested several solutions to the problems of negative and positive externalities. In some instances, market solutions can still occur as a result of these externalities. However, when markets fail, only some form of government intervention can solve these problems.

One form of market solution is the Coase Theorem. This was formulated by the great Nobel Prize—winning economist Ronald Coase at the University of Chicago. According to his theory, government is not needed to provide a solution for externalities where: (a) property ownership is clearly defined; (b) the number of people involved is small; and (c) bargaining costs are insignificant. Under this situation, the government should limit its role to making sure that the bargaining process is still efficient between the parties involved. Property rights place a tag on an externality, creating opportunity costs for all parties. The bargaining process can be a mutually beneficial solution to the externality problem, especially if the economic interests of the parties are at stake.

Property rights can often affect the incentive to produce or to reduce pollution. One way of thinking about the problem of pollution and property rights is that in unregulated markets, no one has a property right to clean air. If nobody has a property right to clean air, then nobody needs to compensate you for infringing on your property right to clean air. If you have a property right to your land, somebody cannot come onto your front yard and dump garbage because you own that property. But you do not own the air over your property in the same sense. If you had property rights that were clear and enforceable, then one party or another would have the appropriate incentives to avoid creating the negative externality of pollution. So, let us think about how you might have property rights that could be used in a way to avoid getting the dirty air.

Coase said that what you want to do is to think about a train that goes past a farmer's field, and that train is emitting sparks. Sometimes, the parks start a fire in the farmer's field. So, we want to think about this as an example of pollution. The train is emitting sparks; the farmer's field is burning. How do we figure out a way to deal with this through property rights? We can approach this in two different ways. First we could say, "Look, a train has a property right to emit sparks, in which case, farmer, it is up to you to figure out how to reduce the chance of fire starting in your field." Alternatively, we could say, "Look, farmers, you have a property right not to have your field set on fire by sparks from the train, in which case the railroad has to find a way to reduce the chance of fire or else pay the farmer when fires break out." Whether you give the property right to the railroad and let it emit sparks or you give the property right to the farmer and say he or she is protected from the emission of sparks determines who has to pay. But, either way, if the property right is clear, then one party has a reason to find a way to reduce the chance of fire, preferably a low-cost method.

When the property rights are clear, often there will be some reason to try to prevent pollution from happening. A classic example is the ownership of federal lands. Oftentimes no one really owns federal lands, so they end up being abused for recreational, logging, hunting, or other purposes. No one has a reason, in terms of property rights, to protect them.

MARKET FAILURE AND GOVERNMENT INTERVENTION

Market failure occurs when the competitive market system does not allocate any resources whatsoever to the production of certain goods, or either under-allocates or over-allocates resources to the production of certain goods. When a market fails, an economic role for the government sector arises.

The role of the government is not an easy task, especially in performing its economic function. Governments should set the rules and regulations, redistributing income when desirable and stabilizing the economy, especially if there are shocks in the market, as there were in the recent financial crisis. The economic role of the government is defined in the context of its leadership's political perspective.

A good example of market failure is the health care industry in the United States. The U.S. health care market can be characterized by rising prices of health care services in general. If we look closely in terms of the demand and supply for health care, there are a lot of factors that can be attributed to causing these rising prices. From the supply side, resources are fixed and do not adjust to the market efficiently because these resources are heavily regulated. For example, doctors need to get training for a minimum of ten years before they can even practice as a medical resident intern. The cost of training is prohibitive, and licensure is based on the rigorous American Medical Association criteria. From the demand side, the demand for health care services is ever increasing thanks to an aging baby boomer population and an increase in the general population. Because of these distortions, market prices for health care services are increasing and are sometimes unaffordable for a typical middle-income person. One governmental policy suggestion to remedy this is the call for a universal health care system. This means that the government would be responsible for offering the service to the public. This is an example in which government can intervene in order to allocate the resources more efficiently than the private market does.

From a political perspective, public goods such as health care services are sometimes produced not because their benefits exceed their costs, but because their benefits accrue to firms located in states served by powerful elected officials. The result of such situations is market inefficiencies because of the lack of an incentive to hold down costs. The failure of programs to achieve their goals may lead to huge costs. Furthermore, policies to correct negative externalities such as these can be blocked politically by the very parties whose decisions produced the externalities.

REFERENCES

Council of Economic Advisers, "Chapter 9: Protecting the Environment," in *Economic Report of the President,* February 2004.

"The Global Environment: The Great Race," *The Economist,* July 4, 2002.

Asch, Peter, and Gary A. Gigliotti, "The Free-Rider Paradox—Theory, Evidence and Teaching," *Journal of Economic Education,* Winter 1991, pp. 33–38.

Coase, R. H., "The Lighthouse of Economics," *Journal of Law and Economics,* October 1974, pp. 374–376.

Name ______________________ Date ______________

Chapter 11

DEFINITIONS

1. Market failure
2. Private goods
3. Public goods
4. Coase Theorem
5. Negative externalities
6. Positive externalities
7. Externalities
8. Cost-benefit analysis
9. Non-rival goods
10. Non-excludable goods

MULTIPLE CHOICE

1. An externality is
   a. an overall cost to a society of producing an additional output of goods and services.
   b. the amount of dollars that a consumer pays to consume a given commodity.
   c. a cost or benefit borne by a third party not involved in a given market transaction.
   d. a problem intrinsic in private goods.
2. Air pollution is an example of
   a. a negative externality.
   b. a moral hazard.
   c. adverse selection.
   d. a positive externality.

3. Education is an example of
   a. a positive externality.
   b. a negative externality.
   c. a moral hazard.
   d. adverse selection.
4. A firm that is overproducing or under producing in a given market is an example of a(n)
   a. externality.
   b. public good.
   c. market failure.
   d. moral hazard.
5. The Coase Theorem states that
   a. under some conditions, private parties can agree on a solution without government intervention.
   b. the public sector will fail to produce an efficient amount of public goods.
   c. if there are external costs in production, government must intervene in the market.
   d. the public good should be produced when marginal costequals marginal benefit.
6. The Coase Theorem will only apply if
   a. the courts can be used to determine the amount of damages given to a party.
   b. the amount of compensation is small enough.
   c. the number of people involved is small enough.
   d. an individual who is not affected by the externality can negotiate a settlement.
7. If the production of a good generates external benefits, the government could increase efficiency by
   a. regulating the sale of the product.
   b. mandating licensing for the production of the commodity.
   c. subsidizing production of the good to increase the amount produced.
   d. taxing the production of the commodity.
8. Public goods are
   a. rival in production and their benefits are non-excludable.
   b. non-rival in consumption and non-excludable in benefits.
   c. rival in consumption and their benefits are non-excludable.
   d. rival in consumption and benefits.
9. If one person's enjoyment of the benefits of a commodity does not interfere with another's consumption of it, the good is said to be
   a. non-rival.
   b. non-excludable.
   c. rival.
   d. excludable.
10. The free-rider problem arises when
    a. government produces a good.
    b. there is a shortage of the product.
    c. people realize they will still receive the benefits of a good whether they pay or not.
    d. there is a surplus of the product.

Gross Domestic Product

What is gross domestic product? Why is the calculation important? In this chapter you will:

- Define GDP
- Calculate GDP using expenditure approach
- Calculate GDP using income approach
- Calculate net domestic product, national income, personal income, and disposable income
- Calculate real GDP
- Examine items not included in the calculation of GDP

■ ■ ■

Gross domestic product is the market value of final goods and services produced in a country in a given period. A final good is a new good (new car, new refrigerator). An intermediate good is a good produced by one firm and purchased by another firm. The good is then used on the final good or service. For example, a BMW is a final good. The Firestone tires on the BMW are considered an intermediate good. The computation of GDP only includes final goods and services. The inclusion of intermediate goods would overstate the value of GDP.

EXPENDITURE APPROACH

The two ways to compute GDP are the expenditure approach and income approach. The expenditure approach considers spending of consumers, businesses, the government, and individuals in foreign countries. Let's examine each component.

Personal Consumption Expenditures: Purchases of goods and services made by households. Goods are classified as nondurable and durable. Durable goods last more than three years. Cars, refrigerators, or washing machines are examples of durable goods. Nondurable goods last less than three years. Food and clothing are examples of nondurable goods. Services are provided by lawyers, doctors, and educators.

Gross Investment. Firms purchase equipment for the purpose of producing goods and services. Purchasing equipment for the business is known as investments. Firms must consider additions to inventory as an investment. Suppose Andrew's Wood Company produced 900 tables in June. If Andrew only sold 800 tables, he will add 100 to his inventory. The 100 unsold tables are now considered an investment.

Gross investment includes purchases of new equipment (capital) and depreciation. Net investment includes the new capital only (gross investment minus depreciation). Depreciation is the wear and tear of capital; it causes the equipment to lose value. The calculation of GDP includes gross investment.

Government Purchases. The government purchases goods and services from firms. Government expenditures fall under two categories: expenditures for public services and expenditures for privately owned capital.

Net Exports. The calculation of GDP includes purchases made by individuals in countries outside of the United States. Net Exports equals exports minus imports. The United States exports when goods are sent to other countries. Importing occurs when the United States receives goods from other countries.

Calculation. Gross domestic product equals personal consumption expenditures plus gross investment plus government purchases plus net exports. $C + Ig + G + Nx$.

INCOME APPROACH

The income approach measures the income of firms and households. Let's first consider the first half of the income approach. National income includes several categories:

- Compensation of employees
- Proprietor's income
- Rent
- Interest
- Corporate profits
- Indirect business taxes

Compensation of employees includes the wages households receive as take home pay. It also includes taxes withheld and fringe benefits. Proprietor's income is the income earned by business owners, partnerships, and unincorporated businesses. Rent is the payments received for the use of land. Rent payments include the money landlords receive for leased property and money received from leased office space. Interest includes the amount of money households receive on certificates of deposit and savings accounts. Interest also includes the amount suppliers of loans receive in addition to the principal amount. Corporate profits are the profits paid to consumers in the form of dividends. Corporate income taxes and undistributed corporate profits are two additional categories of corporate profits. Indirect business taxes include excise taxes, property taxes, and sales taxes.

Compensation of employees, proprietor's income, rent, interest, corporate profits, and indirect business taxes make up national income. Now let's consider a few more accounts needed to arrive at GDP using the income approach.

Net Foreign Income. GDP only considers income generated domestically. National income includes money made by Americans in the United States and foreign countries. We must subtract the income of Americans made in other countries from national income.

Consumption of Fixed Capital. As you learned before, consumption of fixed capital is known as depreciation. Depreciation is a cost of production considered in the computation of GDP.

Statistical Discrepancy. The expenditure and income approach must equal. At times, a discrepancy may occur. To offset the discrepancy, NIPA accountants use a number known as statistical discrepancy to equalize both approaches.

Personal Consumption Expenditures	283	Corporate Profits	48
Compensation of Employees	240	Dividends	15
Net Investment	128	Transfer Payments	15
Rent	15	Social Security Contributions	40
Interest	13	Net Foreign Factor Income	10
Exports	25	Undistributed Corporate Profits	13
Proprietor's Income	56	Government Purchases	68
Indirect Business Taxes	30	Corporate Income Taxes	20
Imports	20	Statistical Discrepancy	92
Consumption of Fixed Capital	36	Personal taxes	30

Expenditure Approach		Income Approach	
Personal Consumption Expenditures	283	Compensation of Employees	240
Government Purchases	68	Proprietor's Income	56
Gross Investment	164	Rent	15
Net Exports	+ 5	Interest	13
GDP	**520**	Corporate Profits	48
		Indirect Business taxes	+30
		National Income	402
		−Net Foreign Income	−10
		+Consumption of Fixed capital	+36
		+Statistical Discrepancy	+96
		GDP	**520**

FROM GDP TO NDP

Net domestic product subtracts depreciation from GDP. NDP is useful because it considers the new output available for consumption and any additions to the stock of capital.

GDP − consumption of fixed capital = NDP
520 − 36 = 484

FROM NDP TO NATIONAL INCOME

As demonstrated before, national income equals compensation of employees plus proprietors income plus rent plus interest plus corporate profits plus indirect business taxes. If net domestic product is known, simply subtract the statistical discrepancy from NDP and add net foreign income.

NI = NDP − statistical discrepancy + net foreign income
484 − 92 + 10 = 402

FROM NATIONAL INCOME TO PERSONAL INCOME

The income received by households is known as personal income. Personal income includes transfer payments. Transfer payments are payments households receive from the government, which include unemployment compensation and social security payments received by retired or disabled individuals. Personal income excludes earnings made by corporations.

PI = NI − SS contributions-indirect business taxes-corporate taxes-undistributed corporate profits + transfer payments
402 − 30 − 40 − 20 − 13 + 15 = 314

FROM PERSONAL INCOME TO DISPOSABLE INCOME

Disposable income is personal income minus any personal taxes paid by households.

DI = PI − personal taxes
314 − 30 = 284

NOMINAL AND REAL GDP

GDP measures the market value of final goods and services produced in a given time period within a country. Nominal GDP does not consider inflation. To account for inflation, we must convert nominal GDP to real GDP.

Real GDP = Nominal GDP/price level

The price level is a measure of the average prices of goods and services. The GDP deflator is a type of price level.

GDP Deflator = (nominal GDP/Real GDP)*100

CALCULATING REAL GDP

Year	Nominal GDP	Price Level	Real GDP
2010	550	1.25	440
2011	680	1.15	591.30

ITEMS NOT INCLUDED IN GDP

GDP is not a perfect measure. The calculation of GDP excludes the following:

- Financial transactions
- Underground economy
- Leisure time

Financial transactions. Trading on the stock market does not affect GDP.

Underground Economy. The underground economy consists of activities hidden from the government. Underground economic activities include illegal drug production and paying employees under the table. Individuals participating in the underground economy do not pay taxes on the illegal activities.

Leisure time. Individuals participate in a number of activities during free time. Leisure time activities help decrease the amount of stress individuals may experience. Leisure time contributes to economic welfare; however, it does not contribute to GDP.

Economic Growth Unveiled

LEARNING OUTCOMES

By the end of this chapter, you will be able to:

- Discuss the importance of the slope of demand-based growth strategies.
- Identify sources of economic growth, which are the factors that can shift the aggregate supply curve and improve productivity.
- Describe how growth in the labor force affects economic growth.
- Understand the supply-side policies relating to taxes, transfers, and regulation.

INTRODUCTION

Imagine it is 2010 and you have just graduated with a degree in management. Considering that the United States is slowly recovering from a 2-year recession and the global economic crisis is also at play, job prospects for the average high school or college graduate

are dismal. The class of 2010 had some of the worst experience in trying to land jobs related to their education since the class of 1981 walked off campus 31 years earlier into 9% unemployment. The Great Recession of 2007–2009 was much less severe, but recovery of the job market has been slow. What happened to the "good old days" when a college diploma from a respectable college combined with reasonably good grades was a ticket to a good job? Will those days ever return?

Jobs are closely linked to economic growth. In the United States and most other industrial nations, economic growth during the last few decades has been rather uneven, averaging 2.5% in the 1980s and slowing down to a crawl (0.7%) in 1990–1992. From 2000 to 2007, growth averaged 2.7%, before turning negative in 2008. In 2010, real gross domestic product (GDP) bounced back to 2.4%. In this chapter, we will examine the causes of economic growth and policies to encourage growth.

PRE-TEST

1. The real business cycle is caused by random shocks to the aggregate demand curve.
   a. True
   b. False
2. Productivity will increase with an increase in the quantity of capital.
   a. True
   b. False
3. Spending on education and training can be compared to investment in machinery and equipment.
   a. True
   b. False
4. The United States does not have an industrial policy.
   a. True
   b. False

Answers

1. b. False. *The answer can be found in Section 13.1.*
2. a. True. *The answer can be found in Section 13.2.*
3. a. True. *The answer can be found in Section 13.3.*
4. b. False. *The answer can be found in Section 13.4.*

DEMAND-BASED GROWTH STRATEGIES

A steady rate of economic growth is the most central of macroeconomic goals. Like any goal, the goal of economic growth involves some trade-offs. Growth is often accompanied by inflation, which redistributes income. Growth may benefit the rich but fail to trickle down to the poor. Growth may come at a cost in terms of leisure, environmental quality, or security. A society must weigh these costs against the benefits of growth. Growth allows a society to absorb a growing labor force without rising unemployment. Growth increases the standard of living. Out of the "growth dividend," a society can (if it chooses) provide for people who are elderly, homeless, or poor—needs that can be addressed less painfully out of new resources and new income. While there are still concerns about environmental effects, leisure, and quality of life, there appears to be a consensus in favor of encouraging growth by either increasing aggregate demand or increasing aggregate supply.

A **demand-based growth strategy** is an attempt to create a long-term increase in output and employment by shifting aggregate demand to the right. Demand-based growth strategies are based on the long-run effects of the lost output during periods when the economy is operating significantly below its potential. The output that is lost during that time includes some valuable investment in research and development, physical capital, and human capital (both formal education and on-the-job training). These lost investments could be the inputs into future growth. The usefulness of demand-based growth strategies depends on the length of the time period that divides the short run from the long run.

The Aggregate Supply Curve Revisited

The debate over aggregate supply has concentrated on the alternatives of vertical versus upward sloping. Most economists agree that the short-run aggregate supply curve is upward sloping rather than vertical. The upward slope results from imperfections in the marketplace, such as immobile resources, imperfect information, long-term contractual agreements, incorrect expectations, or delayed responses to information. Rational expectations suggest that the short run is not a very long period of actual time, and that the long-run aggregate supply curve is vertical or at least very steep. Adaptive expectations suggest that the short-run aggregate supply curve could be fairly flat and that the short run itself may be a long period of time.

Short Run and Long Run

The link between demand management policies and economic growth arises from opportunities for real (short-run) profit created by a rising price level. Workers, entrepreneurs, investors, and consumers who can respond more quickly than others gain from rising prices. Suppose, for example, you are a shoe manufacturer. Prices in general are rising, and you can get a higher price for your shoes. Your contracts with workers and suppliers include prices that are fixed for 6 months. If, during those 6 months, you can obtain resources at fixed prices and sell the shoes for higher prices, you can increase your profits. At the end of 6 months, your contracts will be up for renewal. You know that wages and prices of materials will rise, and your temporary profit surge will end in the long run. In the meantime, however, you have an incentive to expand output. In fact, if you expect more such surges in the future, each with a short-run profit opportunity, you may respond by investing more in new equipment, more modern technology, and upgrading employee skills.

The long-run and short-run aggregate supply curves are shown in Figure 13.1. The long-run aggregate supply curve, AS^{lr}, is vertical at Y^*, which is the real output level corresponding to the natural rate of unemployment. The short-run aggregate supply curve, AS_1, is upward sloping. Initially, the economy is in short-run and long-run equilibrium at P_1 and Y^*. Then aggregate demand shifts from AD_1 to AD_2. Moving along AS_1, output increases to Y_2 and the price level begins to rise to P_2. Producers raise prices and expand output in response to increased demand.

Eventually, however, the rising price level affects the prices of productive inputs: workers, capital, and raw materials. The real value of workers' earnings falls. As soon as resource owners have an opportunity to renegotiate wages and prices, those wages and prices rise. Rising costs produce an upward shift in the short-run aggregate supply curve to AS_2. Once again the economy is in short-run and long-run equilibrium at a higher price level, P_3. However, there has been no permanent increase in the level of output and employment.

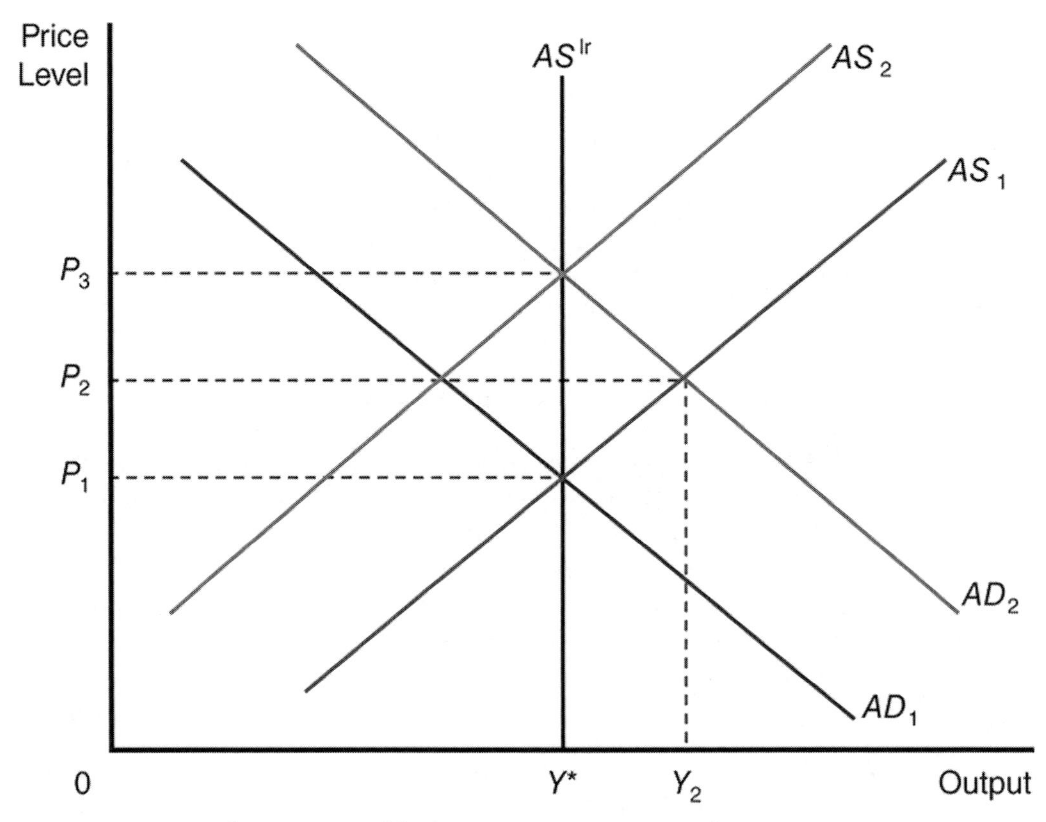

FIGURE 13.1: Short-run and long-run aggregate supply
When the *AS* curve slopes upward in the short run but is vertical in the long run, an increase in aggregate demand results (the shift from AD_1 to AD_2). Real output returns to Y^*, and only the price level increases.

The important question is how widespread these short-run profit opportunities are and how long it takes the market to eliminate them. If imperfections are substantial, and it takes a long time for the market to adapt to change, then an increase in aggregate demand can increase profit opportunities and real output for a fairly long period of time. This higher output represents growth not only of consumption but also of the resource base of human and physical capital acquired during the interim. Expanding aggregate demand can be a growth strategy as well as a stabilization strategy.

The longer the contract period, the longer the original short-run upward-sloping aggregate supply curve will be valid. When contracts expire, the short-run aggregate supply curve will shift upward. A new short run will begin on a new curve at the old level of output associated with the natural rate of unemployment. Once again, economists are faced with this question: How long is the short run? Economists in the Keynesian tradition argue that the short run is very long indeed because these imperfections are large and the market works slowly to overcome them. Economists of the classical tradition claim that the short run is really not a very long period of time. They are more optimistic about people's ability to acquire and process information and about the ability of buyers and sellers to respond quickly by changing prices, quantities, or suppliers. Consequently, they see little role for demand-based growth strategies, and concentrate instead on shifting aggregate supply.

REAL BUSINESS CYCLES

A growing economy typically exhibits some instability because innovations resulting from research and development and investment spending do not occur at a steady pace. Thus, such an economy would be expected to exhibit business cycles. The Keynesian model explains such cyclical fluctuations in output, employment, and the price level in terms of shifts in aggregate demand combined with a relatively stable aggregate supply curve that gradually moves rightward over time.

Another explanation of cyclical fluctuations, in the classical tradition, was developed in the 1980s. Its roots go back to such early-20th-century economists as Wesley Clair Mitchell (who first measured business cycles) and Joseph Schumpeter. This explanation holds that cyclical economic fluctuations result from changes in aggregate supply rather than in aggregate demand (or changes that affect both at once). The cyclical pattern is called the real business cycle. If changes in aggregate supply as a result of technology shocks and other disturbances occur irregularly in large bursts, the result is cyclical fluctuations in output (Mankiw, 1989).

These cyclical fluctuations arise because workers and owners of firms take advantage of temporarily high returns to investment, production, and work effort when such shocks occur. Later, when the returns to such efforts are lower, workers will catch up on leisure and firms will slack off until the next shock begins. Intertemporal substitutions of effort (shifting economic activity between periods to take advantage of the time period with higher returns) will lead to fluctuations in output. Note, however, that in this model unemployment is largely voluntary, caused by the substitution of work effort between time periods to take advantage of the higher wages when productivity is higher.

A supply-induced explanation of fluctuations was a response to the experience of the 1990s and early 2000s. At that time, supply influences, such as a less experienced labor force and higher oil prices, seemed to shift the aggregate supply curve to the left. Such a shift would result in the usual decline in output and employment that indicates a recession. Unlike most recessions, however, there would be no fall in the price level (or the inflation rate). In a supply-induced recession, in contrast to a demand-induced recession, real output can fall while the price level rises. A subsequent shift of the aggregate supply curve to the right would expand both employment and real output. What happened to the price level during such an expansion would depend on whether aggregate demand also shifted to the right during that period.

In general, a real business cycle—one based on shifts in aggregate supply—implies rising price levels or higher inflation rates during recessions and lower price levels or lower inflation rates during expansions. This pattern is somewhat consistent with the experience of the 1990s but does not generally describe cyclical fluctuations for longer periods or any of the more recent business cycles like the one from 2007 to 2009. Evidence to support a real business cycle on a regular and recurring basis has been weak, but some recessions or expansions may be triggered by factors shifting the aggregate supply curve.

KEY IDEAS: GROWTH STRATEGIES—AGGREGATE DEMAND OR AGGREGATE SUPPLY?

- Demand-based growth strategies try to create a long-term increase in output and employment by shifting aggregate demand to the right. These strategies are particularly useful when the economy is operating significantly below its potential.
- Keynesian economists argue that market imperfections are large and as a result the short run can be very long.
- Demand-based growth strategies are appropriate and effective.
- Classical economists claim that the short run is really not very long.
- They tend to focus instead on shifting aggregate supply.

SHIFTING THE AGGREGATE SUPPLY CURVE

Although economists disagree about many things, they do agree about what makes aggregate supply shift. The long-run aggregate supply curve will shift to the right in response to increases in the capital stock, improvement in the size or quality of the labor force, additional natural resources, improvements in productivity, or technological advances. Increases in resources or productivity will shift the aggregate supply curve to the right. Encouragement of production through reduced taxes or regulations that lower costs to firms will also shift the curve to the right. Anything that shifts the aggregate supply curve to the right is a source of economic growth because it will produce a rise in real output and income.

The aggregate supply curve can also shift to the left, indicating negative growth or a decline in a nation's standard of living. Factors that can shift the curve to the left include resource depletion, a decline in the size or quality of the labor force, and public policies (taxes or regulations) that discourage productive activity.

Long-term economic growth requires steady rightward shifts of the aggregate supply curve. Economic growth has been a major concern in the United States for at least 50 years. Economists are constantly examining the growth rate of the U.S. economy to make sure that the standard of living is rising, and economic journalists are always comparing that growth rate to economic growth in other nations, such as China. Economists are also concerned that output expands fast enough to create enough jobs for a growing labor force. The antigrowth voices of the early 1970s became muted when Americans started realizing the costs of not growing—in terms of inflation, unemployment, and a lower standard of living when the population grew faster than real output. During the 1990s and early 2000s, the continuing debate has not been over *whether* to grow but rather *how* to grow. Economists try to determine what strategies are most successful for shifting aggregate supply to the right.

Between 1962 and 2011, real output increased over 300% in the United States. Some of that growth was a result of increased resources, specifically labor and capital. Even coming out of a recession, gross investment in constant dollars was over 400% higher in 2011 than it was in 1962 (www.bea.gov, n.d.). However, recall from Chapter 12 that a large (and increasing) part of gross private domestic investment goes to replace worn-out capital. After correcting for depreciation, real net investment in 2011 was only 12% higher than in 1962! Thus, the real growth rate of investment has been much lower than the rate of economic growth.

Because investment is so volatile, year-to-year comparisons must be treated carefully. Figure 13.2 plots both gross and net investment expenditures as percentages of GDP from 1967 to 2011. The growth of gross investment over that whole period was greater than the growth of total GDP but was very erratic. Net investment—which consists of new plants, equipment, and housing, as opposed to replacement of worn-out facilities and equipment—actually fell relative to GDP during several periods of time. Note that in recession years, such as 1975, 1982, 1991, and 2009, investment declined even more than GDP, reducing the stock of capital available for future economic growth.

Private Saving

The most commonly used indicator of what is happening to saving is the **savings rate,** or saving by households, business, and government combined as a percentage of GDP. The current U.S. rate is low compared to past experience and to savings rates in many other industrial countries. However, saving has fallen in other industrial countries as well in the last four decades, due to the emphasis on consumer spending in an effort to try and bolster the flailing global economy. From 1960 to 1980, the United States saved 19.6% of

GDP, somewhat below the average for 17 industrial countries, which was 23.4%. (Japan, at 35%, had the highest rate.) Demographic factors, such as the maturing of the baby boomers, are just now beginning to contribute to a higher savings rate in the United States. Although the savings rate hit lows of 1.5% in 2005 and nearly zero in early 2008, it surged to 6.9% by 2009. The deep downturn in the economy and the high unemployment figures were partly the reason that U.S. Americans began saving more ("Amid Recession," 2009).

Private saving is the major source of funding for investment to expand future output. Saving by households and business firms, which provides the funds for investment, has not kept pace with the growth of GDP in recent years. Figure 13.3 shows the amount of private savings in billions of dollars and as a percentage of GDP from 1990 through 2011. Although the total amount of private saving has generally increased over time, the amount of private saving as a percentage of GDP has declined. The average rate in the 1990s was 3.25%, as compared to 2.7% in the 2000s.

Private Investment

A higher level of investment would shift both the aggregate demand curve and the aggregate supply curve to the right. Such a shift would increase employment without more inflation. More specifically, business investment in new equipment is a key source of economic growth. Additional equipment gives each worker more capital with which to work and thus increases productivity. New equipment embodies new technology, which also

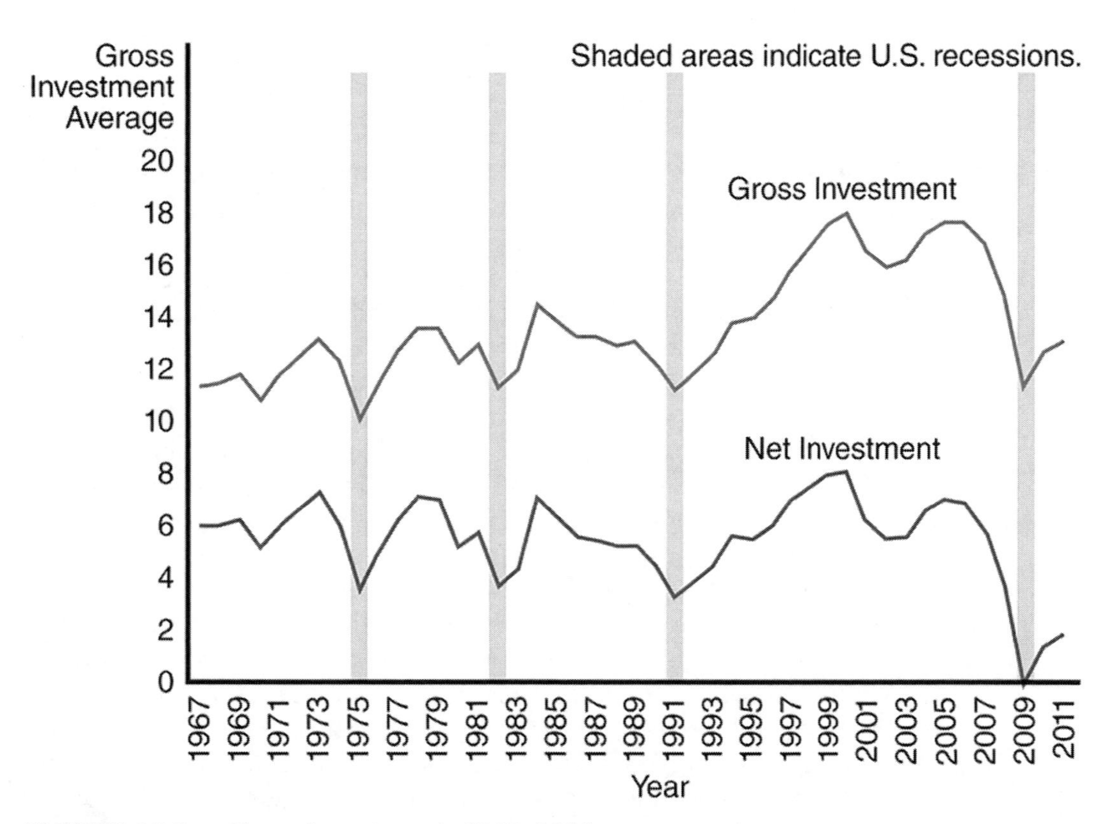

FIGURE 13.2: Gross investment, 1967–2011
Gross investment has averaged about 13.5% of GDP and new investment about 5.5%, with both dropping relative to GDP during the recession years 1975, 1982, 1991, and especially 2009, when net investment fell to 0%.

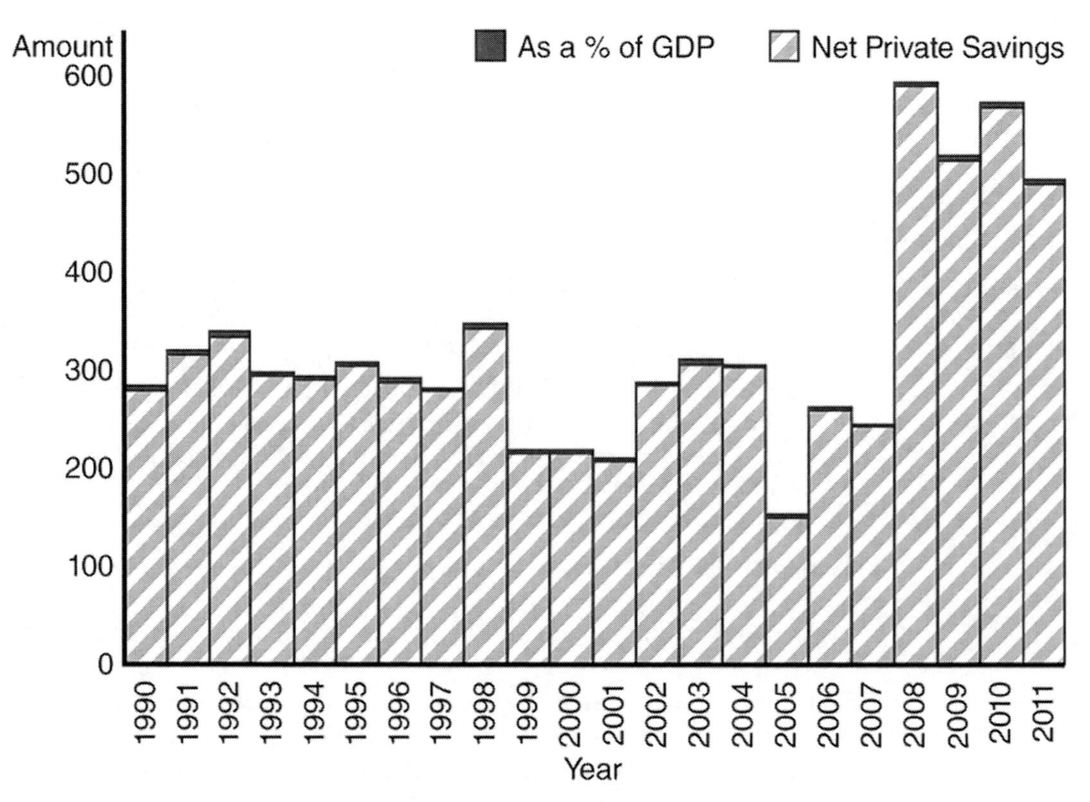

FIGURE 13.3: Net private savings, 1990–2011
The amount of private saving as a percentage of GDP has declined from the 1990s to the 2000s.

Source: Bureau of Economic Analysis, www.bea.gov

increases productivity. Thus, the slowdown in investment in the 1970s, 1980s, and 2000s led to a search for policies that would stimulate investment. Tax incentives of various kinds were proposed and implemented. Since 1986 there have been numerous efforts to restore the special tax treatment of capital gains, which are currently taxed as ordinary income. Capital gains are "profits" that result from the sale of assets at a higher price than they cost. Many policy makers argue that favorable tax treatment of capital gains would stimulate more sales of business firms and corporate stock. However, capital gains taxes are paid by owners of capital, who tend to be more wealthy individuals, making it somewhat of a progressive tax. In any case, the debate surrounding changes to the capital gains tax are controversial and still a hot button issue in the late 2000s.

Public Investment

The policy emphasis in the last few decades has been on private capital as a way to increase economic growth. However, the role of infrastructure as capital should not be overlooked. Most of this capital is in the state and local public sector, where the growth of the capital stock has slowed considerably from earlier decades. The transportation network of highways and airports on which private business depends is provided in the public sector. Investment in human capital also requires local public-sector investments in schools and health care facilities. Some researchers have examined public-sector investment in a number of countries to see if it enhances growth or discourages growth by crowding out private investors. Research has shown that public and private investments can be complementary. Public investments, especially in transport facilities (roads,

KEY IDEAS: AGGREGATE SUPPLY AND ECONOMIC GROWTH

The long-run aggregate supply curve will shift *to the right* in response to

- increases in the capital stock,
- improvement in the size or quality of the labor force,
- additional natural resources,
- improvements in productivity or technological advances, and
- reduced taxes or regulations that lower costs to firms.

A rightward shift of the aggregate supply curve is a source of economic growth, producing a rise in real output and income.

The aggregate supply curve can also shift *to the left,* in response to factors including

- resource depletion,
- a decline in the size or quality of the labor force, and
- taxes or regulations that discourage productive activity.

A leftward shift of the aggregate supply curve indicates negative growth, or a decline in a nation's standard of living.

Long-term economic growth requires steady rightward shifts of the aggregate supply curve.

bridges, airports, and mass transit) enhance the productivity of private-sector capital and contribute to economic growth.

GROWTH IN THE LABOR FORCE

Another source of economic growth is a larger or more skilled labor force. Increases in both the size and the quality of the labor force can contribute to economic growth. If only the size of the labor force increases, as occurred during the 1970s, real GDP may increase but there will be little if any increase in real per capita GDP, which measures improvements in the standard of living. A more skilled and productive labor force, which has more capital and better technology to work with, is the essential ingredient for an increase in real per capita GDP.

The Size of the Labor Force

During the 1970s, the labor force grew by 22%. A large part of that increase reflected the entry of the baby boom generation into the labor force. In 1970, 16% of the population was between 16 and 24 years old, the age group that makes up most of the new entrants to the labor force. Another large part of the increase was due to the increased participation of women, many of whom were entering the labor force for the first time. Thus labor force growth was much more rapid than before, but the average level of workers' skill and experience fell. This fall slowed the growth of GDP and the rightward movement of the aggregate supply curve. Since 1980, labor force growth has dropped, increasing only 16% between 1980 and 1990. By 1990, those in the 16–24 age group made up only 18% of the working-age population. By 2000, that number fell to 16%; in 2010, it was 13.5%. Projections for the 16-to-24-year-old group are estimated to be just 11.2% of the total labor force by 2020 (www.bls.gov).

Although the average worker now has more experience than a decade ago, the retiring baby boomers may add to a substantial slowdown in labor force growth in the coming years. Economists are anticipating a slowdown for the 2015–2025 period as the baby boom generation retires.

Changes in the Face of the Labor Force

In the 2000s and 2010s, increased competition, globalization, and outsourcing have really changed the face of the labor force as well as the location of production facilities. The Bureau of Labor Statistics has been collecting key economic data since 1884, but their data collection and analysis do not fully encompass the changing nature of today's job market and labor force. As seen in Table 13.1, the United States's rate of labor force participation is slowly declining over the decades, while in other countries, such as Germany and Spain, the rate is increasing.

Outsourcing has also been a factor in the changing labor growth rates since the turn of the twenty-first century. **Outsourcing** (or offshoring) is when a company decides to contract an existing business process that was previously performed internally and pay another independent organization to take over that function. In today's terms, this usually means that jobs are being sent overseas because there is cheaper labor to be found there. A form of outsourcing is present in any modern economy, but the outsourcing of business functions gained popularity around 2000. As the decade went on, more manufacturing jobs and production functions were being outsourced; job losses in informa-

Table 13.1: Rates of Labor Force Participation

	1970	1980	1990	2000	2005	2006	2007	2008	2009	2010	2011
United States	60.4	63.8	66.5	67.1	66.0	66.2	66.0	66.0	64.7	64.7	64.1
Australia	62.1	62.1	64.7	64.4	65.4	65.8	66.2	66.7	66.5	66.5	66.5
Canada	57.8	65.0	67.4	66.0	67.3	67.2	67.5	67.7	67.2	67.0	66.8
France	57.5	57.2	56.8	56.3	56.2	56.1	56.2	56.3	56.6	56.5	56.3
Germany	56.9	54.7	55	56.7	57.5	58.1	58.3	58.4	58.5	58.6	59.2
Italy	49.0	48.1	47.2	49.5	48.7	48.9	48.6	49.0	48.4	48.1	48.1
Japan	64.5	62.6	62.6	61.7	59.5	59.6	59.8	59.5	59.3	59.1	58.7
Mexico	n/a	n/a	n/a	57.1	57.1	58.0	58.0	57.8	57.9	57.7	57.8
Netherlands	n/a	55.4	57.0	63.0	64.2	64.5	65.2	65.4	65.2	63.7	63.3
New Zealand	n/a	n/a	63.9	65.3	67.8	68.3	68.5	68.5	68.2	68.0	68.4
Republic of Korea	57.6	59.0	60.0	61.2	62.0	61.9	61.8	61.5	60.8	61.0	61.1
South Africa	n/a	n/a	n/a	n/a	n/a	n/a	n/a	58.0	56.1	54.3	54.3
Spain	n/a	49.9	50.5	53.3	57.0	58.1	58.6	59.6	59.7	59.8	59.8
Sweden	64.0	66.9	67.4	63.8	64.8	64.9	65.3	65.3	64.8	64.9	65.1
Turkey	n/a	n/a	n/a	n/a	n/a	44.9	44.9	45.5	46.2	47.2	48.4
United Kingdom	n/a	62.8	64.3	62.8	63.1	63.5	63.4	63.5	63.4	63.2	63.2

Source: International Comparisons of Annual Labor Force Statistics, Adjusted to U.S. Concepts, 16 Countries: 1970–2011, by the U.S. Bureau of Labor Statistics, 2012. Retrieved from http://www.bls.gov/fls/flscomparelf/tables.htm#table08_lfpr.

tion technology and related areas were being reported more frequently. By 2004, offshoring, outsourcing, and the resulting job losses in the United States were a regular topic of debate for politicians and workers alike (Clayton & Mousa, 2004).

Investment in Human Capital

Investment in human capital includes any spending that increases the health or productive skills of the individual worker. Both individuals and firms can invest in human capital. An individual's decision to seek additional education is very similar to an entrepreneur's decision to purchase a new piece of equipment. In both cases, the investment is productive if the return over time exceeds the cost over the same time period.

The largest investment in human capital in the United States is in the public schools, which offer "free" education through Grade 12. This education is supplemented by postsecondary education in colleges, universities, and technical schools; vocational training programs; adult literacy and retraining programs; and on-the-job training.

The median amount of education (years of schooling completed) of people 25 years old and over has also risen steadily in the United States, from 10.5 years in 1960 to 12.7 years in 1991. In 2011, 87.5% of the adult population had at least a high school diploma. As older workers with less education retire, average worker schooling continues to rise.

The United States spends about 5.5% of GDP on education at all levels as of 2007. A large share of this investment is in elementary and secondary education. In 1959, expenditures per pupil were $1,635. By 2011, this figure had almost quadrupled to $6,065 per student. This amount compares favorably with educational expenditures in other developed nations. Of other major industrial nations, only Switzerland and Denmark spend more per pupil. The other nations of Western Europe, Canada, Japan, and Australia all spend less (see Figure 13.4).

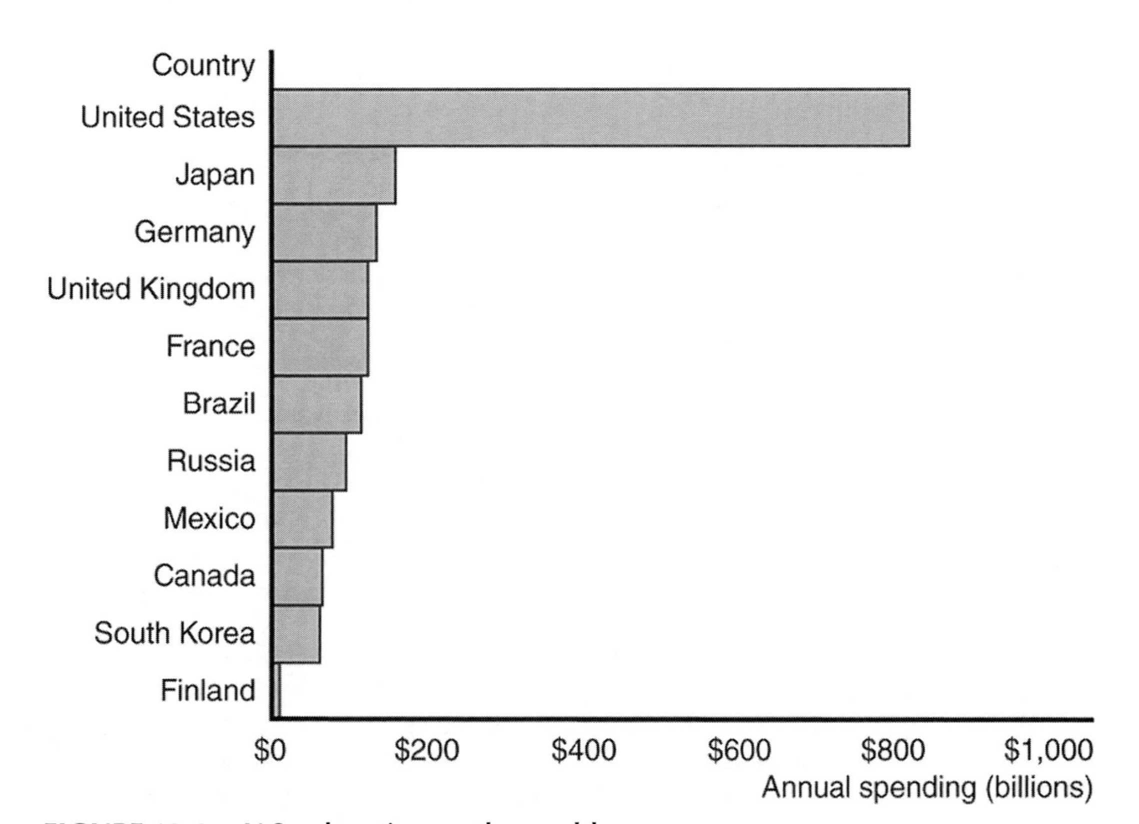

FIGURE 13.4: U.S. education vs. the world

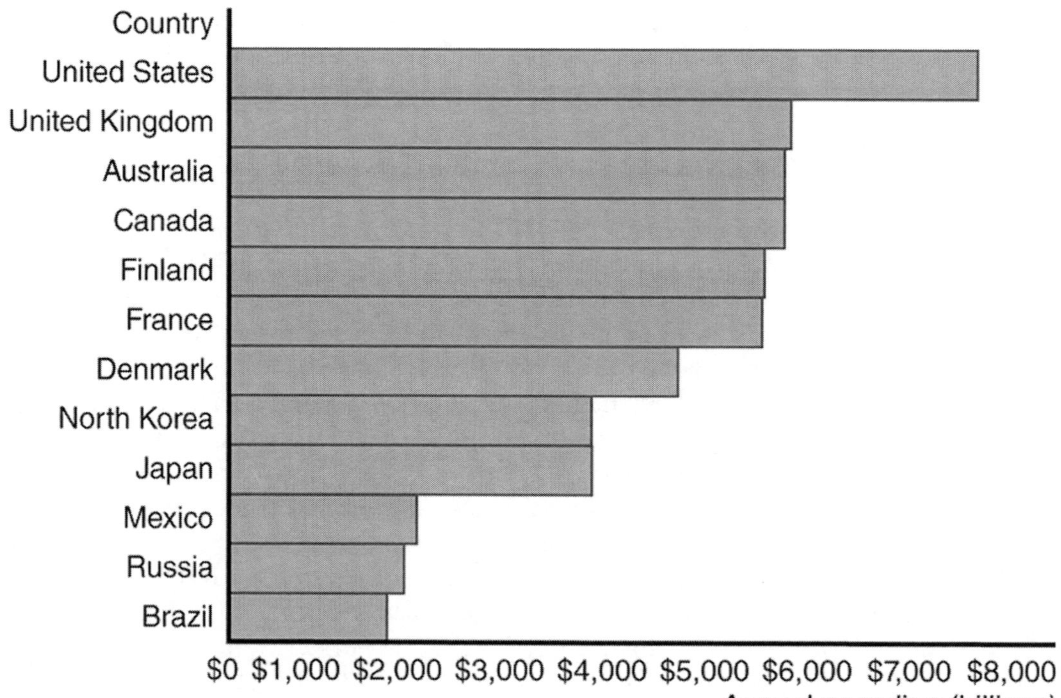

FIGURE 13.5: Annual spending per school-aged child
Investing in human capital helps the economy in many ways. What does an educated workforce offer to its country and the rest of the world?

Source: https://www.cia.gov/library/publications/the-world-factbook/index.html; http://www.geographic.org/country_ranks/educational_score_performance_country_ranks_2009_oecd.html; http://www.un.org/esa/population/publications/2003monitoring/WorldPopMonitoring_2003.pdf.

The U.S. educational system has come under much criticism for failing to produce a well-educated labor force. Public schools were among the scapegoats for the slow economic growth in the 1970s and 1980s as well as more recently in the early 2000s. Parents, taxpayers, and educators pointed to falling SAT scores and high dropout rates (Gottlob, 2009). Employers complained about a lack of basic skills in writing and computation.

The result of these complaints has been a careful examination of how effectively resources invested in education are being used. At the elementary and secondary levels, a number of states have enacted reforms in order to use those resources more effectively. Those reforms include tougher attendance laws, stricter teacher certification, basic skills testing for students, and other measures designed to improve the quality of public education. A few business leaders have even offered to provide college funds for those who make it through 12th grade in certain inner city schools. That guarantee has lowered the dropout rate in those schools. President George W. Bush introduced legislation in 2001 called the No Child Left Behind Act (NCLB). NCLB required all government-run schools receiving federal funding to administer a statewide standardized test annually to all students. If the school's results were repeatedly poor, then steps would be taken to improve the school, like asking the state office of education to run it directly, or to close the school. Although the efficacy of NCLB has been questioned, steps like these are attempts to improve the quality of human capital. If successful, the result would be an increase in aggregate supply and an improvement in the U.S. standard of living.

Growth in Natural Resources

The last category of inputs that can shift the aggregate supply curve is natural resources. During the 2010s, the most significant demand for natural resources is coming from China. China's enormous population (1.3 billion people, or 19.6% of the world population, as of 2011) is demanding more and more natural resources such as energy, oil, gas, and so on. This pull on the natural resources available has a serious impact on the aggregate supply curve because it goes back to supply and demand. Additional demand for these resources leads to price increases, which impact aggregate supply by increasing the cost to produce goods and services. One major resource where prices impact GDP growth is oil, which had a tenfold price increase in just 7 years from 1973 to 1980, leading to a temporary leftward shift of the aggregate supply curve. In that case, even with a dramatic price increase of a widely used natural resource, producers and consumers adapted. More fuel-efficient cars, alternative energy sources, insulation, modified production methods, and other responses minimized the long-run effect on the economy. Cheaper energy supplies shifted the aggregate supply curve back to the right to some extent, but as the demand for oil and other natural resources continues to grow, the U.S. economy will certainly feel the impact.

Research and Development

Increased productive resources are not the only source of increases in aggregate supply. If new ways of using resources can create more output, then those technological changes can also shift the aggregate supply curve to the right. New technology may be embodied in new capital or in a change in methods of production. Research and development, or R&D, consists of efforts to develop new products and new production methods and put them to use. In the United States, R&D is supported by both the private and the public sector. Overall spending on R&D in the United States was $400.5 billion as of 2009 (Boroush, 2012).

Total research and development spending, public and private, accounts for about 2.8% of GDP as of 2011. This figure is comparable to levels in Germany and South Korea, and higher than the share of GDP that goes to R&D in France, the United Kingdom, and China. The goal of research and development is to allow the United States to compete in the world economy. One vital area of research is in new technologies.

Technological change is a two-step process. The first step requires investment in research into new products and new methods. This step results in inventions. The second step is to translate those inventions into something that is commercially feasible and cost effective. This second step is **innovation,** or the translation of new methods and products into actual production and marketing.

Technological change is difficult to measure in the aggregate. It is possible to measure changes in spending on research and development, and on new equipment that embodies the latest technology. There is no easy way, however, to measure the extra output due to the new technology. The United States does spend heavily on R&D. Of the 2.8% of GDP going to R&D in 2011, much of it was funded by the federal government and carried out by industry and universities. In the 1970s and 1980s, however, about 25% of U.S. spending on R&D was directed to defense-related research, which has limited applications to other markets. Other countries (especially Japan) have historically put much more effort directly into industrial research.

Research and development spending usually requires investment in new capital that embodies the newly developed technology. Thus, R&D spending and new capital spending go hand in hand to shift the aggregate supply curve to the right and promote economic growth.

POLICY FOCUS: MILITARY SPENDING, DEFENSE CONVERSION, AND ECONOMIC GROWTH

As the United States continues to increase its military spending, economists have taken the opportunity to explore the impact of the defense buildup of the last 50 years on economic growth. In 2011, the U.S. federal budget included $683.7 billion for military expenditure by the United States Department of Defense. In 1992, that figure was just $265 billion.

Has military spending helped or hindered the growth of U.S. output? There has been a lot of literature written on this subject—from both sides of the argument (Heo, 2010). One side states that military spending reduces growth through the disproportionate allocation of scientific and engineering talent to military research. This argument notes that the rate of commercial innovation has declined appreciably since the late 1960s. Rising prices and deteriorating relative quality have made U.S.-produced goods increasingly noncompetitive in both world and domestic markets, forcing production cutbacks and plant closures in the United States and creating additional inflationary pressures (Heo & Eger, 2005). On the other side of the argument, however, it has been reported that military spending helps stimulate the economy, as this defense spending helps create jobs (Cuaresma & Reitschuler, 2004). These jobs are formed in the military sector as well as generating private-sector employment via defense contracts and subcontracts.

This observation pinpoints an essential concern about the relationship of military spending to the economy. Has defense spending displaced infrastructure investment or funding for human capital? Has military research and development benefited private industry?

The United States concentrates a much larger share of research and development spending in defense than most other industrial countries. The distinction between military and civilian R&D spending would be less important if there were substantial spillover benefits between the two. Two examples of military R&D success that were translated into profitable civilian applications are the transistor and the microwave. However, Hewlett-Packard has argued that defense has been a net user of civilian-created technology in electronics, rather than the other way around (Gansler, 2011). The military is generally more interested in performance than in price. The civilian market is sensitive to both concerns. Machine tool manufacturing in the United States has been stimulated by military demand, but the result has been an industry that has been more attentive to high performance than to cost.

Some military innovations with spinoffs to the private sector have been not in technology but in management. Cost-benefit analysis, operations research, and planning-programming-budget systems originated in the military and spread quickly to private industries. Overall, however, it is difficult to evaluate whether high levels of defense spending have increased, reduced, or had no impact on U.S. economic growth.

Public Policy Toward Research and Development

Because the federal government plays a major role in the allocation of research and development funds, it has an important direct influence on the activities of invention and innovation. In addition to direct expenditures, the federal government also finances the education of many scientists and engineers, protects property rights to inventions through the patent system, and offers special tax breaks for R&D spending in the private sector.

Profits are the incentive to engage in research and development. The outcome of an R&D effort will be more profitable if the resulting product reaches the broadest possible market. One effort to increase the return to research and development, therefore, has concentrated on opening foreign markets to new U.S. products and better protecting patents and copyrights on a worldwide basis (protecting rights in "intellectual capital").

KEY IDEAS: SOURCES OF ECONOMIC GROWTH

Aggregate supply shifts to the right and real output grows as a result of:

- Increased investment and saving
- Private saving
  - Private investment
  - Public investment in infrastructure and human capital
- Growth of the labor force
  - Increased numbers of workers
  - Improvements in worker skills
  - Growth of natural resources
  - Discovery versus depletion
- Research and development
  - Invention
  - Innovation

Table 13.2: Productivity change in the nonfarm business sector, 1947–2011

Years	Average Annual Percentage Change
1947–1973	2.8
1973–1979	1.1
1979–1990	1.4
1990–2000	2.1
2000–2007	2.5
2007–2011	1.8

Source: Labor Productivity and Costs, by the U.S. Bureau of Labor Statistics, 2012. Retrieved from http://www.bls.gov/lpc/prodybar.htm.

The Productivity Dilemma

Between recession and slow growth, increases in real per capita GDP have been small—about 2% a year from 1979 to 2011, or from $14,183 to $48,442. In real terms (using constant 1982–1984 dollars), the average weekly earnings for workers in the private sector in the United States has only slightly increased, from $315.44 in 1972 to $352.26 in 2012 (www.bls.gov). After exactly 40 years of economic growth, this 11.7% increase in earnings paints a dismal picture of real gains for U.S. workers.

Increases in real wages depend on increases in productivity. **Productivity** is the measure of real output per worker hour. Like the price level, productivity changes are measured by an index. Table 13.2 shows the increase in productivity by decade for the United States.

The slight increase and then decrease in productivity growth in the last two decades is concerning, although this problem is not unique to the United States. A similar slowdown in productivity growth has plagued many developed industrial countries. The concern over productivity, slow growth, and the combination of rising prices and rising unemployment led to many efforts to explain what was occurring and to devise suitable policies to get the economy moving again.

One type of policy to increase productivity consists of various types of incentive, bonus, or profit-sharing schemes to encourage labor to work harder and become more skilled. Under such plans, workers are paid for output rather than input. Their pay is based on what they produce, rather than being an hourly wage or annual salary. A number of studies on productivity incentives that have concluded that there is some persuasive statistical evidence that they do increase productivity (Durant et al.).

Some economists question the accuracy of the productivity data. Productivity is much harder to measure in services than in goods production, and the share of services in total output has been rising for at least two decades. For example, in banking, output is measured by the number of checks processed or deposits taken. With widespread use of automatic teller machines and electronic banking, the number of checks is significantly down, yet productivity is up. Other observers feel that we are at the point of a productivity payoff to the development and adoption of new technology in information processing and management techniques that have taken place over the last 30 years. The payoff to new technology is delayed somewhat because it takes a while for workers to learn to use it and for management to figure out how to adapt the technology to their particular line of production (Casolaro & Gobbi, 2007). However, increased productivity has resulted in more job opportunities, especially for skilled workers who can work with computers. The next challenge will be how to measure intangible goods like social networking and electronic gaming, which have become increasingly popular in the 2010s.

SUPPLY-SIDERS: PUBLIC POLICIES TO SHIFT AGGREGATE SUPPLY

In the late 1970s and early 1980s, it was proposed that the United States adopt policies that would be aimed at shifting aggregate supply to the right. **Supply-side economics** was the work of a group of economists and business journalists who advocated a specific group of policies relating to deregulation, tax incentives, and work incentives.

In designing these policies, supply-siders emphasized certain microeconomic foundations of aggregate supply. They insisted that economic incentives are important and that the driving force behind economic decisions is the self-interested behavior of individuals. Recall the importance of incentives and response to the role of interest rates in money demand, bank lending, and business investment decisions on the aggregate demand side of the market. The response of individuals in their roles as workers, managers, investors, and savers to changes in the reward structure of their environment is also important for aggregate supply. Supply-siders pointed out that the government has a great deal of influence on this reward structure.

In a broader sense, all economists are supply-siders in that they believe that factors that can shift the aggregate supply curve are important for long-term economic growth. In fact, a Keynesian or a monetarist is often an advocate of some supply-side policies.

For the most part, what President Reagan did in his first term (1981–1985) was a textbook application of supply-side economics. Congress and the President reduced some nondefense programs, such as grants to state and local governments, and enacted a three-stage, 25% cut in personal income taxes in 1981. Accompanying the tax cuts were some incentives to save and invest. Also, efforts were made to reduce the burden on business of complying with government regulations. The goal was to shift aggregate supply to the right, increasing saving, investment, productivity, output, and employment while reducing inflation.

At first, U.S. supply-side policies seemed to be out of step with much of the rest of the world. European countries were committed to demand management policies, and the United States was pursuing supply-side policies. In the latter part of the 1980s, however, supply-side policies became more popular in France, Denmark, New Zealand, Canada, and the United Kingdom. All of these countries adopted a less progressive tax system aimed more at incentives and less at redistribution of income. These changes may be the most lasting legacy of supply-side economics.

Regulation and Deregulation

Supply-siders were very critical of government regulations in environmental and health and safety areas that increase costs of production and drive up prices without increasing output. In addition to the direct costs of compliance, these regulations place a heavy burden of paperwork on industry. Although the purposes of the regulations might indeed be desirable, they divert real resources from producing goods and services to complying with regulations and filing forms. These higher costs shift the aggregate supply curve to the left. Deregulation, ideally, should shift it back to the right.

Deregulation was a central feature of the policies of the Reagan administration. Some regulations were repealed. Others were simply not enforced. Experiments with deregulation in the 1980s in the airline industry, telephone service, and banking, however, generated mixed results. For example, the Airline Deregulation Act of 1978 removed government control over fares, routes, and market entry (of new airlines) from commercial aviation. The goal was to allow market forces to encourage entry into air transportation by new carriers, entry into new markets by current carriers, and generally reduce the rigid practices previously enacted by the Civil Aeronautics Board. Although the average fare per passenger mile did fall from 33.3 cents in 1974 to 13 cents in 2010 (in real terms), deregulation also brought about a wave of bankruptcy filings, union disputes, and a sky-high number of passenger complaints (Breyer, 2011).

Many economists also point to deregulation as one of the primary causes of the housing bubble, subprime mortgage financial crisis, and subsequent Great Recession of 2007–2009 (Palley, 2010). The Financial Services Modernization Act of 1999 removed a restriction of the Glass-Steagall Act of 1933, allowing banking, securities, and insurance companies to act as a combination of investment bank, commercial bank, and insurance company. This led to lax lending practices as companies grew larger and took greater risks in order to reap financial gain. Although many economists argue that deregulated banks were not the cause, or at least not the main cause of the crisis, it is clear that too much regulation was definitely not the problem.

Taxes, Transfers, and Incentives

Supply-siders were particularly concerned about the effects of taxes and transfer payments, especially personal income taxes, on incentives and productive activity. They argued that the growth of the tax-transfer system reduces incentives to work, save, invest, and innovate, all of which contribute to productivity. Higher taxes drive up costs of production and consumer prices. Taxes to support government activity create a **tax wedge,** which is the gap between prices paid by consumers and the prices (incomes) received by sellers (resource owners). Thus, the tax wedge discourages both consumption and production. If the government borrows instead of raising taxes to finance additional spending, this action raises the cost of borrowing to private firms. The rise in the cost of borrowing drives up their costs and discourages private-sector investment. Either way, supply-siders argue, the growth of government contributes to rising costs.

Taxes and Work Effort High marginal tax rates discourage individuals from putting forth extra effort and encourage tax avoidance. Under a progressive income tax system, increases in nominal income push workers into higher marginal tax brackets (the U.S.

federal income tax is considered progressive—see www.irs.gov/taxstats for the different tax rates). As a result, a significant portion of the return to increased effort and productivity is taxed away. Consequently, workers are likely to opt for more leisure (longer vacations, increased absenteeism, less moonlighting, and earlier retirement). Consider Ruth Perez, a skilled accountant who earns $55 an hour. She is considering either putting in an extra 4 hours for a client on Saturday morning or spending that time cleaning her carpets. If she works, her gross income will be $220. A commercial carpet cleaner charges $160. Without considering taxes, it makes sense for her to work 4 hours, pay the carpet cleaner, and come out $60 ahead. Resources would be efficiently allocated. The value of her time as an accountant is higher than the value of her time as a carpet cleaner. However, taxes may change her decision. If her marginal income tax rate (federal plus state) is 40%, then after taxes she will earn only $132. It would be cheaper to clean her own carpets. A lower tax rate would induce her to use her time where it is most productive—as an accountant, not as a carpet cleaner. These concerns about the incentive effects of high marginal tax rates were reflected in the tax cuts of 2001 and 2003. Both of these policy actions sharply reduced marginal income tax rates for individuals.

Looking at Figure 13.6, you can see that the total federal tax rate has fallen for many taxpayers, but the group with the most significant decline in share of taxes paid is the top 0.01% of earners. In 2012, this disconnect between the wealthiest individuals and the other "99%" became a major source of contention in the general public, leading to a wave of protests referred to as Occupy Wall Street. The trade-off between high tax rates that reduce the incentives to work and the glaringly large income inequality in the United States is an ongoing issue.

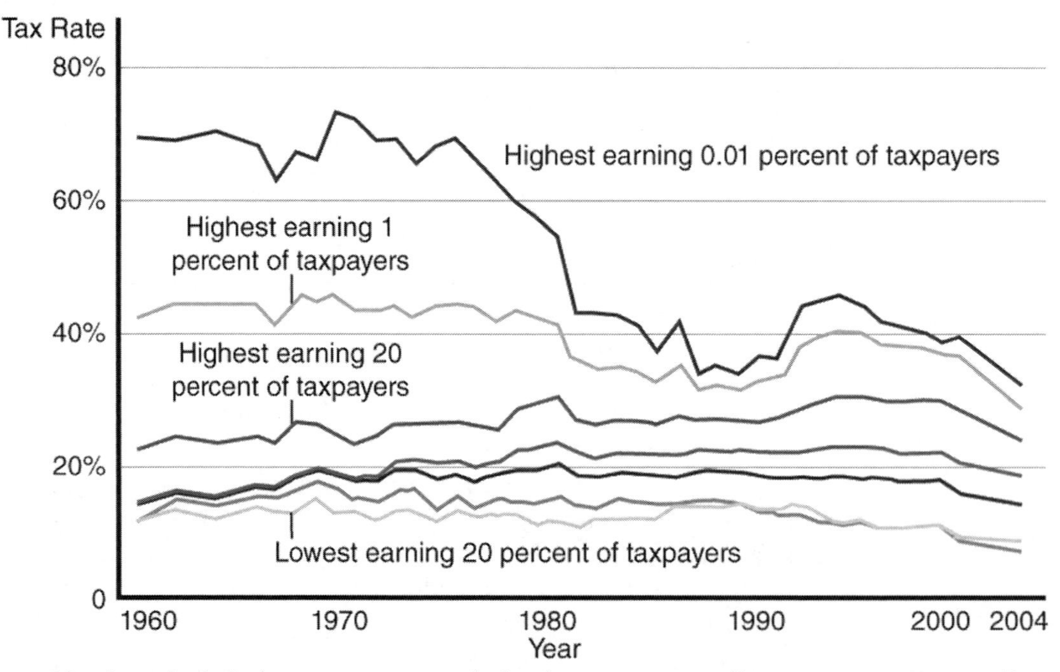

FIGURE 13.6: Lower taxes for the higher earners

Since the 1960s, the total federal tax rate has fallen for low earners, risen for relatively high earners, and fallen significantly for very high earners.

Source: visualizingeconomics.com/blog/2007/11/03/nytimes-historical-tax-rates-by-income-group.

Taxes, Saving, and Investment An individual's reward for saving depends on both the interest rate and the marginal tax rate on the next dollar of income. For any given interest rate, there is less incentive to save additional dollars at a higher marginal tax rate. Less credit will be available to borrowers. Thus, a progressive income tax discourages saving and—indirectly, through the higher cost of borrowed funds—discourages investment.

Supply-siders also applied this argument to entrepreneurial or managerial risk taking. In deciding whether to expand productive facilities or to implement new technologies, owners or managers must weigh the risks that are involved against the expected profits *after taxes.* The higher the marginal tax rate, the smaller the expected profit will be, and the less eager investors will be to assume risks. As a result, less new technology is adopted, and both output and productivity growth are stunted.

Transfer Payments and the Income Tax Supply-siders also argue that transfer payments discourage productive work. Unemployment compensation programs encourage workers to stay unemployed until their benefits are exhausted. Welfare programs, including not only cash transfers but also food stamps, subsidized housing, and Medicaid, discourage people from taking low-wage jobs. The wages they could earn may barely offset the loss of welfare payments plus other benefits. Consider Bruce Thompson, who currently receives $320 a week in welfare benefits. A job becomes available that would require Bruce to work 40 hours a week at the minimum wage of $9.25 an hour. If he takes the job, he loses his welfare benefits. He will earn $370 a week instead of $320. Is it worth working 40 hours a week to earn $50 more? When designing welfare programs supply-siders argue that it is important to consider the disincentives that may be created.

Resource Allocation Supply-siders also argue that progressive taxes cause resources to be allocated inefficiently. Resources flow to certain sectors of the economy, such as real estate, that enjoy tax advantages. A fair amount of depreciation, taxes, and interest expenses are deductible on real estate investments. Individuals in high marginal tax brackets find that their after-tax yields are higher from investing in real estate than in other assets. Thus, supply-siders argue that too many financial resources flow into the real estate market, instead of more productive uses.

KEY IDEAS: SUPPLY-SIDE POLICIES

Supply-siders would recommend the following policies:	Supply-siders would predict the following results:
Deregulation of industries	Increased work effort by high-income workers
Reduction in taxes on highly productive workers	Increased work effort by former welfare recipients
Reduction in taxes on business firms	Increased saving
Reduction in tax disincentives for welfare recipients	Increased investment and risk taking
Tax incentives for saving and investment	Improved resource allocation
	Reduced tax avoidance

GLOBAL OUTLOOK: INDUSTRIAL POLICY IN EUROPE AND JAPAN

Supply-side economics was a politically conservative growth strategy, relying on private market forces. A politically liberal competing growth strategy began in response. This strategy, known as **industrial policy,** calls for government to identify and encourage promising industries and to cushion the decline of old industries. Japan and the European Union offer good examples of two very different approaches to industrial policy. Japan pursues a more positive policy of identifying and promoting industries that seem to have growth potential. Since Japan had one of the best records of economic growth of any industrial country from World War II until very recently, other countries have shown much interest in its policies. As a general rule, the nations of the European Union (EU) have pursued a more negative approach. This approach consists of protecting and supporting declining industries, trying to get them back to a competitive level.

The key to Japan's program has been the Ministry of Trade and Industry (MITI), which selects the industries to assist. Methods used in the 1950s and 1960s included organizing cartels, providing loans at low interest rates to targeted industries, and controlling imports. In the 1970s and 1980s, the government did offer some aid to declining industries in the form of tax breaks and loan guarantees. However, overall industrial policy in Japan has been directed much more at supporting promising industries through accelerated depreciation allowances, tax benefits, research support, and loans. The U.S. government usually makes such benefits available to all firms, but Japan is more selective in deciding which industries to favor. Critics have argued, however, that the MITI is not always successful in identifying which industries to promote. It has backed some losers and missed some potential winners, such as the auto industry. Although the Japanese strategy is mostly positive, selected industries, such as agriculture, are heavily protected.

The EU's primary strategy has been to slow structural changes that cause losses and unemployment in declining industries. Low-interest loans and import restrictions play a key role. Agriculture has benefited from subsidies and import controls, despite its comparative disadvantage. Other declining industries that have been singled out for special treatment are shipbuilding, steel, textiles, and footwear. It is difficult to support, subsidize, and protect specific industries against competition within a unified (currently) 27-nation market with uniform product standards, no trade barriers, and a free flow of goods and productive resources.

U.S. policy makers interested in industrial policy have been attracted to the Japanese model because of Japan's high growth rate over three decades. However, most of the policy proposals as well as actual practice in the United States seem to more closely resemble the European model. They have emphasized protection from foreign competition and focused on rebuilding declining industries rather than developing promising new ones.

Tax Avoidance Finally, supply-siders stress that high marginal tax rates cause too many scarce resources to be devoted to avoiding taxes. Time spent looking for tax loopholes (by individuals and their hired attorneys and accountants) could be used more productively.

Did Supply-Side Economics Work?

It is difficult to evaluate supply-side policies because it is impossible to conduct ceteris paribus experiments. There is some support for the argument that marginal tax rates affect those at the bottom of the ladder. There is also some weak support for a similar effect on those in high tax brackets. In the late 1980s, economists Gary Burtless and Robert Haveman (1987) summarized a variety of studies of the effects of taxes and transfers, concluding that the loss of welfare benefits was a deterrent to work effort in some experimental programs to test work incentives. More recent studies have agreed with this conclusion (Garfinkel, Rainwater, & Smeeding, 2006). Labor supply responses to lower tax rates were also modest, although different researchers have found different results. Combining work from several sources suggests a labor supply response to tax cuts of 2% or less (Akhtar & Harris, 1992; Romer & Romer, 2007).

Crowding out within the budget, which was impacted by reduced tax revenue and increased Social Security payments, is at least partly responsible for reduced public-sector capital formation and reduced spending on nondefense research and development. These two negative effects on growth offset some of the potential gains from work and investment incentives.

The Reagan supply-side program was often criticized on distributional grounds. Opponents argued that the package of tax cuts and incentives was "welfare for the rich," who received the biggest tax cuts and benefited the most from saving and investment incentives. Supply-siders countered that the rich were paying the most to begin with! In addition, as a group they tend to include the most productive workers (measured by their high salaries) and the individuals most willing and able to save and invest. Thus, any program aimed at encouraging work effort, saving, and investment has to focus on incentives for individuals with higher incomes. But, the defenders argued, the resulting economic growth, lower inflation rates, and higher productivity will eventually benefit everyone.

The ongoing debate over supply-side economics tends to focus on the massive federal budget deficits, increased income inequality, and failure to promote growth. The most notable critics of supply-side policies include Nobel Prize-winning economist Paul Krugman, who even wrote a book called *Peddling Prosperity* (1995), which attacks the theory. He argues that although any policy that leads aggregate supply to shift to the right would be beneficial to the economy, the policies prescribed by supply-side economics are questionable in both their efficacy and motives.

CONCLUSION

The U.S. economy is many things to many people, but for most of those over 18 and under 65, it is first and foremost a job-creating machine. The experience of 2010 was very discouraging, not only for new high school and college graduates but also for older workers displaced by downsizing (especially middle managers), blue-collar workers, and unskilled workers. The prospects for the rest of the decade are generally somewhat brighter, although there will be regions of slow growth, particularly those that face closure of defense plants and military installations.

Brighter prospects come not only from demand factors—like growth in Latin America, recovery in Europe, a backlog of demand for autos and appliances, and low interest rates—but also from some long-term supply factors. The labor force is getting more experienced. The productivity payoff from the investment in information technology is being realized. The savings rate is picking up after three decades of abnormally low saving. Companies that went through the trauma of mergers, acquisitions, and bankruptcies in the 1990s and early 2000s are now leaner, more efficient, and ready to invest and grow. Those new workers who have studied the market and matched their skills to emerging job opportunities should be poised to succeed.

Name ______________________ Date ______________

Post-Test

1. A growth strategy that focuses on the long-run costs of lost output and lost spending on investments in physical and human capital is called
   a. a demand-based growth strategy.
   b. a supply-based growth strategy.
   c. an output-based growth strategy.
   d. a cyclical growth strategy.
   e. a classical growth strategy.
2. Which one of the following is NOT part of the real business cycle explanation of economic fluctuations?
   a. oil price shocks
   b. a less experienced labor force
   c. a change in money supply growth
   d. improved technology
   e. a decline in human capital
3. Which one of the following will NOT shift the aggregate supply curve to the right?
   a. lower prices for natural resources
   b. a bumper crop of grain
   c. a higher average level of education
   d. a larger defense budget
4. Long-term economic growth requires
   a. steady rightward shifts of the aggregate demand curve.
   b. steady rightward shifts of the aggregate supply curve.
   c. centrally administered industrial policy.
   d. falling prices for natural resources.
5. Which of the following is an example of investment in human capital?
   a. roads and bridges
   b. research and development
   c. tax breaks for the working poor
   d. technical training
   e. export promotion spending
6. If the quality of human capital increases, then
   a. the *AS* curve shifts to the left.
   b. the standard of living increases.
   c. the *AD* curve shifts to the right.
   d. the *AD* curve shifts to the left.
   e. productivity falls.
7. Which one of the following is NOT a tool of industrial policy?
   a. subsidies
   b. tax incentives
   c. free markets
   d. import restrictions
8. A criticism of industrial policy is that
   a. the government replaces the market as decision maker.
   b. owners of productive resources become the decision makers.
   c. it inevitably leads to deregulation.
   d. it often discourages saving.

Answers

1. a. a demand-based growth strategy. *The answer can be found in Section 13.1.*
2. c. a change in money supply growth. *The answer can be found in Section 13.1.*
3. d. a larger defense budget. *The answer can be found in Section 13.2.*
4. b. steady rightward shifts of the aggregate supply curve. *The answer can be found in Section 13.2.*
5. d. technical training.*The answer can be found in Section 13.3.*
6. b. the standard of living increases. *The answer can be found in Section 13.3.*
7. c. free markets. *The answer can be found in Section 13.4.*
8. a. the government replaces the market as decision maker. *The answer can be found in Section 13.4.*

KEY IDEAS

1. Monetary and fiscal policies to stimulate demand can be considered growth strategies because they attempt to increase output by ensuring that what is produced will be sold. Such strategies increase demand in the face of an upward-sloping short-run aggregate supply curve, and will increase both output and the price level.
2. The slope of the aggregate supply curve and the length of the time period that separates the short run from the long run have important implications for the effects of a change in aggregate demand on prices, output, and employment. If the aggregate supply curve is vertical, at least in the long run, and the short run is relatively brief, demand management policies will have little impact on economic growth. If the aggregate supply curve has a flatter slope in the short run and the short run is a fairly long period of calendar time, demand management policies will have more effect on growth of GDP.
3. The aggregate supply curve can be shifted by changes in the quantity and quality of resources available or by changes in technology. Increases in capital, including human capital and improvements in technology, increase worker productivity. Productivity growth in industrial countries has been slower in recent decades than in earlier periods.
4. Supply-side economics is a group of policies intended to shift the aggregate supply curve to the right. These policies include work incentives, saving and investment incentives, and deregulation. The Reagan administration implemented a supply-side program in the 1980s. These policies had some modest effects on work effort but little impact on investment and saving, and are partly responsible for the growth of the deficit.

Name ________________________________ Date ____________________

CRITICAL THINKING QUESTIONS

1. How are demand-based growth strategies different from supply-based growth strategies?

2. Does business investment shift aggregate supply or aggregate demand? How do you think increased business investment will affect prices and real output?

3. Why have natural resources not been a serious constraint on economic growth?

4. How would each of the following affect measured productivity?
   a. new and better capital equipment for many workers

   b. a sharp rise in the labor force participation rate

   c. higher prices for natural resources in general

5. What are some of the factors that can increase labor productivity?

6. Marilyn Karcher is retired and receiving Social Security benefits, but she is considering working part-time. If she works part-time, she will pay about 15% of her earnings in federal income tax, 4% in state income tax, and 7.3% in Social Security tax. What is her marginal tax rate on earnings? If she works 20 hours a week, she will earn a gross income of $145 a week. What is her net income and her net hourly wage? Should she take the job?

7. Robert Stewart is trying to decide whether to work on Saturday for 3 hours at an hourly rate of $20 or to spend the 3 hours cleaning his garage. He can hire two neighborhood boys to clean the garage, but they charge $35. What should he do if his combined tax rate (federal income tax, state income tax, and Social Security tax) on the additional income totals 30%? What if the combined tax rate totals 50%?

8. How can a tax cut be both a demand-side (Keynesian) and a supply-side policy? Does it make any difference what kinds of taxes are cut?

9. The United States has had an extensive, federally funded program of research and technical assistance to agriculture through the Cooperative Extension Service and the agricultural experiment stations located in each state's land-grant universities. Is this industrial policy? Do you think it has been successful?

What Goes Up Must Come Down: The Business Cycle

LEARNING OBJECTIVES

- Explain the nature of the Business Cycle and the problem of economic instability.
- Describe the causes of Inflation using the Aggregate Supply/Aggregate Demand model and explain the effects of Inflation on the economy.
- Describe the causes of Recession using the Aggregate Supply/Aggregate Demand model and explain the Effects of Recession on the economy.
- Explain the various Types of Unemployment and how they are measured.
- Describe the social impact of Economic Instability (Inflation and Unemployment).
- Use the Major Economic Models to demonstrate an understanding of the chain reactions resulting from human choices and how they move through an economy. Demonstrate an understanding of the Tradeoffs that result.

■ ■ ■

INTRODUCTION

A major macroeconomic problem for modern nations is the tendency toward periodic instability—the (seemingly) constant threat of economic conditions turning toward either inflation or recession. In this lesson, we will define and discuss instability—the business cycle—relative to the causes, expected effects and possible remedies. In later lessons, we will explore the counter-cyclical mechanisms of government fiscal and monetary policy, which are the policy weapons available to deal with recession and inflation.

BUSINESS CYCLES

Business cycles are the ups and downs (usually short-term) of real GDP or fluctuations in economic activity. Attempts to maintain constant or increasing business activity are not always successful. Macroeconomic instability describes the irregular, unexpected changes in business activity. The economic result of these fluctuations will vary depending on the phase of the cycle. We may experience periods of **recession** and unemployment (or even depression), which may be followed by **inflation** and an overheated economy. Figure 14.1 presents a hypothetical **business cycle.** A larger version is available in the Interactive Exercises.

Business cycle phases can be divided into the peak, which is the maximum point of economic activity, and the trough, which is the lowest point of business activity. A recovery is a period of renewed economic activity between the trough and the peak. A recession is a period of decreasing economic activity between the peak and trough.

Cyclical Variations

A downward slope in economic activity results in decreases in output, income and employment and may lead to a longer-term recession. The Bureau of Economic Research (NBER) is the accepted authority deciding when a recession begins or ends. This prominent group of economists is considered to be nonpolitical. The NBER officially declares a recession in the United States after two consecutive quarterly declines in real national income; however, the NBER may judge a recession to exist with any combination of other business activity changes.

The major causes of cycles include war, monetary policy changes, speculation, political events and even technological changes. War is devastating to individuals and to the economy because it reduces available resources and diverts existing resources to the war effort. Too much available money relative to the supply of goods and services causes inflation, which initiates a new business cycle. Speculation in the stock market may drive prices to an unsustainable high, and political actions or reactions may overly stimulate or depress business activity. Technology improvements can increase economic activity,

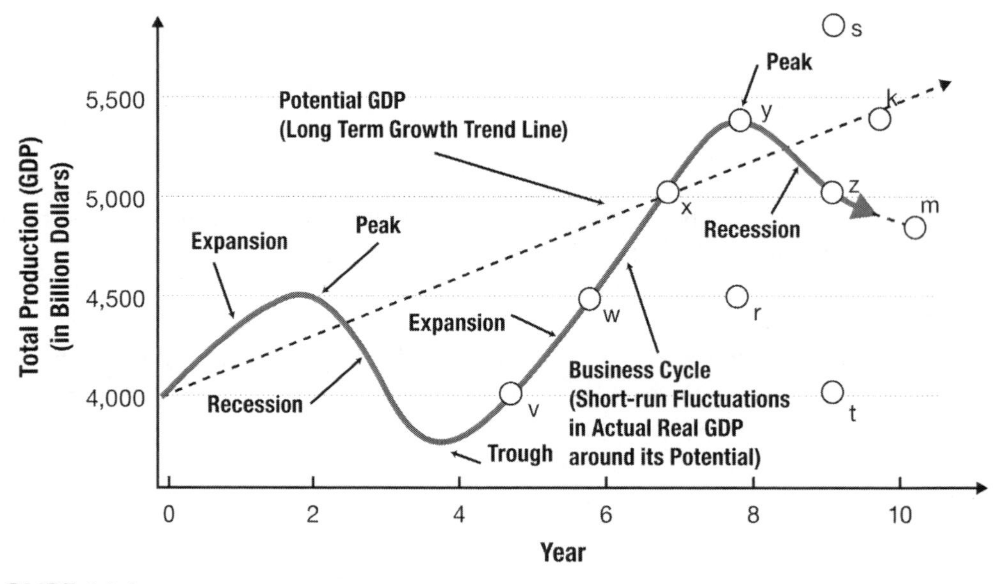

FIGURE 14.1
Business cycle phases and turning points

provided that production costs are reduced and the economy can absorb those workers who become unemployed as a result of technological improvements. All these events may trigger a business cycle.

Inflation

Inflation is one of the most difficult problems of business cycles. Inflation is a rise in the general price level. Inflation can reduce real income, employment and output because of its affect on business investment and the general economy.

CAUSES OF INFLATION

Inflation is often a result of changes in the business cycle but economists can isolate different types of inflation. There are many theories of what causes inflation in an economy.

Demand-Pull

The demand-pull theory argues that inflation is caused by too much money in an economy with too few goods. If the growth of money is faster than the growth of goods and services, pressure is placed on producers to sell more than they can efficiently produce. Increasing output often causes unit costs to increase and, thereby, prices to rise. When demand in our economy is greater than our ability to meet that demand, the usual result is inflation.

The demand-pull theory is illustrated by Keynesian analysis comparing prices (inflation) on the Y-axis and real national output on the X-axis, as shown in Figure 14.2. Keynes assumed that an economy with high unemployment (Stage 1) would have a flat aggregate supply (AS) line, with an intersecting decreasing sloped aggregate demand (AD) line. As the aggregate demand line shifts right (increases from AD1 to AD2), there

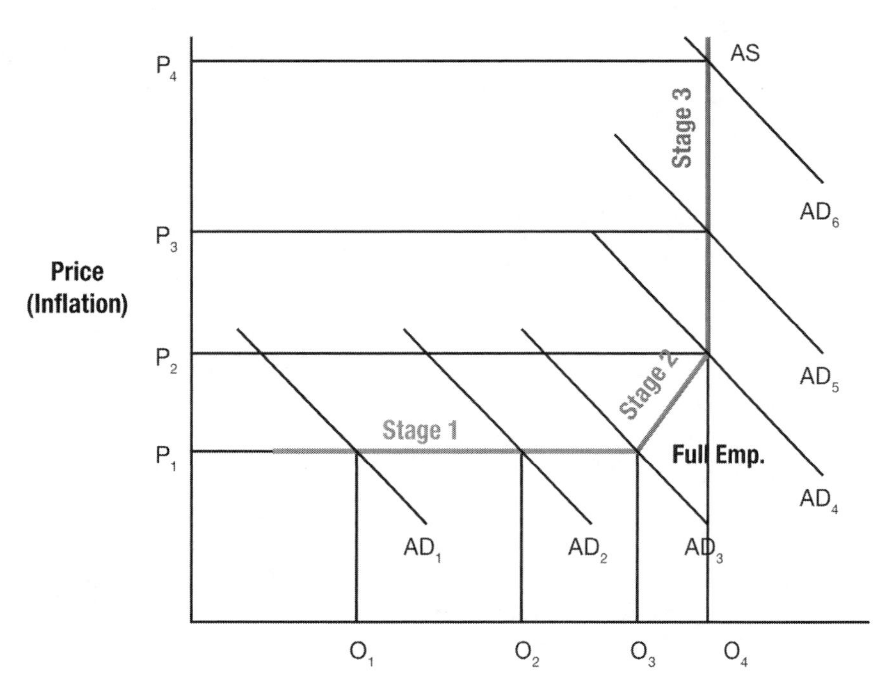

FIGURE 14.2

would be no inflation. In Stage 2, as AD shifts right (increases from AD3 to AD4) along an upward sloping AS line, both output and prices increase (P1 to P2). However, as the aggregate demand line approaches the capacity on the aggregate supply vertical line (Stage 3), inflation occurs (price increases from AD5 to AD6), with no increase in output. At full employment, increases in aggregate demand will only cause inflation with no increase in real national output.

Cost-Push Inflation

Cost-push is another theory of what causes inflation. In this model, inflation is determined by owners of resources increasing their prices, which causes cost increases for all producers and eventually consumers. This action effectively "pushes up" prices throughout an economy.

Three Types of Cost-Push Inflation:

Increasing Resource Prices Perhaps the leading cause of **cost-push inflation** is the scarcity of basic resources. In our world today, increases in oil prices represent the best example of how a basic commodity can cause inflation throughout producer and consumer allocations.

Wage-Price Spiral Although we have not seen very much of this type of inflation in recent years, it has to do with labor unions' demands for higher wages when **demand-pull inflation** is occurring. When (or if) these demands are met, it increases the cost of production, resulting in more inflation, which, in turn, may again increase union demands.

Monopoly Power If there is very little competition in a given market, producers may raise prices simply to increase profits. This is difficult to do in a competitive market or in a recession, but we are seeing increasing levels of market power exhibited in many parts of our economy.

There are other theories of inflation that argue inflation is likely if the economy is nearing capacity and therefore resources are in high demand. We may also see labor moving from one job to another that pays more. Thus, resources are attracted through higher compensation but higher output is not attained—only higher prices.

INFLATION—OVERALL EFFECTS

Inflation is normally associated with the expansionary side of the business cycle. The definition is simple. Inflation occurs when there is a general and sustained increase in prices. The major measures of inflation are the **Consumer Price Index (CPI)** and the **Producer Price Index (PPI).**

Both indices relate to the idea of a "general and sustained price increase." The CPI notes inflation for a family of four in a city, while the PPI notes inflation at the wholesale level of business. These measures are statistically complex but result in a very useful tool for analysis. Each index weighs (gives measured component value to) a wide diversity of purchases by consumers or businesses to provide an aggregate cost value for a given month. This value is then compared to the same value in the following month to determine the change in prices for the aggregate of the purchases.

- According to the U.S. Bureau of Labor Statistics (BLS), "Prices for the goods and services used to calculate the CPI are collected in 87 urban areas throughout the country

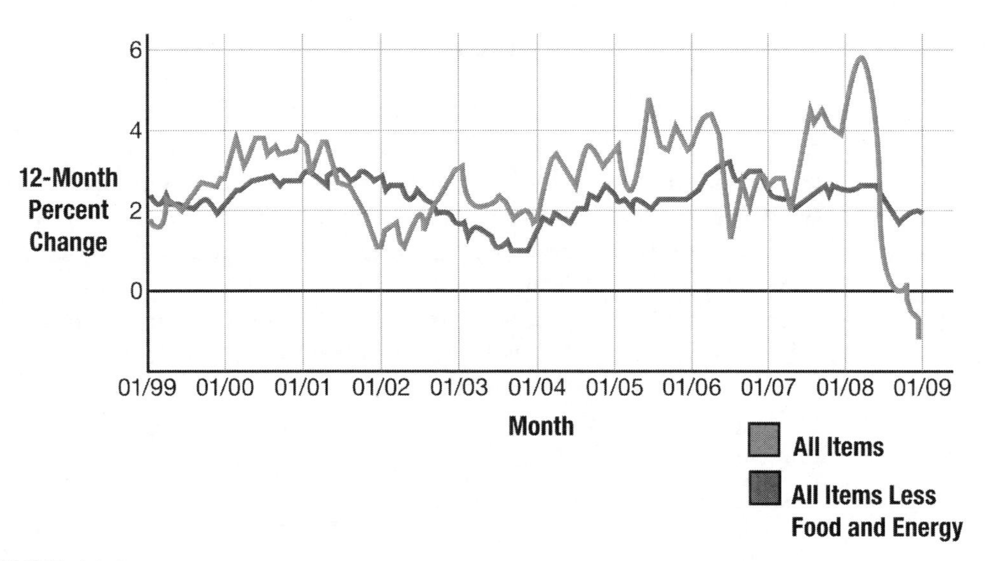

FIGURE 14.3
Consumer Price Index for All Urban Consumers: U.S. City Average, All Items and All Items Less Food and Energy
SOURCE: U.S. Department of Commerce, Bureau of Economic Analysis

and from about 23,000 retail and service establishments. Data on rents are collected from about 50,000 landlords or tenants.

- The weight for an item is derived from reported expenditures on that item as estimated by the Consumer Expenditure Survey." Source: www.bls.gov/cpi/

The CPI is computed with and without food and energy because of the volatile nature of food and energy. Notice the high inflation of food/energy followed by deflation (decrease in prices) in 2007 and 2008.

U.S. inflation rates are generally lower than most industrialized nations; however, the inflation rate has varied from 2 percent recently to 13 percent in 1979. Other national rates vary widely, from a low rate in most of Western Europe to a high rate in an African nation of more than 4000 percent.

Inflation Arithmetic

The impact of inflation on prices over time can be calculated by the **rule of 70.** The rule of 70 is a measure of how long it will take for prices to double at a given annual inflation rate. The compounded inflation rate is divided into the number 70 to find the number of years for prices to double. For example: if a nation's prices are inflating at 10 percent per year, it will take seven years for the prices to double (70/10 5 7 years). However, if inflation is 2 percent, it will take 35 years for prices to double (70/2 5 35 years).

Inflation Basics

Although numerous theories attempt to explain inflation, we have previously discussed the two major causes of inflation. Demand-pull inflation, which is "too much money chasing too few goods," meaning that there is excessive demand (see Stage 3 in Figure 14.2). Money is available but supply is usually limited in the short run so prices are bid up. The other major theory of inflation is the cost-push model. With cost-push, the costs of production are increasing, which "pushes" up overall prices.

Redistribution of Income and Wealth

When the rate of inflation exceeds wage or profit increases, wages and profits are reduced in real terms. This process rewards those workers or firms with market power and penalizes those without. With market power, one can increase prices to keep up with increasing costs or even gain through inflation by increasing prices more than the general price level increases. In contrast, people living on a fixed income will decrease their purchasing power by the amount of inflation.

For example, if you receive a monthly $1,000 pension for life and after one year inflation is 10 percent, then your monthly income in real terms is only $900. Nominal vs. real income is the issue of inflation's effect on purchasing power. Real income is current income divided by the price index at a base year times 100. For example, assume in 2010 that your income was $20,000 and in 2011 your income increased to $22,000; how did your real purchasing power change?

If prices increased from 100 in base year 2010 to 110 in 2011 (a 10 percent increase), then your actual real income stayed the same—$22,000 divided by 1.10 5 $20,000 in real 2010 dollars.

Borrowers May Gain at the Expense of Lenders

Unanticipated inflation reduces the value of the money that is paid back to the lender. Assume you borrowed $100,000 at a fixed rate of 7 percent for 30 years to purchase a house. If the inflation rate increases to 7 percent or more, you are repaying with funds less valued than the interest rate because the lender did not anticipate such inflation. Through unanticipated inflation, lenders actually lose purchasing power. You borrowed something (money) that was worth more at the time than the money that you later returned to the lender.

The effect of inflation (if anticipated) will result in savers earning higher interest rates to accommodate for inflation. If banks (savers) anticipate an inflation rate of 5 percent and require a return of 5 percent, then interest rates are set at 10 percent. If unanticipated inflation rises from 5 percent to 10 percent and interest rates are set at 10 percent, banks (savers) will lose their expected return of 5 percent.

Real Interest Rates

Real interest rates are the actual return a saver receives for loaning money. The real interest rate is the nominal interest rate minus the inflation rate.

Real Interest Rates = Nominal Interest Rate minus Inflation Rate

If interest rates for a given loan are 12 percent but there is 4 percent inflation, the real rate of interest is (12–4) 8 percent.

Inflation Discourages Saving

If you are being paid a 5 percent return on your savings and inflation is running at 7 percent, it is not logical to save money for a purchase. The value of your money is declining in real terms while in your account. In addition, the item that you may be saving to purchase is increasing in price as inflation takes place. It may be a more sound decision to borrow the money now to buy the item that is increasing in price rather than save to purchase it in the future.

Inflation Encourages Speculation

As mentioned, if the value of your saved money is declining, it is logical to put your money into an investment that is keeping pace with inflation. Inflation interrupts the normal borrowing-saving relationship and results in speculative investments with market power to increase prices without increasing output. During 2007–2008, as seen in the CPI graph of oil, oil markets were representative of this speculative process (Figure 14.3).

The impact of inflation creates a great deal of uncertainty and risk. To accommodate for possible inflation increases, savers/lenders may require a premium interest rate to hedge against a possible loss from unanticipated inflation.

Creeping (Anticipated) Inflation

A slower rate of inflation (creeping) will not have as negative of an effect as those just mentioned. Most businesses would argue that a small amount of inflation (2 percent or 3 percent) might actually be beneficial for the economy. **Creeping inflation** may encourage some economic growth and profits as investors anticipate stable returns.

Noncyclical Changes

Noncyclical fluctuations are economic fluctuations other than business cycles. **Seasonal variation** and **secular trends** are two examples of such fluctuations.

Seasonal fluctuations form a regular (predictable) pattern of economic activity during a year. Retail activity, for example, follows a seasonal pattern, higher in November and December and lower in January, while farm output is higher in the summer and lower in the winter.

A secular trend is a long-term average of economic activity. Examples are the ownership of cell phones and iPods over a time period. Secular trends illustrate long-term movements. A secular trend is illustrated on the cycles graph (Figure 14.1) by the dashed line.

Aggregate Supply Implications for Growth

The secular trend (or Long-Term Trend Line) represents the path of a long-run movement in the economy. Secular trends are driven by the relatively slow rightward shifts of the AS curve. These rightward shifts in AS are also responsible for long-run growth discussed in Lesson 2 (PPF). When AS shifts left with a given AD, prices raise (inflation) and national output declines, but when AS shifts right, prices decline and real national output increases.

The rightward shifts in AS are also responsible for long-run growth of output in our ongoing studies of the Circular Flow diagram that we began in Lesson 1. Although there are technical differences in the graphs, an insight into the factors that cause rightward shifts in the Aggregate (Macro) Supply curve can be gained by reviewing the factors that caused rightward shifts in the Market (Micro) Supply Curves in Lesson 3. The "macro" models of the economy are all strongly linked together (with the AS/AD driving changes in the others.) Supply and demand shifts at the micro level ultimately drive the changes in the "macro" AS/AD. Keep these points in mind along with our ongoing theme of "Making Good Choices for Healthy Growth" as the course continues to unfold.

EFFECT OF RECESSION—UNEMPLOYMENT

Recession is generally defined by the NBER as occurring when two consecutive declines in quarterly GDP occur. This is somewhat inexact but we know that unemployment is one of the major characteristics of a slowing business cycle. Unemployment in economics is normally defined as workers who are willing and able to work for pay but are unable to find work (Lesson Two). The **unemployment rate** is the number of unemployed (those unable to find work) *divided* by the total labor force. The total labor force includes those willing and able to work whether employed or unemployed. Some adjustments to this definition are made by the BLS.

The Three Types of Unemployment

Cyclical unemployment is present when there is insufficient demand for labor in an economy due to a decline in the business cycle. The lack of demand for workers results in increased unemployment.

Frictional unemployment occurs when workers are moving between jobs. There is a period of adjustment as a worker is temporarily unemployed while looking for a job or moving to a new job. Frictionally unemployed can be unemployed by choice. This is quite different from those who cannot find work due to a recession.

Structural unemployment is the most difficult type of unemployment for society to correct. **Structural unemployment** occurs when workers do not have the required skills for

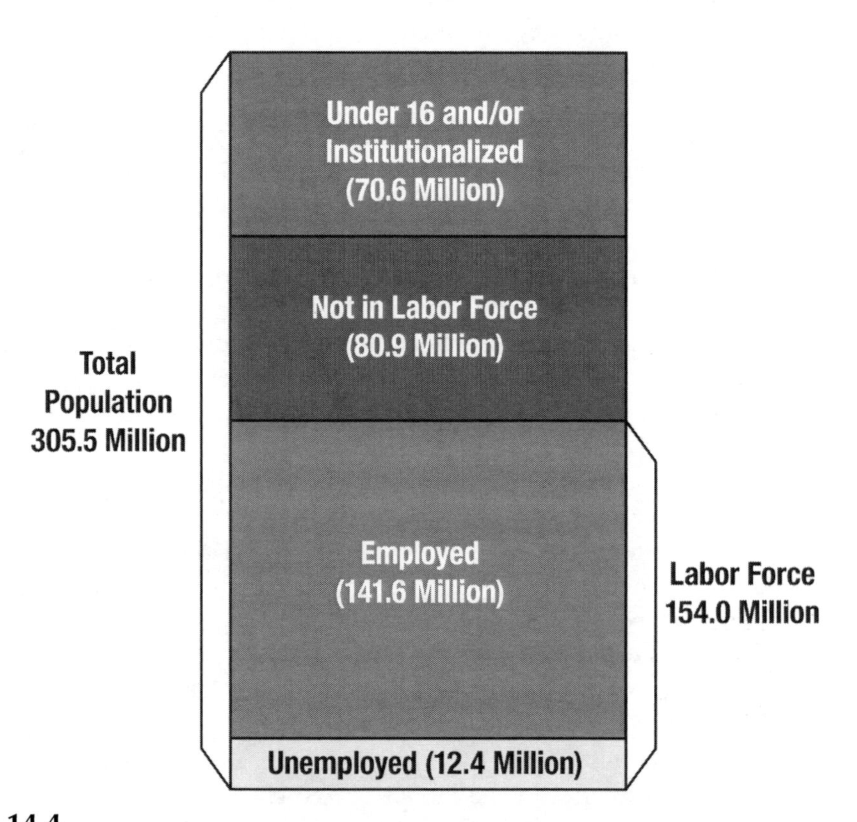

FIGURE 14.4
The U.S. Labor Force, Unemployed Workers, and Employed Workers in 2008
SOURCE: Bureau of Labor Statistics

existing jobs. If workers' skills do not keep up with job demands or, more broadly, workers lack basic reading, writing and computational skills, an expanding job market may not benefit this group.

Calculating Unemployment

The unemployment rate is calculated by the BLS monthly figures based on a sample survey of 60,000 households. A person in this survey is classified as employed if the person did any work for pay or profit during the survey week. Part-time and temporary workers are considered employed even if they work for only one hour.

To be considered unemployed, an individual must be:

1. Able to work
2. Willing to work
3. Seeking a job during the previous month
4. Not retired, under 16 years of age, or institutionalized

Individuals who are under 16, retired or institutionalized in prison or hospitals, as well as homemakers, are not considered part of the labor force so they cannot be unemployed.

Unemployment rates are often criticized because these values do not consider the above groups, who may wish to work but are unable to find jobs, nor do they consider people who do not actively seek work.

People who have not made active efforts within a month before the survey are considered **discouraged workers** and not unemployed. Also, self-employed workers and retired workers without work who wish to work are not considered unemployed. **Underemployment** may also occur as workers are forced to take available jobs below their skill levels, but these workers are not defined as unemployed.

Costs of Unemployment

An economy experiences many negative individual and social consequences from unemployment. There are lost goods and services but also personal and social costs as well as government costs associated with unemployment.

The social and individual costs include the inability of people to pay bills, mental stress resulting in illness, loss of self esteem, and even increases in crime and suicide. The individual and social costs, combined with the loss of goods and services, increases in governmental costs for unemployment, welfare and health services, and the loss of tax revenues, illustrate the high cost of unemployment. These economic costs are unlikely to be recovered once lost.

The "Expected Rate of Unemployment"

The **natural rate of unemployment** is the unemployment rate at full employment. The natural rate of unemployment is the combined frictional and structural unemployment rate excluding **cyclical unemployment.** The current goal of the natural unemployment rate is 4 percent. At this rate, production output is assumed to be at a maximum. The natural unemployment rate varies with social conditions over time. This rate has decreased from 6 percent in 1980 as more employment opportunities exist within the workforce.

High unemployment rates (rates above the natural rate) cause a gap between what is produced and what is possible at full employment. The **GDP gap** is the difference between potential output at full employment and current output.

HISTORY OF THE NBER

Founded in 1920, the National Bureau of Economic Research (NBER) is a private, nonprofit, nonpartisan research organization dedicated to promoting a greater understanding of how the economy works. The NBER is committed to undertaking and disseminating unbiased economic research among public policymakers, business professionals and the academic community.

Over the years, the NBER's research agenda has encompassed a wide variety of issues that confront our society. The NBER's early research focused on the aggregate economy, examining in detail the business cycle and long-term economic growth. Simon Kuznets' pioneering work on national income accounting, Wesley Mitchell's influential study of the business cycle, and Milton Friedman's research on the demand for money and the determinants of consumer spending were among the early studies done at the NBER.

The NBER Today

The NBER is the nation's leading nonprofit economic research organization. Sixteen of the 31 American Nobel Prize winners in economics and six of the past chairmen of the President's Council of Economic Advisers have been researchers at the NBER. The more than 1,000 professors of economics and business now teaching at universities around the country who are NBER researchers are the leading scholars in their fields. These NBER associates concentrate on four types of empirical research: developing new statistical measurements, estimating quantitative models of economic behavior, assessing the effects of public policies on the U.S. economy and projecting the effects of alternative policy proposals.

The NBER source: http://www.nber.org/info.html

Unemployment and Lost GDP

Economists often use **Okun's Law** to estimate the loss of GDP associated with an increase in unemployment. Okun's Law estimates that for every 1 percent increase in unemployment above the natural rate, a GDP gap of 2 percent occurs. Thus, if an economy has 5 percent unemployment when 4 percent is the estimated natural rate, a 1 percent gap yields a 2 percent loss of GDP.

5% 2 4% 5 1% gap times 2 5 2% loss of GDP

The average annual unemployment rate of the United States is less than in most industrialized nations of the world. A comparison of unemployment rates throughout the world can be found at the International Monetary Funds Internet website or at the CIA World Book website.

POLICY TRADE-OFFS OF INFLATION AND UNEMPLOYMENT

There are inevitable trade-offs that are always at play in our economy. If we have inflation, it normally means that we have a rapidly growing, overheating economy but we have more jobs (at least with demand-pull inflation). If we have recession, it normally means that the economy is slowing with fewer jobs, but at least we don't have to worry about inflation.

In the 1970s, and more recently, we have (unfortunately) experienced the "worst of both worlds." With the oil price shocks of 1972–1973 and 2007–2008, we seem to see history repeating itself. The new word in the mid-70s was **stagflation** and we currently fear repeating this cycle.

Stagflation

This term was coined by combining two different words to describe a perplexing economic problem. If our economy is "stagnant" or not growing but is experiencing, at the same time, a significant degree of inflation, the result is "stagflation."

Some economic theories suggest that we cannot have high unemployment and high inflation at the same time. If we look at the demand-pull model, this would appear to be true. However, most of our price shocks, then and now, have resulted from cost-push factors that center on the price of oil.

In the mid-1970s, a barrel of oil increased from $1.75 at the wellhead to $8. While this seems incredibly cheap today, it still represented a quadrupling of oil prices. From 2007–2009, we have seen oil prices vary by a similar multiple—from approximately $35 per barrel to more than $140 and then back to under $100.

With this kind of price change for such a critical commodity, varying inflation is the inevitable result—regardless of other economic variables.

SUMMARY

Business cycles are a common problem for capitalism. Both inflation and unemployment present hazards for an economy but are inevitable occurrences over time. There are significant costs associated with both inflation and unemployment that ultimately affect the national economy.

KEY TERMS

Anticipated or Creeping Inflation: A small amount of inflation—less than 3 percent.

Business Cycle: Unexpected changes in overall GDP. Fluctuations in spending.

Consumer Price Index: Measuring inflation by tracking the costs of a market basket of consumer goods (i.e., 80,000 items) month to month.

Cost-Push Inflation: Inflation caused by increasing costs of production, which may come from resource price increases, labor demands or simple monopoly power.

Cyclical Unemployment: Those unable to find a job because of the decline in economic activity.

Demand-Pull Inflation: A theory that attempts to explain inflation by saying that when demand is excessive, relative to supply, prices are "pulled" up by the level of spending that is occurring.

Discouraged Worker: Someone who is no longer looking for work and is not counted in the unemployment statistic.

Frictional Unemployment: Those who are unemployed by choice and may be in school or training to improve skills.

GDP Gap: The difference between potential GDP (100 percent) and actual GDP for a given year.

Inflation: A general and sustained price level increase. Measured by the CPI.

Natural Rate of Unemployment: The combined frictional and structural rate of unemployment.

Okun's Law: A method of estimating changes in GDP based on changes in unemployment.

Producer Price Index: A calculation similar to the consumer price index that traces increases in production cost.

Recession: When GDP declines for two successive quarters.

Rule of 70: A measure to determine how long it will take inflation to double prices.

Seasonal Variation: An expected change in overall spending during certain times of the year such as pre-Christmas or back to school.

Secular Trend: A fundamental change in our economy that is occurring over a much longer period of time. Example: Over the past 30 years, there has been a secular trend in the United States toward a service economy rather than manufacturing.

Stagflation: When there is rapid inflation and a high rate of unemployment occurring at the same time. The word was coined by combining stagnant and inflation.

Structural Unemployment: Those whose skills do not keep up with changing job requirements or do not possess very basic skills.

Unanticipated or Galloping Inflation: A relatively high degree of inflation (over 5 percent) when the negative effects of inflation begin to occur.

Underemployed: A worker who settles for a job that is below his skill and normal pay level.

Wage-Price Spiral: Inflation caused by labor demand for higher wages.

Name ______________________________ Date ______________

Applied Exercises

1. Given the data below, find real GDP in each year. On the basis of this information, can we conclude that there was real growth or recession in 2009 and 2010?

Year	Nominal GDP	Price Index
2008	$500	100
2009	$550	105
2010	$575	110

2. Answer the following as True or False.
   ___ The production of durable goods is more stable than the production of non-durables over the business cycle.
   ___ People who work part time, but desire to work full time, are considered to be officially unemployed.
   ___ The natural rate of unemployment in the United States is about 5 percent.
   ___ Unanticipated inflation benefits some groups in the economy.
   ___ During the past 10 years, the U.S. economy has experienced three recessions.

3. If we assume that the natural rate of inflation for Nation X is 5 percent but the current economy has 11 percent inflation, according to Okun's Law, what is the loss in GDP?

Applied Exercises: Answers

1. Given the data below, find real GDP in each year. On the basis of this information, can we conclude that there was real growth or recession in 2009 and 2010?

Year	Nominal GDP	Price Index	Real GDP
2008	$500	100	**500/100 × 100 = $500**
2009	$550	105	**550/105 × 100 = $523.8**
2010	$575	110	**575/110 × 100 = $522.7**

   Real growth occurred between 2008 and 2009 as real GDP increased by $23.8 but declined between 2009 and 2010 by $1.1.
2. **Numbers 1, 2, 5 are False.**
3. If we assume that the natural rate of inflation for Nation X is 5 percent but the current economy has 11 percent inflation, according to Okun's Law, what are the costs to GDP?
   The opportunity cost or lost goods and services according to Okun's Law would be 11 percent 2 5 percent 5 6 percent times 2 for a loss of GDP of 12 percent per year.

The Aggregate Nature of Economics

We now need to turn our attention supply and demand for the economy as a whole. We will examine the following concepts in this chapter:

- Aggregate demand and supply
- Determinants of aggregate demand and supply
- Equilibrium

AGGREGATE DEMAND

The aggregate demand curve shows the relationship between the price level and real GDP. An inverse relationship exists between the price level and real GDP. As the price level increases, real GDP decreases. As the price level decreases, real GDP increases.

GDP consists of consumer spending, government spending, and net exports. An increase in the price level causes overall spending to decrease. The indirect relationship between the two variables results in a downward sloping aggregate demand curve.

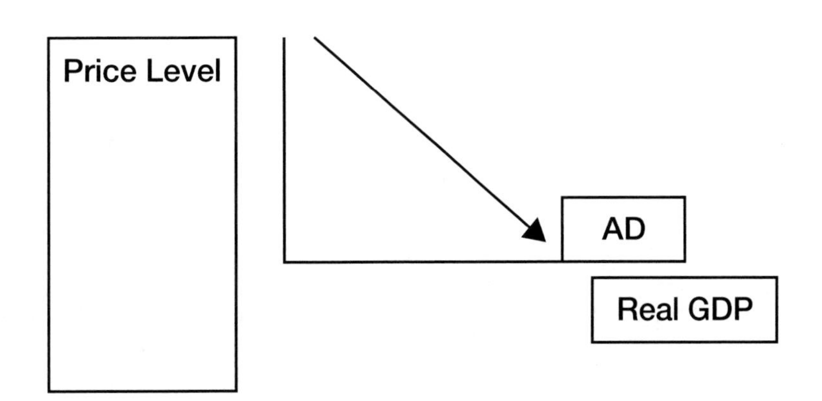

DOWNWARD SLOPING AGGREGATE DEMAND CURVE

The aggregate demand curve slopes downward for three reasons: real balances effect, interest rate effect, and foreign purchases effect.

Real Balances Effect. An increase in the price level decreases a consumer's purchasing power for goods and services. If the economy is in an inflationary time period, the value of the consumers' money income decreases. It is more expensive to purchase goods and services.

Interest Rate Effect. A change in the price level affects investment spending. Producers may purchase equipment on credit or use a loan to purchase equipment. An increase in the price level may cause producers to apply for more loans. An increase in the amount of loans will drive up the interest rate for loans. Once the interest rate increases, less producers will apply for a loan. A decrease in borrowed money decreases aggregate demand.

Foreign Purchases Effect. An increase in the price level will increase the price of U.S. exports. If it is more expensive to have goods exported to other countries, consumers in foreign countries will decrease the demand for U.S. made goods.

Shifts in Aggregate Demand Curve

So far we discussed the shape of the aggregate demand curve. Now let's consider the shifts in the aggregate demand curve. Take a look at the graph. The original curve is shown as AD. An increase in aggregate demand shifts the curve to the right (AD′). A decrease in aggregate demand shifts the curve to the left (AD″).

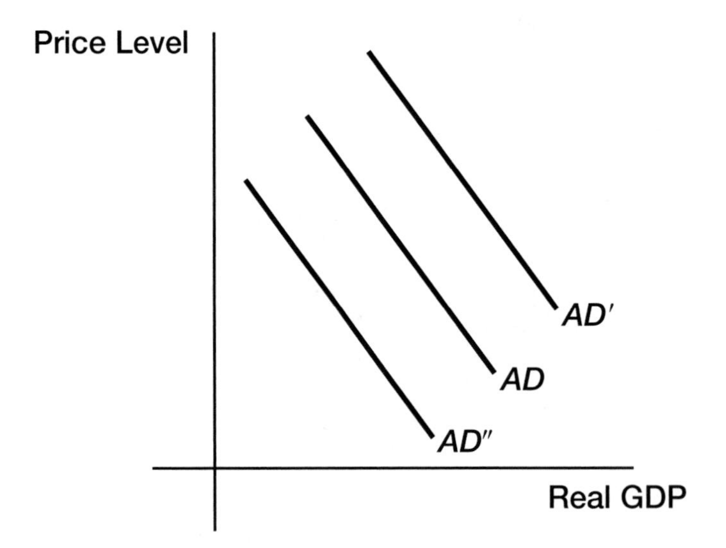

Consumer spending. Consumers' wealth, debt, expectations, and interest rate paid on borrowed money will cause a shift in aggregate demand.

- An increase in wealth will increase aggregate demand.
- Increases in consumer debt cause consumers to spend less. Less spending leads to a decrease in aggregate demand.
- Expected increases in income causes consumers to spend more money (increases AD).

Investment Spending. A foreseen increase in profitability will cause producers to spend more money on capital goods.

Government Spending. If the economy is experiencing an expansionary time period, the government will spend more money (increase in AD). If price levels rise, the government will spend less money (decrease in AD).

Net Export Spending. Consumers in foreign countries purchase goods and services in the United States. We must consider the exchange rate in foreign countries. If the dollar appreciates in terms of a foreign currency, net exports decrease. If the dollar depreciates in terms of a foreign currency, net exports increase.

AGGREGATE SUPPLY

Producers examine the relationship between price level and real GDP as it relates to aggregate supply. Let's take a look at the long run and short run.

SHORT RUN

The short run aggregate supply curve is upward sloping. A direct relationship exists between the price level and real GDP. Let's consider the reasons why the short run aggregate supply curve slopes upward.

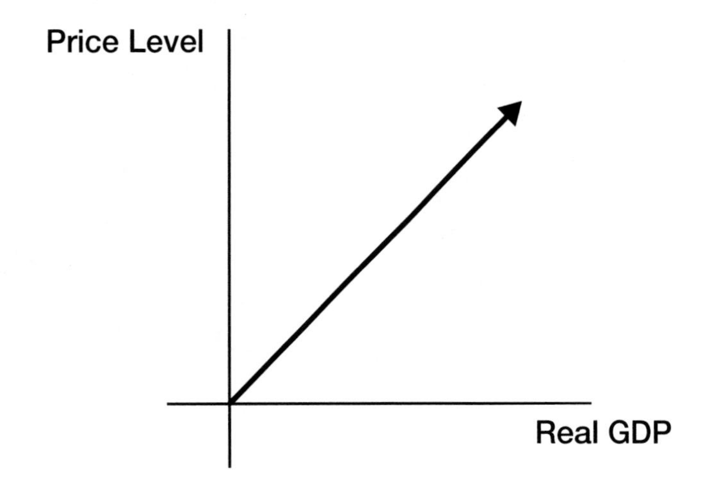

1. Sticky wages. In the short-run employers do not have enough time to adjust wages. Employees are resistant to a decrease in wages. Some employees have labor contracts. What would happen if an employer told his employees he was decreasing wages by 10 percent? The employees would not have a positive reaction to the news.
2. Sticky prices. Producers cannot change prices immediately. Price changes require money and additional time. Take McDonalds, for example. Price changes have to occur on the menu in the store, on the kiosk at the drive-thru, and on all of the registers. The managers must pull someone from his regular responsibilities to complete the price changing task.

Long Run. The long run aggregate supply curve is vertical at full employment. Changes in the price level do not affect the aggregate supply in the long run.

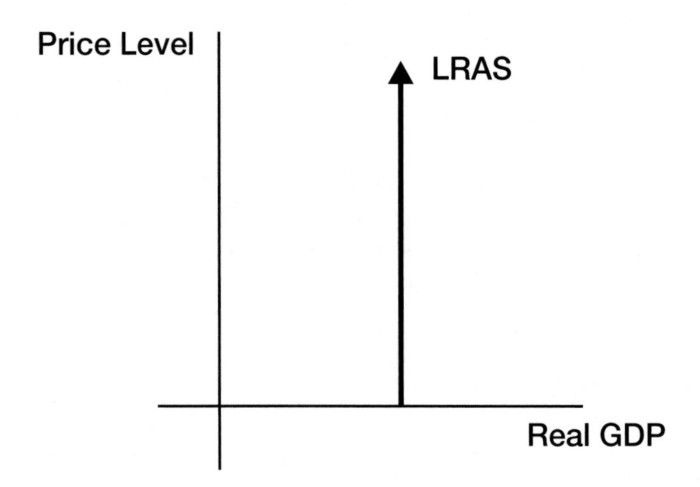

Next, let's examine the things that cause a change in aggregate supply. An increase in aggregate supply shifts the curve to the right. A decrease in aggregate supply shifts the curve to the left.

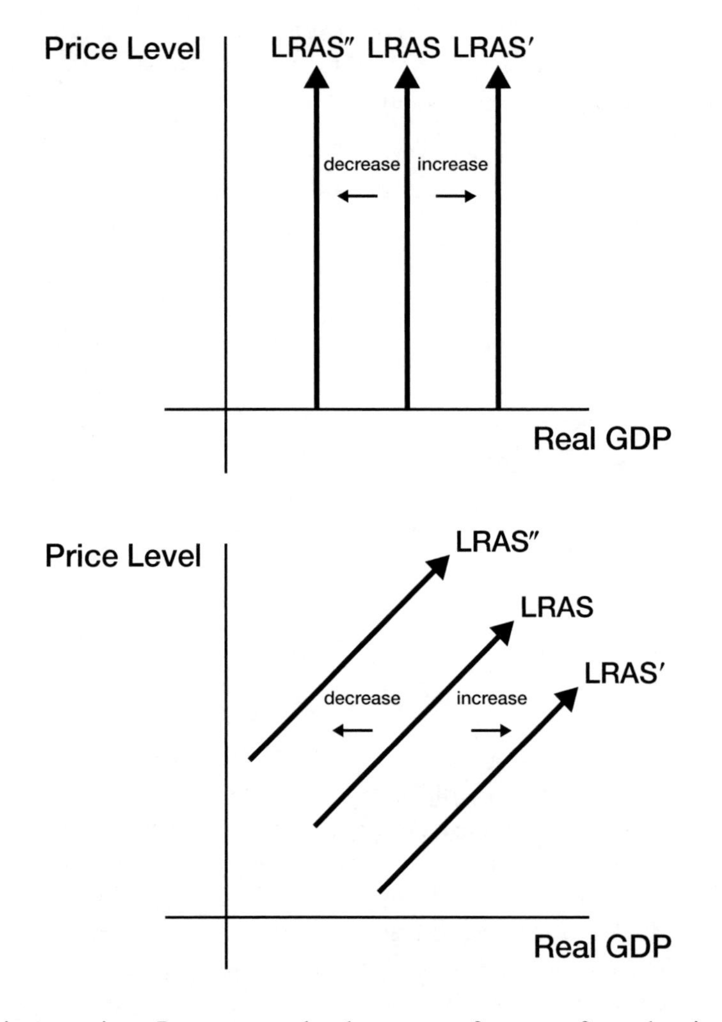

1. Change in input prices. Inputs are also known as factors of production. The factors of production include land, labor, human capital, physical capital, and entrepreneurial ability. Suppose producers experience an increase in wages paid to employees. An increase in wages increases the costs of production. Increases in costs of production decreases aggregate supply.

2. Changes in productivity. An increase in productivity increases the supply of a good or service. If employees experience a decrease in morale, productivity decreases. A decrease in productivity decreases aggregate supply.
3. Changes in taxes and subsidies. Subsidies are grants provided by the government. An increase in subsidies will decrease the cost of production. Decreases in costs of production will increase aggregate supply.

EQUILIBRIUM

So far we have discussed aggregate demand and aggregate supply. Now let's put the three curves together. We reach equilibrium when aggregate demand, short run aggregate supply, and long run aggregate supply are equal at the same price level. Ideally, we want the economy to reach equilibrium. Let's examine a few cases.

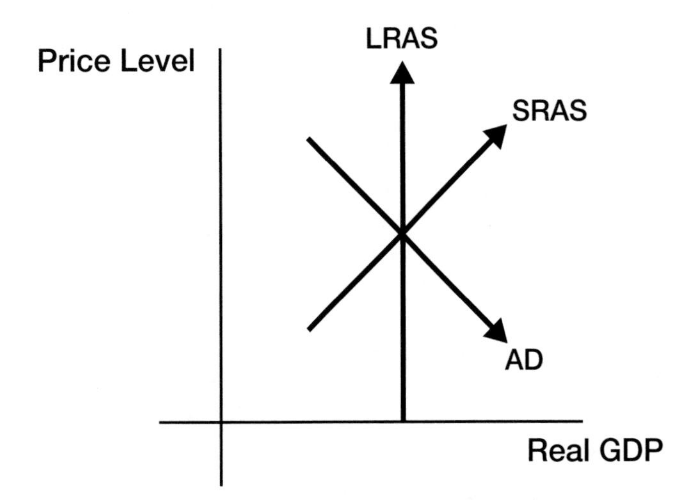

1. Suppose consumers experience an increase in money income. Consumers are willing and able to purchase more goods and services. An increase in aggregate demand shifts the curve to the right. As demonstrated in the graph, the price level and real GDP increase. An increase in the price level leads to demand pull inflation.
2. Suppose consumers fear a recession is coming. Consumers stop spending money and begin to save more money. A decrease in spending shifts the aggregate demand curve to the left. A decrease in spending leads to a recession and cyclical unemployment.
3. Suppose input prices increase for producers. An increase in input prices increases the price level for goods and services. An increase in prices will lead to a decrease in aggregate supply. The increase in price level leads to cost push inflation.

CHAPTER SIXTEEN

Fiscal Policy

LEARNING OBJECTIVES

- Describe Fiscal Policy and the objectives of Fiscal Policy.
- Explain the Mechanics of Fiscal Policy and how it works.
- Describe the Budget Implications of surpluses and deficits.
- Describe Discretionary and Nondiscretionary Tools.
- Describe Public Debt and the true burdens and myths associated with it.
- Use the Major Economic Models to demonstrate an understanding of the chain reactions resulting from human choices and how they move through an economy. Demonstrate an understanding of the Tradeoffs that result.

■ ■ ■

"The temptation to form premature theories upon insufficient data is the bane of our profession."

SHERLOCK HOLMES

INTRODUCTION

While the world's greatest detective was undoubtedly referring to a frequent failing on the part of criminologists, the temptation to make premature declarations on sketchy information plagues the economics profession as well. With economic decision making, there are even more clues and variables to contemplate.

All theories—ultimately—come from our belief about our world and our behavior as we interact with that world. As we have seen in our discussion in this unit, Classical Theory was the first real attempt to theorize about our economic behavior from the macro standpoint. Based on observation and data, Classical Theorists reached certain conclusions about the predictability of our economic behavior and the effects that would follow. Later theorists would conclude that the Classical Theorists were asking the correct questions but did not provide the correct answers.

By the late 1930s, Keynesian Economics became the set of ideas that would challenge the older theory (Classical). While this new school of thought was still looking at the old questions, the answers were different and seemed to be more supported by data and empirical evidence. These emerging ideas promised a new way of looking at economics and, even more importantly, suggested that there were "counter-cyclical tools" that could help us manage the periodic instability that had long plagued our system.

In this lesson, we will be focusing on Keynesian Theory and how these ideas attempted to provide insight into the most perplexing area of macroeconomics—how do we maintain a stable, growing economy without slipping toward inflation or recession? As a part of this model, it will also be necessary to gain some understanding of the way our federal budgets are managed and the role of public debt.

Normative Economics

As we have seen a number of times, the normative elements in economics are numerous. As we look at the impact of budget deficits, surpluses and the many political decisions that govern both discretionary (by our actions) and nondiscretionary (by adjustments with) policy, we must recognize that the decisions to use these models come from the beliefs of policymakers and have much to do with their perception of the world and their beliefs about the role of government. As we have also seen in earlier discussions, all economic theories require assumptions.

FISCAL POLICY

Although **fiscal policy** is relatively complex, the definition is fairly simple: It is the action taken by government (usually federal) to change tax rates and/or spending levels for the purpose of stabilizing our economy. While the definition is simple, the discussion between our elected policy makers that usually predicates governmental action is quite a different story. Keep in mind that fiscal policy is largely a political answer to an economic problem and involves many different normative judgments.

The presentation of the principles in this lesson will be consistent with the assumptions of Keynesian Theory. As Keynes viewed the world, he came to several conclusions:

- A market economy is inherently unstable.
- There are no built-in economic devices in a market economy that will guarantee stability.
- Government has the ability, and the responsibility, to attempt to steer our economy toward price stability, growth and full employment.

Objectives of Fiscal Policy—Employment Act of 1946

The objectives of fiscal policy were identified by federal legislation that was passed in 1946. This legislation really did not do that much—it contained no regulations or appropriations. However, it did say that the federal government should make every effort to:

- Help maintain a stable economy relative to recession or inflation
- Encourage economic growth
- Promote full employment

These three simple objectives don't sound very difficult individually, but accomplishing all three at the same time is a major challenge. Although this legislation was passed in 1946, it would not be until the early 1960s that an active attempt would be made to carry out these objectives through fiscal policy. Legislation introduced by President Kennedy proposed an across-the-board tax cut to stimulate a sluggish economy. This policy action was based on an application of Keynesian Theory.

DISCRETIONARY FISCAL POLICY

The overall intent of fiscal policy is very direct—the government is attempting to influence aggregate demand. If you think back to our model, we know that aggregate demand is what drives our economy in the short run. If the economy is moving too slowly, AD has to increase for us to move from recession. If it is moving too rapidly, it must be slowed to reduce the possibility of inflation. According to the Keynesian model, managing AD, during recession or inflation, can (in the short run) achieve our objectives of stability, growth and full employment.

As we look back to our bathtub model in Figure 16.1, we know that raising or lowering taxes has a predictable effect on AD as does a change in government spending. However, we must also consider the effect on the federal budget with any of these actions and, more importantly, understand the implications of the effects of these decisions for the longer run.

Summary: Discretionary Fiscal Policy with Less Than Full Employment

If taxes are raised-AD declines and the overall economy slows
If taxes are lowered-AD increases and the economy grows
If governmental spending is raised-AD increases and the economy expands
If government spending is lowered-AD declines and the economy slows

If we apply the Keynesian model and our economy is in recession, we must use fiscal policy to stimulate aggregate demand, which means that we would lower taxes and/or

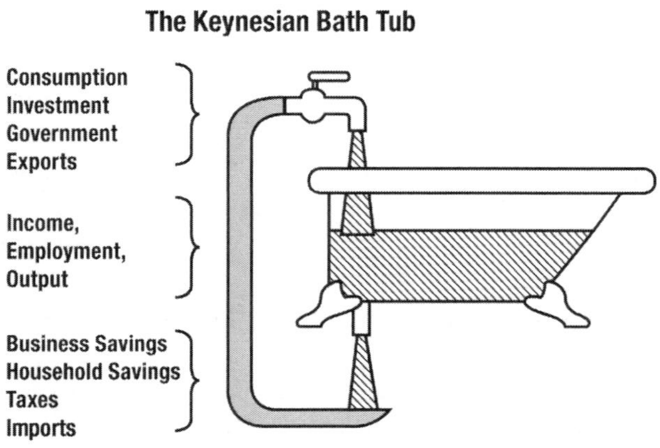

FIGURE 16.1
The Keynesian Bath Tub

increase government spending. When the desired result is accomplished—an increase in AD to create an expanding economy—it would also normally result in a budget deficit.

If we are suffering from inflation, the opposite policy would be appropriate—raise taxes and/or lower spending. This would reduce aggregate demand and slow the economy. With higher tax revenues and less spending, we might then incur a budget surplus.

BUDGETARY IMPACT

As we look more closely at the finer points of fiscal policy, it is important to understand that some of these elements are counterintuitive—they may not seem logical. Could it be beneficial in some situations if the federal government did not maintain a balanced budget? Keynes would say yes, if incurring a short-term deficit or surplus would help promote our longer-term objectives of stability, growth and employment. In a Keynesian approach, the federal government is the only entity in our system that can assume this responsibility. State governments do not have the ability nor do corporations or consumers.

When the economy is stable and at full employment, a balanced budget would seem to be appropriate because it would not create an expansion or contraction. During a period of instability, however, the federal government can attempt to provide the impetus for a change in aggregate demand. If the economy is slowing, then fiscal policy would call for policy action to encourage an increase in AD, which would mean a cut in taxes and/or an increase in federal spending.

The result of this action is potentially a budget deficit because of less federal tax revenue (because of the tax cut) or the increase in spending. The net effect is an increase in AD as less money flows out of the tub because of lower taxes and more flows into the tub through greater federal spending. In effect, there is more water in the tub as a result of the budget deficit.

When inflation in the economy is accelerating, the opposite action would be appropriate and the goal will be to try to slow the right shifting AD. This would mean a cut in government spending and/or an increase in taxes. This action would translate into a budget surplus (or a smaller deficit)—more money flowing into the tub and less flowing out. The political consequences could be considerable, however, when elected officials tell taxpayers that raising their taxes will have a positive economic benefit.

What does President Kennedy's quote about a rising tide really mean? His message was that if the economy is growing and improving, then everyone benefits. All boats respond to a rising tide. One of the main problems, however, with fiscal policy (as envisioned by Keynes) was public perception and opinion. Many questions have to be answered and many normative judgments must be made. Does government have the right to take these actions and the right to spend more money than tax revenues allow? How could spending more money than you have available be a good thing? What will the money be spent for? Whose taxes will be raised or lowered?

In responding to some of these questions, Keynes would argue that deficits year after year would not be appropriate any more than constant surpluses. However, if an economy was in a severe decline, government policy should provide a "jump-start." If this did help to get the economy moving again and increase employment, then the longer-term benefit outweighs the short-term deficit. He argued equally about the benefits of a budget surplus to deal with inflation—this action would decrease AD at the appropriate time.

Popular opinion about Keynesian economics centers on the mistaken conclusion that Keynes believed that a nation could spend its way to prosperity with deficits as far as the eye could see. This was never his belief. Keynes argued that a deficit was only appropriate for recession situations and a budget surplus was needed for inflation situations and to pay off the previously incurred deficits. For elected officials to follow both sides of the Keynesian theory can require significant political courage.

Financing Budget Deficits

The federal government, as previously mentioned, is in a singularly unique position to influence business cycles. The federal government can spend more than it takes in, for a rather extended period of time. The primary reason for this is that the federal government largely controls our money supply—or at least the ability to refinance indebtedness as stated in the U.S. Constitution, Article I.

The federal government has two methods available to finance deficits. It can borrow the money through the issuance of bonds (a promise to pay), or it can virtually create money through interaction with the Federal Reserve (the United States' central bank). Either process involves the interaction of the U.S. Treasury and the Federal Reserve.

The Treasury has generally chosen to finance deficits through borrowing (issuing bonds). When the borrowed money is spent, it does expand our economy in the Keynesian sense and does not have quite the inflationary risk of money creation. Contrary to some political statements that have been made in the past few years, the debt that is incurred by selling more bonds is real. It is not just numbers on a page—it must be repaid to the person or institution that loaned the government the money. Given the minimal (or even negative) savings rate in this country, it has been necessary to borrow increasing amounts of money from foreign investors and institutions. In recent years, the majority of this lending has come from China, Japan and Europe. See Figure 16.2.

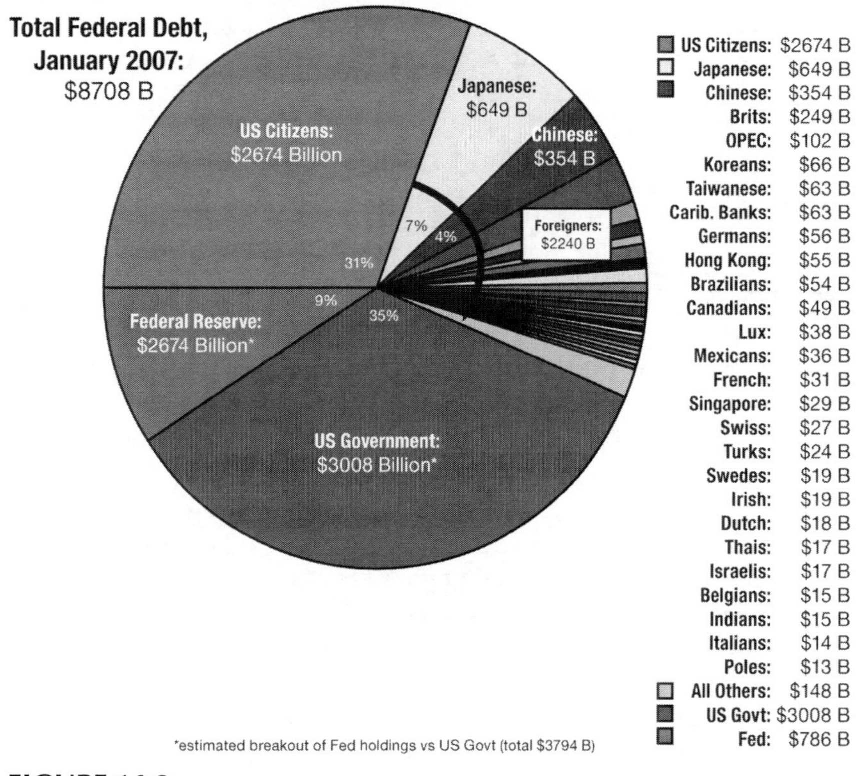

FIGURE 16.2
Pie Chart of Who Owns the National Debt

SOURCES: est. foreign holdings http://www.teas.gov/tic/mfh/txt
total and intragov http://www.treasurydirect.gov/NP/BPDLogin?application=np
Fed portion of intragov http://www.bondmarkets.com/story.asp?id=121
[extrapolated to Jan'07]

Budget Philosophies

There is much political discussion about budget deficits and public debt and, not surprisingly, a great deal of confusion on the part of voters. The idea of requiring an **annually balanced budget** seems reasonable and even mandatory to many people. Some have suggested a constitutional amendment that would dictate that requirement. The problem is that such a requirement would remove fiscal policy as a major tool to combat severe instability. Further, forced balancing of the budget would actually be procyclical. When there is a surplus, government spending would have to increase and when there is a deficit, spending would have to decrease. Required spending to do away with a surplus would likely be inflationary and decreasing spending with a deficit would intensify a recession.

A **cyclically balanced budget** would seem more logical than a requirement to balance the budget each and every year—but it can be more difficult to administer. The idea here is to balance the budget over the course of the business cycle, but these cyclical fluctuations are very irregular in length and intensity. A downturn or upswing may last for six months or as much as three or four years. There is no way to know the duration of the cycle until it is completed.

Functional finance is the budgetary philosophy the United States has used since the 1960s. This approach suggests that the federal budget should be managed to focus on the primary objectives of stability, growth and employment—even if this means periodic budget **deficits** or surpluses. Under this philosophy, balancing the budget is a secondary consideration. This approach does suggest that a deficit is appropriate when the economy is slowing and a surplus is needed when the economy moves toward inflation, but there is difficulty in timing such actions. Functional finance is also difficult because of political realities. Taxpayers generally accept tax cuts or increases in spending in a recession but resist tax increases or decreases in spending in an inflationary situation.

NONDISCRETIONARY FISCAL POLICY

The federal government has created a means of *automatically* countering business cycles through **nondiscretionary fiscal policy.** What characterizes nondiscretionary policy from other government action is that no legislative action is required—it is already built in. For the most part, these devices are triggered by changes in the level of employment. We know that employment levels go down during recession and go up during inflation. When this happens, tax revenues and government spending will change automatically.

Consider the counter-cyclical influence of **federal income taxes.** Assume that you were out of work for several months last year because of a recession. When you file your tax return, you will find that your tax rate will be lower because your annual income was lower. The result, although small for the individual, is a tax cut, which is appropriate policy for a recession. During an inflationary period, you probably worked all year plus had overtime pay. Now when you file your taxes, your income is up and so is the tax rate—automatically. Appropriate policy for inflation is such a tax increase.

Unemployment insurance is a very similar counter-cyclical policy. During inflation, when more people are working, premiums are paid into the program. During recession, when fewer people are working, the benefits are paid out. We have money (although a relatively small amount) taken out during inflation and then paid out as "unemployment benefits" during a recession—again appropriate policy.

Government subsidy programs have limited impact on actually changing the level of economic activity in a counter-cyclical way. The primary conclusion here is that most of these programs do not automatically adjust very much (in a counter-cyclical way) when economic conditions are changing. Consider Social Security—it puts a tremendous amount of spending into our economy each month. The business cycle may be trending up or down, but these benefits are relatively constant—or possibly *pro-cyclical.*

Advantages of Discretionary Fiscal Policy

There is no question that **discretionary fiscal** policy is an important and powerful tool to deal with the problem of instability. While we may argue some of the finer points, when it is needed (or not needed) and the particular timing, fiscal policy continues to be used, especially to deal with recession.

Another use of fiscal policy is to target specific groups or different parts of the economy. We may chose to spend our deficit (borrowed money) on defense, health care or training programs or we may choose to cut taxes for specific income groups—lower, middle or upper.

Disadvantages of Fiscal Policy: Timing

Political realities often create a time delay in the passing and implementation of fiscal policy legislation. Our elected officials are obviously concerned about voter's perceptions of a change in policy. In addition, it takes time to accurately identify a change in the cycle—usually at least six months. Also, it takes time to recommend legislative action and actually activate the policy. Finally, it takes time for the economy to realize the effects of changes in taxation or spending. All these delays could postpone the effect of policy actions to well over 18 months. By this time, the natural cyclical adjustments of the market may actually be taking the economy in another direction!

Crowding-Out

The **crowding-out** effect is another possible problem with fiscal policy. If government borrowing becomes so great that it absorbs most of the savings in the economy, then fiscal policy actions can force interest rates to increase. This can then "crowd-out" private borrowing. This crowding-out lowers business investment spending and may affect our long-run competitiveness and growth.

PUBLIC DEBT—Figures 16.3 and 16.4

The definition for **Public Debt** is fairly simple. Public Debt includes an accounting of all past deficits and surpluses from previous years. Public debt is past tense. Budget deficits, on the other hand, refer to the current year and measure how much our government spending exceeds the tax revenues—or vice-versa in the case of a budget surplus. As you can see from Figures 16.3 and 16.4, the data is very straightforward and strictly "positive economics"—no normative judgments. However, it is very difficult to get much further into our analysis without opinion entering the conversation. The questions that immediately come to mind are very direct: Why did debt explode in the early 1980s and why has it continued to grow at such a rapid pace? The political debate that has ensued is similar to many other public issues, with both major political parties blaming each other for the problem.

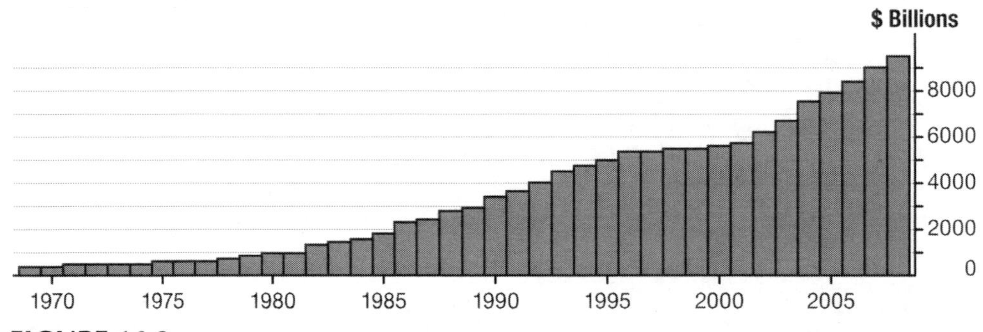

FIGURE 16.3
U.S. National Debt In Current Dollars
SOURCES: White House OMB

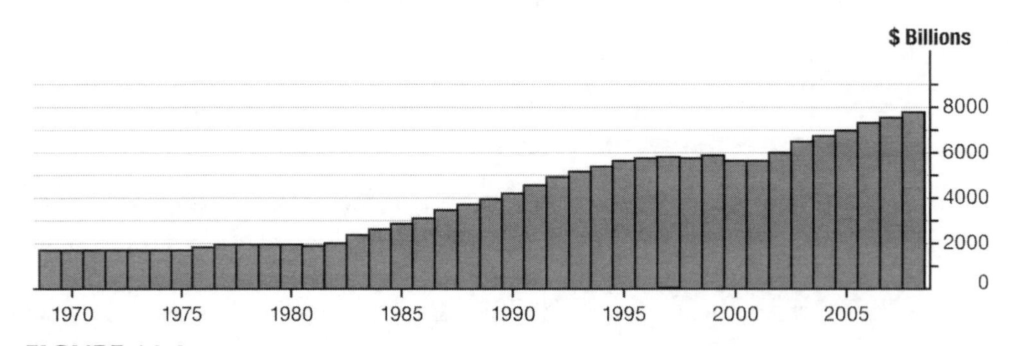

FIGURE 16.4
U.S. National Debt In Constant (2000) Dollars
SOURCES: White House OMB

A History of Deficits and Surpluses—Figures 16.5 and 16.6

There have been historical periods of rapidly increasing deficits in America's history—particularly those associated with WWII. Since the early 1980s, the increase in budget deficits (and public debt) has been unprecedented. The data is fairly clear, as you can see in Figures 16.5 and 16.6 (Figure 16.5 illustrates Current Dollars and Figure 16.6 shows Constant or Real "Inflation Adjusted" Dollars). These tables do not provide answers as to "why" we have made these political choices nor do they convey the impact that they have had. Remember that the term deficit is always describing the current budget year. We incur a deficit when our federal expenditures are greater than tax revenues. A surplus in the budget occurs when tax revenues are greater than government expenditures, as shown in Figure 16.5 from 1998 to 2001.

Presidential Budgets: Deficits and Surpluses—Figures 16.7a & b

Even though the "who is responsible" question may be difficult to answer (Congress is very much involved in the budget process), the data in Figure 16.7A does answer the question of "when." The data in the amended table provides an answer as to who was the U.S. president during the relevant time periods. Again, given the lagging effect of sometimes uncontrollable economic events and Congressional involvement, there is still much disagreement about the question of "who is responsible" for deficits and surpluses during each of those administrations.

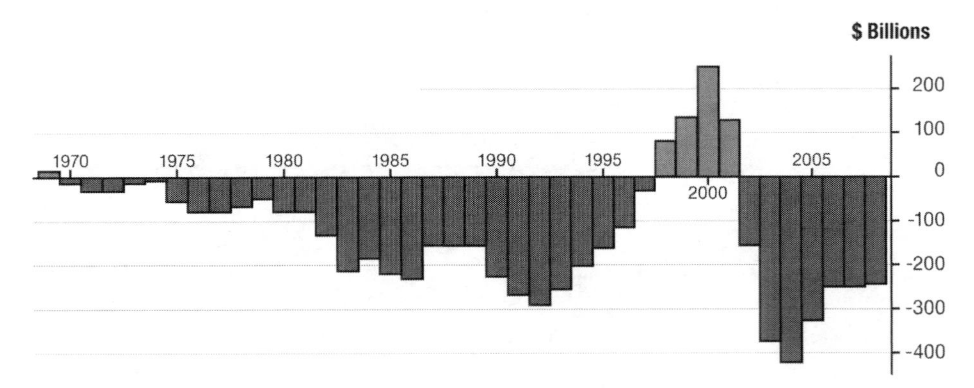

FIGURE 16.5
Federal Deficits and Surpluses In Current Dollars
SOURCES: White House OMB

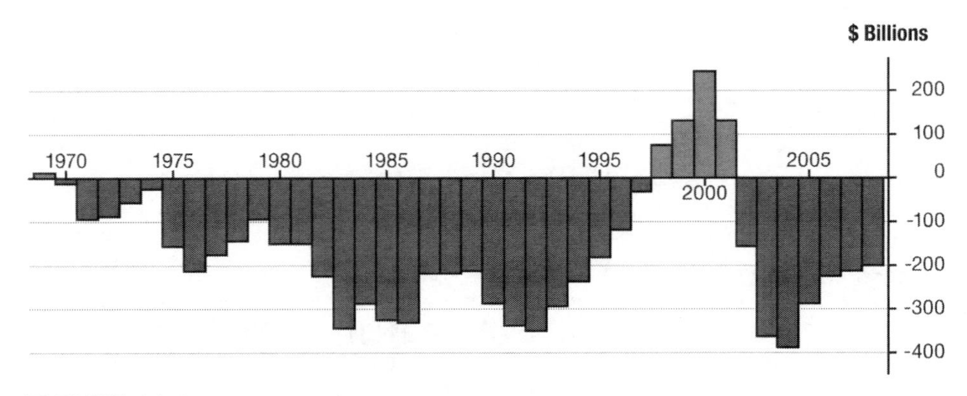

FIGURE 16.6
Federal Deficits and Surpluses In Constant (2000) Dollars
SOURCES: White House OMB

The Balanced Budget Multiplier

With our total public debt exceeding $11 trillion, it is almost impossible not to be overwhelmed by the immensity of the number. The difficulty of comprehending the magnitude can be overcome by breaking the total down and expressing the debt on a per capita or individual basis. If we divide the total debt by total population in this country, we get *per capita* public debt. This figure is for every man, woman and child in the United States and measures their individual portion of the debt. This is a little easier to understand and can be even more shocking to contemplate. Remember that these are constant dollar figures—the price index has been applied so that we can accurately compare year to year without the effects of inflation.

What we see is that per capita debt has grown from about $3,900 in 1980 to roughly $39,000 today in real terms. The national debt has increased at an average of $3.8 billion per day since September 2007. See Figure 16.8.

Growth in Public Debt—Figure 16.9

As we have seen, there are many different opinions about the "why" and "who" questions relative to the debt. It is important that every student and every voter determine their own opinions. Global conflicts have no doubt prompted more government spending, particularly when we are involved in costly wars—(whether a war is justified or not

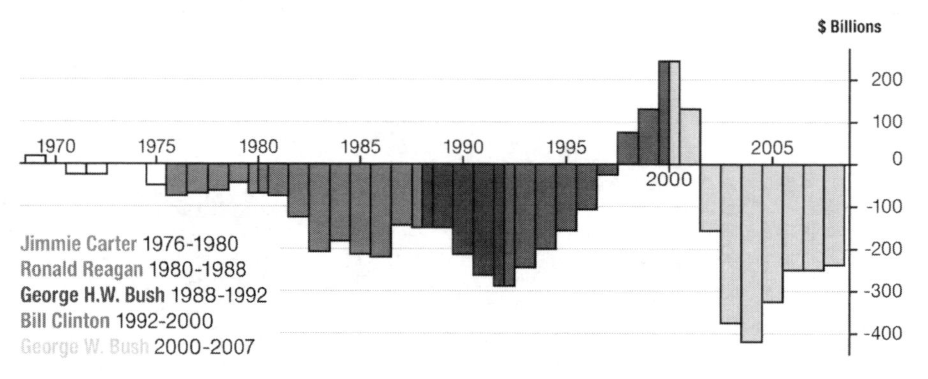

FIGURE 16.7A
Federal Deficits and Surpluses In Current Dollars
SOURCES: White House OMB

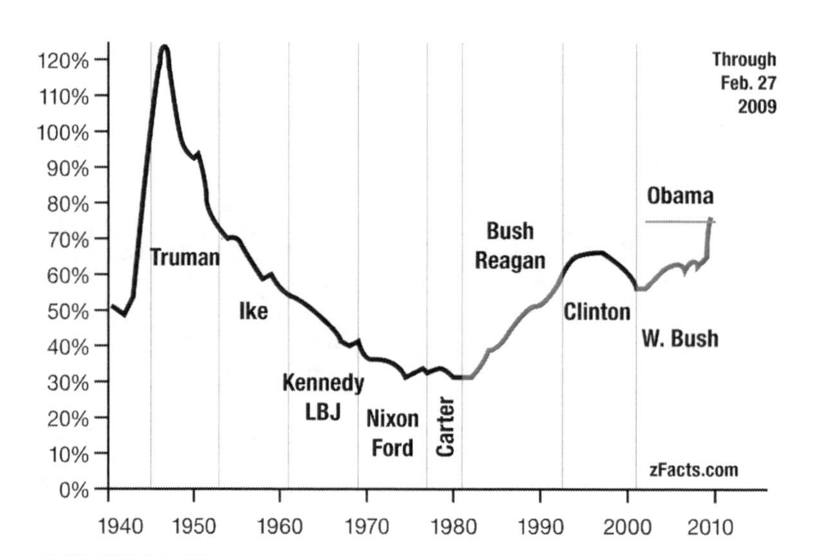

FIGURE 16.7B
The National Debt as a Percent of Gross Domestic Product
SOURCES: data through 2007 is from Bush's whitehouse.gov

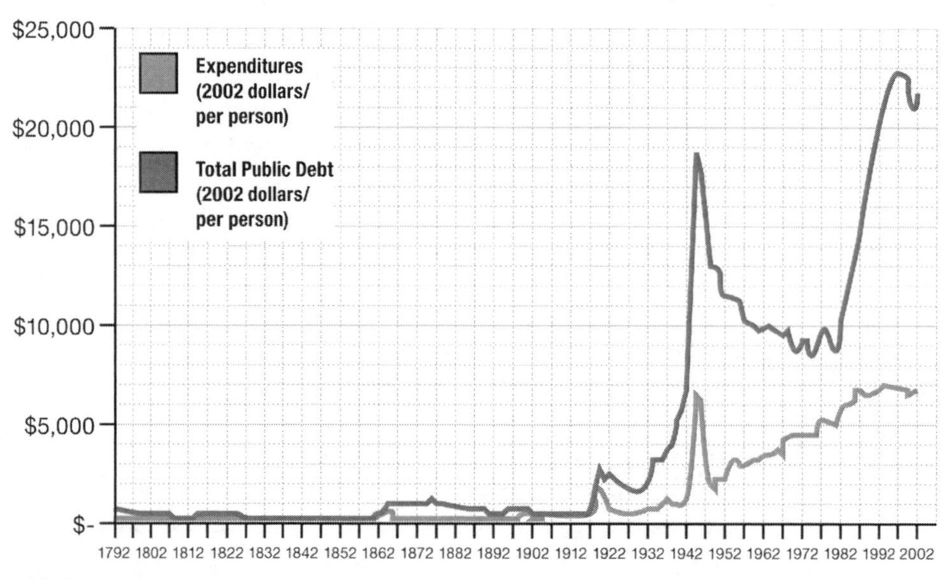

FIGURE 16.8
US National Government Expenditures and National Debt per Person 1792 to 2002, in Inflation-Adjusted (2002) Dollars

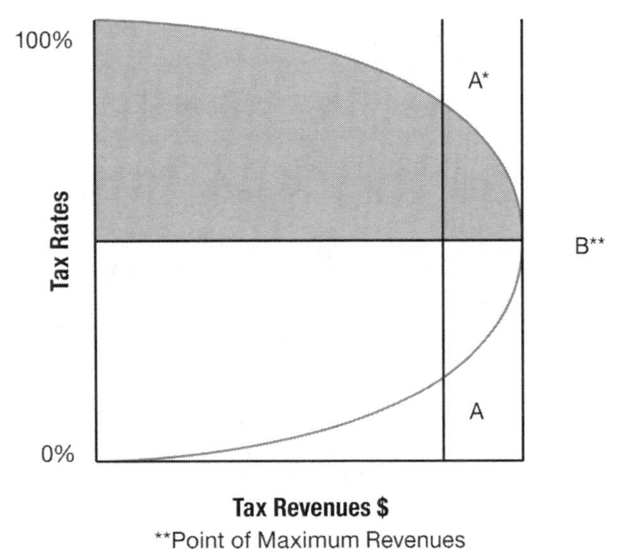

FIGURE 16.9
Laffer Curve

is beyond the scope of the economics, but it is a good example of a normative question). As you should recall from earlier discussion, recessions also have considerable impact on the deficit because a slowing economy reduces the number of jobs and results in lower tax revenues and increases in government transfer payments.

Supply Side Economics

In 1980, Ronald Reagan was elected president and he introduced Supply Side Economics to the nation. This theory was based on classical principles that the supply forces within a nation were primarily responsible for determining employment, output and income. President Reagan introduced legislation to cut taxes and reduce government regulation to encourage increases in productive activity (right shift in the AS). According to Supply Side Economics, increases in aggregate supply would increase output and reduce prices. This effect would multiply through the economy (some would say "lifting all boats" while others would say "trickling down") to lower-income groups through lower prices and increases in employment.

As you look at the impact of Supply Side Economics, most would agree that the tax cuts (without corresponding spending cuts) had significant impact on our increasing debt. The **Laffer Curve,** shown in Figure 16.9, suggested that tax cuts would increase tax revenue if the tax rate was at A* and moved to B**. Supply Side economists argued that a lower tax rate would encourage people to work more (and work smarter). It was also proposed that more people who had avoided (or even evaded) taxes when rates were high would now pay their taxes with the lower rate.

However, if the nation is at B** on the curve, a movement to A* would actually decrease tax revenues. With the record now available, it appears that the nation may have initially been at B** (not A*) and that cuts in tax rates did, in fact, lower tax revenues. However, the debate continues about the impact of changing tax rates on growth and economic activity.

Economic Growth

The discussion above on increasing or decreasing tax rates does have major implications for changes in the aggregate supply curve as well as the aggregate demand curve. All other things remaining the same, a reduction in tax rates would be associated with increased incentives for production and, therefore, a rightward shift in the AS. This would create an outward growth in the PPF, a "larger" Circular Flow and a sustained (or even increased) upward slope in the Long-Term (Secular) Trend Line for the economy.

Conversely, an increase in tax rates would create a decrease in incentives for production and, therefore, a leftward shift in the AS. At the extreme, this could create an inward shift of the PPF, a "smaller" Circular Flow and a negative slope on the Long-Term Trend Line.

Who Owns the Public Debt?—Figure 16.10

Figure 16.10 illustrates national debt ownership. Even though it is accurate to say that the majority of the debt is money that we owe to ourselves—that is, bondholders who reside in this country—we have seen foreign-held debt escalate dramatically in recent years. Foreign-held debt is money that we owe to someone or some entity outside the country. Domestically held debt is somewhat analogous to a person borrowing money from himself or from his family as compared to money that was borrowed from the bank. Repayment to the bank is somewhat different from repayment to "ourselves."

In Figure 16.10, the debt being held by various government agencies is largely because of tax revenues that are being temporarily invested in government bonds. For example, the Social Security Trust Fund holds surpluses of Social Security tax revenues in U.S. Treasury bonds.

Public Debt: Myths

We hear frequent statements about public debt (from politicians and others) that may not be entirely true. One often repeated myth is the idea that the ***federal government can become bankrupt.*** The federal government cannot really go bankrupt because the government largely controls our financial system and can constantly refinance the existing debt (issue new bonds). Of course, the government could mismanage our financial system to the point of financial distress, so the effect could be very similar to "bankruptcy."

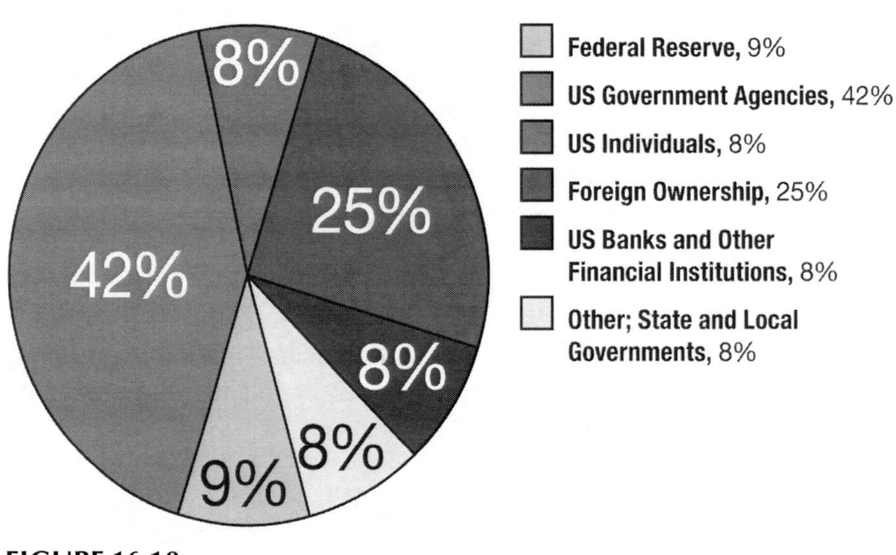

FIGURE 16.10

Shifting the burden to future generations, another phrase popular with some politicians, is also somewhat inaccurate. The impact of rapidly escalating public debt is generally felt in a shorter time period. For instance, if this (shift to future generations) were completely true, we would still be reeling from the effects of the deficits during World War II—we are the children and grandchildren of that generation. If our resources are employed wisely and economic growth is positive over time, then debt can be managed.

Public Debt: True Burdens

Many of these burdens of the debt have already been discussed. We know that some **crowding-out** takes place with deficit financing as private borrowers find it increasingly difficult to borrow money at higher interest rates. The size of the deficits, other current factors in our economic environment and world affairs all affect the relative magnitude of the crowding-out.

Since the mid- to late 1980s, the amount of **foreign-held debt** has increased dramatically. This has been partially due to the very low savings rate in this country. As the deficits escalated in the 1980s, we were faced with only two alternatives because there was not enough savings to buy up the level of debt being issued by the U.S. Treasury. One alternative was to finance by actually creating money. This is nearly always very inflationary. The second, more politically acceptable option, was to keep interest rates high enough to attract foreign investment. The result has been the growth of debt held by foreign investors (from the example above, this is analogous to money that we owe to the bank rather than to ourselves). Repayment of principle and interest may provide a means for foreign ownership of U.S. assets to increase.

Lastly, some **income and wealth redistribution** has occurred. The majority of debt is held by upper-income groups, both foreign and domestic, while the majority of taxpayers are not part of that group. We do see some wealth being redistributed toward those who hold the debt. However, it is also true that the majority (86 percent) of federal income taxes are paid by taxpayers who are in the top 25 percent of income earners. For further information see: http://www.taxfoundation.org/research/show/250.html.

Public Debt and the Net Export Effect

While most of our discussion has been centered on the impact of deficits and debt on our domestic economy, it is important to realize that our budget deficits have also affected our trade deficits. Budget deficits and net exports are seemingly unrelated, but, since the mid-80s, they have become more "linked."

When budget deficits began to escalate in the early to mid-80s, it became apparent that we could not domestically "buy up" the volume of bonds that were being issued. We faced some unpleasant alternatives. We could "create" the money to buy the bonds and monetize the debt (which is very inflationary) or we could elevate interest rates so that we attracted foreign investors to buy our bonds. We chose the latter.

While we cover the basics of international economics in the micro course, there are many macro considerations when we look at international trade. Why are budget deficits and trade deficits linked so closely? When we began to sell more and more of our debt to foreign investors in the early 1980s, there was an "unintended consequence." The value of our dollar went up dramatically. To purchase U.S. securities, foreign currencies must be converted to U.S. dollars, which meant that more foreign investors wanted to "buy" the U.S. dollars. Since exchange rates are largely a factor of simple supply and demand, the effect was not surprising. The U.S. dollar grew much stronger (higher exchange rate) relative to most all world currencies.

SUMMARY

Isn't a strong dollar better than a weak dollar? The answer to this question would seem to be an automatic yes. But while a strong dollar is good if you are buying foreign goods (they are cheaper), it is not so good if you are trying to sell U.S. goods to foreign markets (our goods became more expensive). The result of this process over the past 25 years has been a dramatically escalating trade deficit. The dollar amount of imports over exports has grown from less than $50 billion in the early 1980s to levels approaching $1 trillion more recently. These trade deficits have affected jobs and income in this country as we have imported increasing amounts of consumer goods.

There is a great deal of debate about the overall implications of globalization and trade in our world today—especially as it relates to employment. Take a moment and review the two different viewpoints in Real-World Economics.

KEY TERMS

Annually Balanced Budget: A budget approach that would require that the federal budget be balanced every 12 months—regardless.

Crowding-Out: Excessive government borrowing (usually for deficit financing) that raises interest rates and negatively affects private borrowing needs.

Cyclically Balanced Budget: A budget philosophy that suggests that the budget be balanced in consideration of changes in the business cycle and not just the calendar. Deficit: Usually associated with the federal government, it is simply the amount by which spending exceeds tax revenues—in a given year.

Discretionary Fiscal Policy: Fiscal policy that requires specific legislative action to change existing federal spending levels or tax codes to stabilize the economy.

Employment Act of 1946: Legislation in that year that established economic objectives for our economy and suggested that fiscal policy could help meet the goals of full employment, price stability and growth.

Fiscal Policy: Using changes in taxation and/or spending to affect aggregate demand to have a counter-cycle affect on the business cycle.

Functional Finance: A budget approach that concludes that the federal budget should be used primarily as a counter-cycle tool and one that attempts to promote employment, stability and growth.

Laffer Curve: A method of comparing tax rates and tax revenues.

Net Export Effect: The effect that rapidly expanding domestic deficits has on our trade deficit as we have to borrow from foreign investors. This causes the dollar to strengthen, making imports cheaper and exports more expensive.

Nondiscretionary Fiscal Policy: Policy that is built into our existing federal budget so that there is some automatic counter-cycle affect when the economy slows or speeds up.

Public Debt: This is the sum of all past Federal deficits and surpluses.

Name ______________________ Date ______________

Applied Exercises

1. a. Given the Laffer Curve shown below, how would government tax receipts change if tax rates were increased from A to B**?

   b. How would they change if tax rates were decreased from A* to B**?

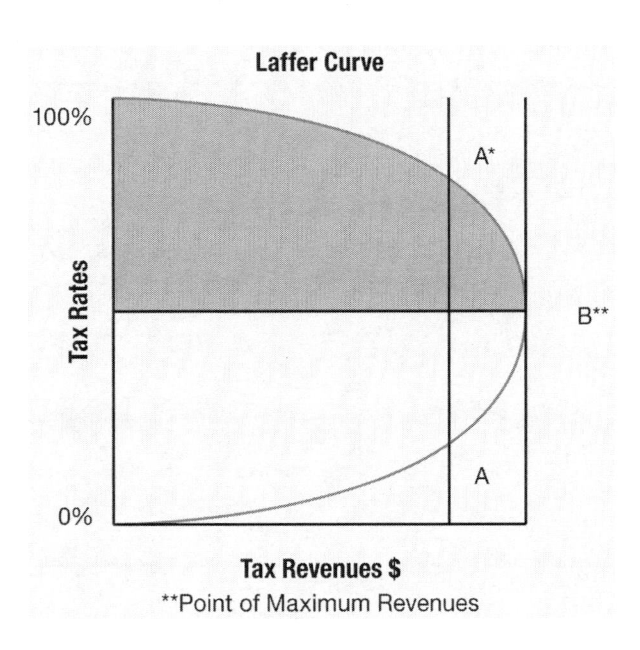

2. a. Consider the three stages of the AS curve and describe appropriate fiscal policy in Stage 1. Why is this called the Keynesian range?

b. What would appropriate fiscal policy be in Stage 3?

c. Why is this called the Classical range?

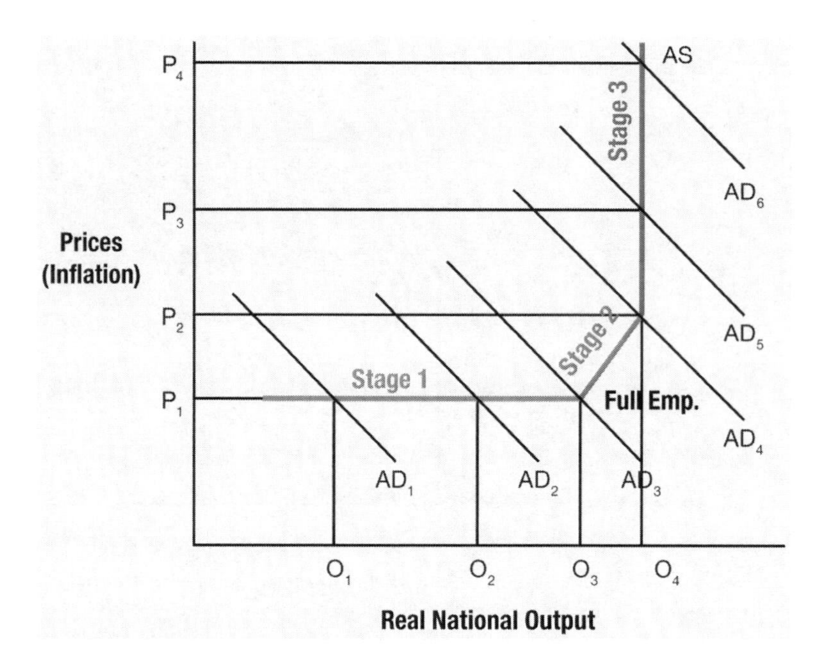

Name ______________________ Date ______________

Applied Exercises: Answers

1. a. Given the Laffer Curve shown below, how would government tax receipts change if tax rates were increased from A to B**?
   Tax revenue would increase.
   b. How would they change if tax rates were decreased?
   Tax revenue would decrease.
2. a. Consider the three stages of the AS curve and describe appropriate fiscal policy in Stage 1. Why is this called the Keynesian range?
   Because Keynes assumed a high level of unused capacity and, therefore, increases in AD would not cause inflation but would increase output.
   b. Why is this called the Classical range?
   Because Classical Theorists assumed that an economy was at full employment and therefore the AS curve was vertical.

Our Money

Have you heard the saying money makes the world go around? Money, money, money. We use money every day. Can you imagine your life without money? What would you do? How would you eat? How would you live? What did individuals do before the existence of money? This chapter contains the following objectives:

- Functions of money
- Definition of money
- Banking system
- Federal Reserve System

FUNCTION OF MONEY

Money serves several functions: medium of exchange, unit of account, and store of value. Let's examine each of the functions of money.

Medium of Exchange. Before the creation of money, consumers exchanged goods for goods (barter economy). Bartering requires a coincidence of wants. Suppose you are a farmer who produces fruits and vegetables. You need more cloth to make pants and shirts for your family. You would have to find someone who produces cloth and who has a need for fruits and vegetables. The creation of money eliminated the need of double coincidence of wants. Individuals now use money as a payment for goods and services.

Unit of Account. Money is used as a measurement of goods and services. A pair of Nikes cost $85.00 at Foot Action. An individual can visit Foot Action and purchase the shoes if he has the money. Suppose the individual brought with him a bucket of apples. Could he purchase the Nikes with the bucket of apples? No, he cannot purchase the shoes because it is hard for the cashier to measure the Nikes in terms of apples.

Store of Value. The consumer can hold money as a savings mechanism. The money is held for use at a later date. Some consumers choose to place the money in a checking or savings account. Others may simply place the money in a jar inside of the home.

DEFINITIONS OF MONEY

Money is a relative term that seems easy to define, right? Let's examine two definitions of money. M1 consists of currency and checkable deposits. Currency consists of coins in circulation and paper money. The deposit in a checking account (checkable deposits) also falls under the M1 definition of money.

M2 contains M1 plus savings deposits, money market mutual funds held by individuals, money market deposit accounts, and small time deposits. The money in a consumer's savings account is included in the savings deposit balance of the M2 definition of money. Small time deposits include certificates of deposit with a value of $100,000 or below. Money market deposits include checking accounts that pay a higher interest rate to consumers and require a higher initial deposit. Mutual fund companies sell shares to investors and then use the money to purchase stocks and bonds.

M1 + savings deposits + money market deposit accounts + money market mutual funds held by individuals + Small time deposits = M2

DEPOSITORY INSTITUTIONS

The main depository institutions include the following: commercial banks, thrift institutions, and money market mutual funds. **Commercial banks** receive deposits from customers and provide loans. **Thrift institutions** are comprised of savings and loan associations and savings banks. *Savings and loan associations* receives checking and savings deposits. The association also provides personal, commercial, and home loans. *Savings banks* accept savings deposits and make home loans. A **money market mutual fund** is a portfolio of stocks and bonds. Financial institutions sell shares of stock and hold liquid assets.

FEDERAL RESERVE SYSTEM

The Federal Reserve System is the central bank of the United States. Functions of the Federal Reserve include:

- Control the money supply
- Issue currency
- Act as the bankers' bank
- Supervises other banks

STRUCTURE OF THE FEDERAL RESERVE SYSTEM

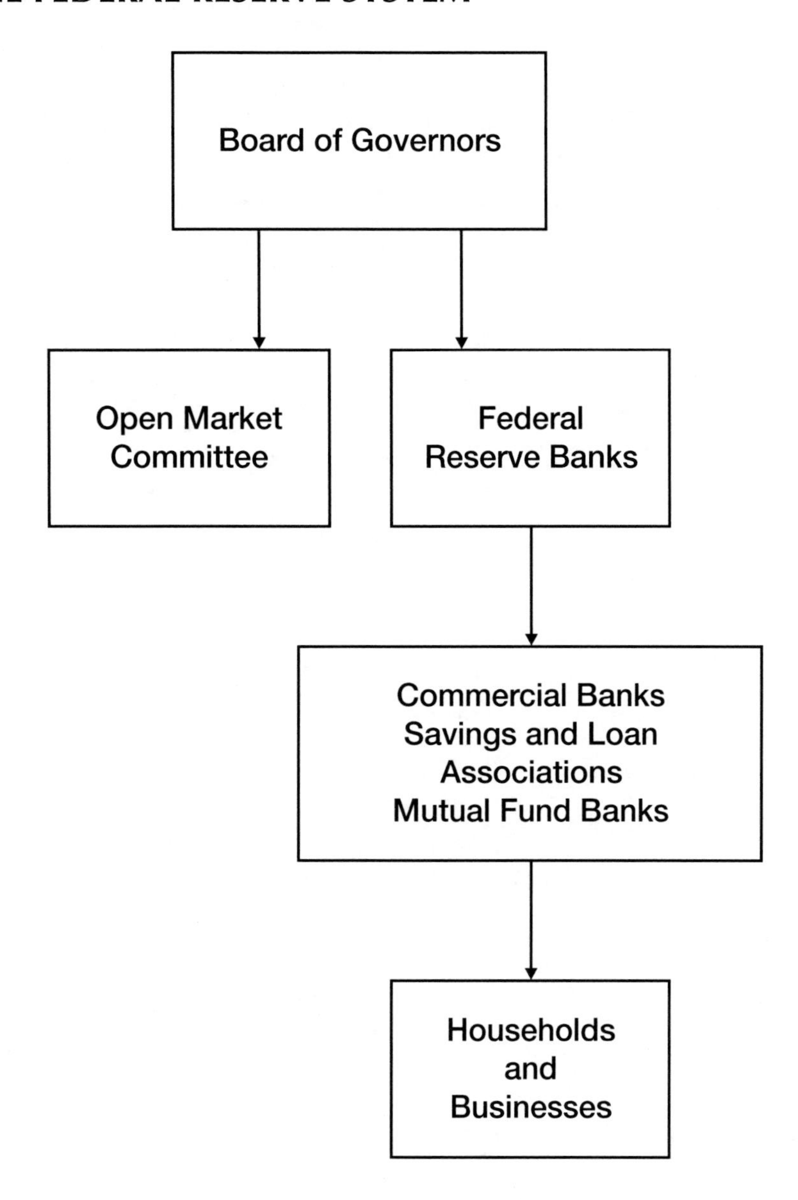

Board of Governors. The Board of Governors consists of seven members appointed by the President of the United States and confirmed by the United States Senate. The members serve a 14 year term. The terms are staggered to allow one seat vacant every two years. The President appoints one of the board members as chairman of the board for a four year renewable term. The current chairman of the Board of Governors is Ben Bernanke. Some of the responsibilities of the board consist of setting the *discount rate* and establishing the *reserve requirement* for commercial banks.

Federal Reserve Banks. Each district of the United States contains a Federal Reserve Bank (12 Federal Reserve Banks). The Federal Reserve Bank of New York implements the policy decisions of the Federal Open Market Committee. The functions of the Federal Reserve Banks include:

- Holding reserves of commercial banks
- Lending money to banks
- Operating as a check-clearing service for commercial banks

Federal Open Market Committee. The primary function of the FOMC is to buy and sell securities to alter the money supply. The voting members of the committee include the seven Board of Governors and president of the New York Federal Reserve Bank. Four presidents of the other Federal Reserve Banks vote on a rotating basis.

The Federal Depositors Insurance Corporation (FDIC) is an insurance program that insures depositors' accounts in commercial banks in the event of bank failure. The FDIC was established in 1933.

Money Creation

The purpose of this chapter is to explore the operations of a commercial bank. The operations of the bank are recorded using a double entry accounting system.

BALANCE SHEET

The commercial bank's balance sheet must balance. All of the bank's assets are on the left side of the balance sheet. Assets are essentially what the bank owns. The liabilities of the commercial bank are on the right side of the balance sheet. Liabilities are what the bank owes. Net worth is also on the right side of the balance sheet. Net worth includes investments made by stockholders of the bank. Let's examine a series of transactions of Justice National Bank.

1. The bank sells shares of stock worth $300,000 to shareholders.
   Shares of stock once purchased belong to shareholders (assets). The sold shares of stock are known as net worth. To balance the transaction, the value of the shares of stock are placed in the cash account of the assets side.

Assets		Liabilities	
Cash	**300,000**	Capital Stock	300,000

2. Justice National Bank (JNB) purchases equipment for $150,000 cash.
   Since the bank used cash to purchase the equipment, the bank can list equipment as an asset.

Assets		Liabilities	
Cash	**150,000**	Capital Stock	300,000
Equipment	**150,000**		

3. Justin deposits $250,000 in his checking account at the bank.
   The $250,000 belongs to Justin. He can withdraw any portion of his money at any time. The $250,000 deposit is a liability to the bank. To balance, we must place the $250,000 in the cash account.

Assets		Liabilities	
Cash	**400,000**	Capital Stock	300,000
Equipment	**150,000**	Checkable Deposits	250,000

It is now important to introduce a few new terms. The Federal Reserve requires commercial banks to place a percentage of deposits in a reserve account. The commercial bank can keep the *required reserves* in the vault or send the amount to the Federal Reserve Bank. Any amount placed above the required amount is known as *excess reserves.* Actual reserves equal required reserves plus excess reserves.

4. The Fed created a 25 percent reserve requirement. JNB places 100 percent in the reserve account.
   The commercial bank owns the reserves. TO create the reserve account, we will move money from the cash account to the reserve account. Once a reserve account is established, we will no longer touch the cash account.

Assets		Liabilities	
Cash	**150,000**	Capital Stock	300,000
Equipment	**150,000**	Checkable Deposits	250,000
Required Reserves	**62,500**		
Excess Reserves	**187,500**		

The commercial bank can provide loans to customers now that excess reserves exist. The bank creates new money when a loan is granted. Granting a loan increases the money supply. Let's examine a transaction when a commercial bank creates a loan.

5. Jennifer requests a loan for $75,000 from JNB.

Assets		Liabilities	
Cash	**150,000**	Capital Stock	300,000
Equipment	**150,000**	Checkable Deposits	325,000
Required Reserves	**81,250**		
Excess Reserves	**168,750**		
Loans	**75,000**		

The loan is a liability to the customer and an asset to the bank. The bank places the loan in the customer's checking account. The checkable deposit account increased. The required reserve is 25 percent. We must recalculate the required reserves (325,000*.25 = 81250). Now we must recalculate excess reserves. Notice on this particular transaction cash and equipment equal the amount in capital stock. Loan, required, and excess must equal checkable deposits. We know the loan amount, required, and checkable deposits. We can find excess by completing the following:

325000 − (81250 + 75000) = 168750

6. The Fed lowers the reserve requirement to 20 percent.
20 percent of 325000 (checkable deposits) is 65000. To find excess reserves take checkable deposits minus (required reserves plus loans).

Assets		Liabilities	
Cash	**150,000**	Capital Stock	300,000
Equipment	**150,000**	Checkable Deposits	325,000
Required Reserves	**65,000**		
Excess Reserves	**185,000**		
Loans	**75,000**		

7. Justin writes a check for $85000 for a down payment for a house.
As stated before, a customer can withdraw money from his checking account at any time. A withdrawal subtracts money from checkable deposits and reserves.

325000 − 85000 = 240000 (new checkable deposits)
240000*.20 (required reserves) = 48000 (new reserve amount)

Now find excess:

240000 − (48000 + 75000) =
240000 − 123000 =
117000 excess reserves

Assets		Liabilities	
Cash	**150,000**	Capital Stock	300,000
Equipment	**150,000**	Checkable Deposits	240,000
Required Reserves	**48,000**		
Excess Reserves	**117,000**		
Loans	**75,000**		

8. The government purchases securities from JNB for $70,000.
Treasury bonds are securities. Bonds are a legal debt obligation. Securities are assets to the bank and a liability to the purchaser. The balance of the security is placed in the customer's checking account. The bank will have an increase in securities and checkable deposits. Required reserves and excess reserves also change.

Checkable deposits plus amount of securities (240000 + 70000 = 310000)
310000*.20 = 62000

To find excess reserves, we must consider the amount required, loans, and securities.

310000 − (62000 + 70000 + 75000)
310000 − 207000 = 103000

Assets		Liabilities	
Cash	**150,000**	Capital Stock	300,000
Equipment	**150,000**	Checkable Deposits	310,000
Required Reserves	**62,000**		
Excess Reserves	**103,000**		
Loans	**75,000**		
Securities	**70,000**		

9. Jennifer pays back the $75000 loan.
   Money is subtracted from checkable deposits and the loan account when the loan is repaid. Money is destroyed when the loan is repaid.

   310000 − 75000 = 235000 new checkable deposit amount
   75000 − 75000 = 0 new loan amount
   235000*.20 = 47000 new reserves
   235000 − (70000 + 47000) = 118000 new excess reserves

Assets		Liabilities	
Cash	**150,000**	Capital Stock	300,000
Equipment	**150,000**	Checkable Deposits	235,000
Required Reserves	**47,000**		
Excess Reserves	**118,000**		
Securities	**70,000**		

Now let's examine the Multiple Banking System. Assume the bank starts with an initial excess of zero and a 20 percent reserve requirement.

1. Customer places $500 in checking account Bank A.

Assets		Liabilities and Net Worth	
Required Reserves	**100**	Checkable Deposits	500
Excess reserves	**400**		

2. Customer requests loan from Bank A. Assume the customer requests the full amount.

Assets		Liabilities and Net Worth	
Loan	**400**		
Required Reserves	**180**	Checkable Deposits	900
Excess reserves	**320**		

3. The customer deposits loan from Bank A in a checking account in Bank B.

Assets		Liabilities and Net Worth	
Required Reserves	**80**	Checkable Deposits	400
Excess reserves	**320**		

4. Customer requests a loan from Bank B.

Assets		Liabilities and Net Worth	
Loan	**320**		
Required Reserves	**144**	Checkable Deposits	720
Excess reserves	**256**		

5. The customer places loan from Bank B in a checking account in Bank C.

Assets		Liabilities and Net Worth	
Required Reserves	**64**	Checkable Deposits	320
Excess reserves	**256**		

6. Customer request loan from Bank C.

Assets		Liabilities and Net Worth	
Loan	**256**		
Required Reserves	**115.20**	Checkable Deposits	576
Excess reserves	**204.8**		

How much money was created from the loans of the banks? First we must find the money multiplier. The money multiplier = 1/required reserve ratio. Next, multiply the money multiplier by the amount of the initial loan.

1/.20 = 5 money multiplier
5*400 = 2000 loans created by banks

Bank	Actual Reserve	Required Reserve	Excess Reserve	Money Created
A	500	100	400	400
B	400	80	320	320
C	320	64	256	256

KEY TERMS

Actual reserves
Assets
Excess reserves
Liabilities
Money multiplier
Net worth
Required reserves
Securities

Monetary Policy

LEARNING OBJECTIVES

- Provide a basic definition of Monetary Policy and describe the primary and secondary tools of Monetary Policy.
- Explain the advantages and disadvantages of Monetary Policy and the concept of "easy money" and "tight money."
- Describe the minor controls of Monetary Policy.
- Demonstrate an understanding of the "Equation of Exchange" and provide a numerical example.
- Describe the Quantity Theory of Money and describe the ongoing debate between Monetarists and Keynesians regarding government involvement in the macroeconomy.
- Use the Major Economic Models to demonstrate an understanding of the chain reactions resulting from human choices and how they move through an economy. Demonstrate an understanding of the Tradeoffs that result.

■ ■ ■

MONETARY POLICY

Monetary policy is the management of the money supply by the Federal Reserve to best achieve price stability, full employment and economic growth. Most of the Fed's policy is directed toward commercial banks and attempts to influence the banks' lending ability by making money (M1) either more or less available to borrowers. The cost of credit or the "rental price" of money is the interest rate. Monetary policy is determined by the Fed but still must be coordinated with the federal government (fiscal policy) through U.S. Treasury operations. Monetary policy is an essential counter-cycle tool.

The Objectives of Monetary Policy

The objectives of **monetary policy** are basically the same but the "tools" (introduced in Lesson 11) are different. The Federal Reserve is attempting to promote a growing economy with more and better jobs within a stable (noninflationary) environment. Although the tools are different, the intent is basically the same as fiscal policy.

The Tools of Monetary Policy

The Fed regulates the money supply by using its major or quantitative tools of operation. As the term "major" implies, these are the primary tools used to meet Fed objectives. All of these primary tools will affect the availability and cost (interest rates) of bank credit. These tools can indirectly affect the lending ability of financial institutions to create checkbook money through loans as well as directly affecting the supply of money through the buying and selling of government securities. The level of required reserves (depositor funds that banks "hold back") is also very important.

The Major Fed Tools are:

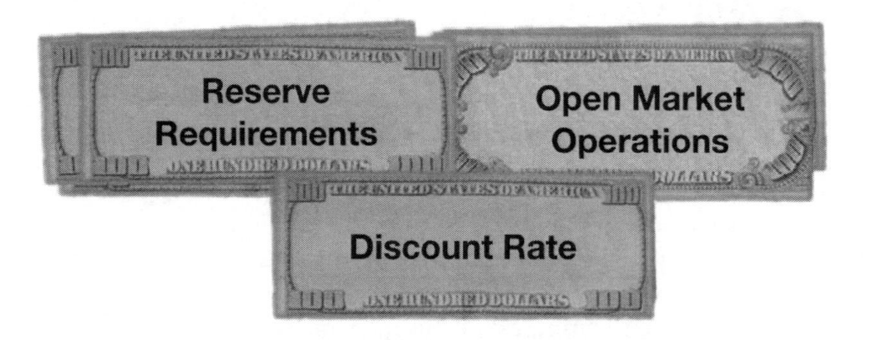

The Fed's most powerful tool is the control of **reserve requirements.** The Fed sets the minimum percentage of depositor funds that must be retained by commercial banks in legal reserves (cash in the vault or deposits with the Fed). The reserve requirement varies according to the size of the financial institution and the type of deposit. Changing this percentage not only changes the availability of excess reserves, but it also changes the money multiplier. With this "double impact," this tool is obviously very powerful and is, therefore, used infrequently by the Fed, which prefers a more gradual approach when possible.

The **discount rate** is the interest rate charged to commercial banks when they borrow from the Fed to meet reserve requirements. The discount rate is set monthly and is a highly visible tool of Fed operations. The Fed is known as the "lender of last resort" for commercial banks. A financial institution with a loss of deposits can usually (but not automatically) borrow from the Fed, if it cannot borrow elsewhere, to maintain its required reserves.

The **Federal Open Market Committee (FOMC)** directs the buying and selling of securities (usually U.S. Treasury securities) to influence the nation's money supply. The **open market operations** of the FOMC are the most frequently used tool of the Fed because they are effective in changing reserves in a gradual manner.

Open Market Operations

In a recession, the money supply can be increased when the Fed buys securities. Through this purchase of Treasury securities, the Fed sends money into the bank's or public's hands and the bank or public sends the securities to the Fed. When the Fed sends the money to the seller's bank account, the bank itself then holds more funds (excess re-

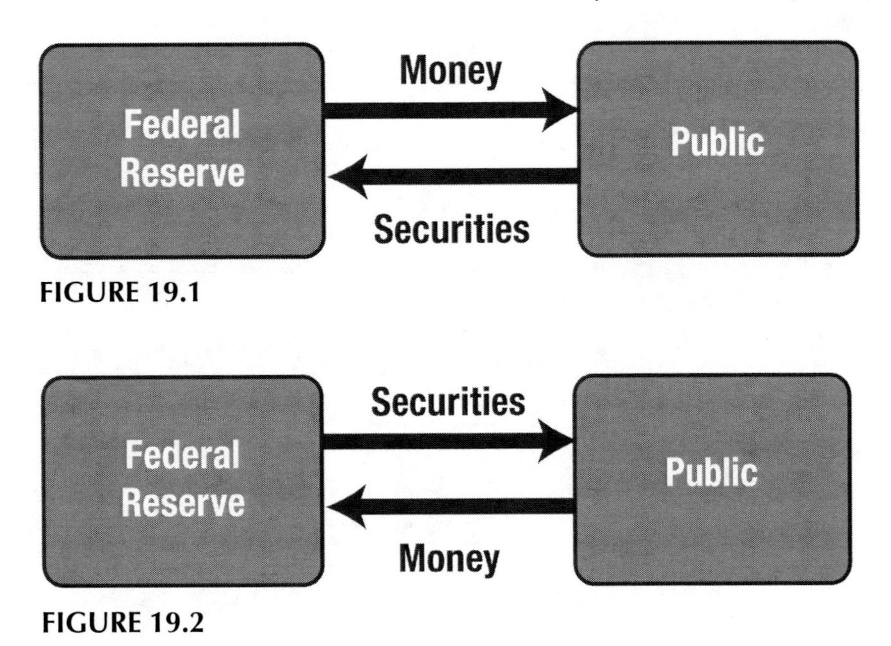

FIGURE 19.1

FIGURE 19.2

serves) from which it can make loans. Purchase of securities directly from a bank results in an increase in the bank's legal reserves and also results in more "excess reserves" and, therefore, the potential for new loans for increases in the supply of money (M1).

In an inflationary period, the money supply can be restrained (or even contracted) by the Fed selling securities. The above process is reversed when the Fed sells securities to then banks (or the public). When the Fed sells securities, banks have fewer excess reserves to make available for loans and the public has less money in their checking accounts, therefore, M1 has declined.

Open market operations (OMO) as described above take place through buy/sell agreements coordinated by the Fed with the Treasury. Each action is targeted for its impact on interest rates and the growth in the money supply. The following quote from the New York Federal Reserve explains the key concepts of OMO.

Open Market Operations: Key Concepts

- "Temporary open market operations involve repurchase and reverse repurchase agreements that are designed to temporarily add or drain reserves available to the banking system.
- Permanent open market operations involve the buying and selling of securities outright to permanently add or drain reserves available to the banking system.
- The federal funds rate is the interest rate at which depository institutions lend their balances at the Federal Reserve to other depository institutions overnight."
  Source: New York Federal Reserve

You notice from the information above that open market operations involve short-term interventions in the financial market to smooth interest rates and also longer-term "permanent open market operations" to change the long- term money supply.

The Fed as a Bank

An understanding of the basic accounts of financial institutions and the Fed is important to grasp the process of monetary policy. Recall from Lesson 11 that the balance

Balance Sheet of the Federal Reserve* (in millions) 2009

Assets	
Securites in Treasury Notes	$1,000,000
Loans to Banks	290,000
All Other Asset	110,000
	$1,400,000
Liabilities	
Reserves of Banks	170,000
Treasury Deposits	280,000
Federal Reserve Notes (outstanding)	900,000
Capital (Net Worth)	
Combined Capital	50,000
Liabilites + Capital	$1,400,000

*All accounts approximate

sheet equation of bookkeeping is Assets 5 Liabilities 1 Net Worth. The Fed, like all financial institutions, has assets that it obtains from stockholders, lenders to the bank or depositors.

The assets of the Fed include investments in U.S. Treasury bills, bonds, notes, loans (at the discount rate) to banks and selected other necessary operating assets. Liabilities include the funds deposited by banks into the Fed, the checking account balance of the U.S. Treasury and the Federal Reserve Notes outstanding. Federal Reserve Notes are the paper money issued by the Fed that is the currency in circulation. The capital account (net worth) includes the investment that the commercial banks are required to make in the Fed as a corporation.

The actions of the Fed were dramatic in 2008 and 2009 as reflected by major changes in the Federal Reserve Balance Sheet. These changes caused the Federal Reserve to issue a statement explaining the positions on the balance sheet at that time. The following statement was released by the Federal Reserve on April 3, 2009 from Chairman Ben S. Bernanke:

THE FEDERAL RESERVE'S BALANCE SHEET

In ordinary financial and economic times, my topic, "The Federal Reserve's Balance Sheet," might not be considered a "grabber." But these are far from ordinary times. To address the current crisis, the Federal Reserve has taken a number of aggressive and creative policy actions, many of which are reflected in the size and composition of the Fed's balace sheet. So, I thought that a brief guided tour to our balance sheet might be an instructive way to discuss the Fed's policy stategy and some related issues. As I will discuss, we no longer live in a world in which central bank policies are confined to adjusting the short-term interest rate. Instead, by using their balance sheets, the Federal Reserve and other central banks are developing new tools to ease financial conditions and support economic growth." See the Fed statement at:

http://www.federalreserve.gov/newsevents/speech/bernanlo200000403a.htm

This statement notes the role of the Fed's balance sheet in reflecting the dramatic changes in monetary policy that were used in an attempt to resist a major recession/depression. The role of the Fed is critical when the economy experiences a financial crisis as it did beginning in 2007. The traditional tools of the Fed together with fiscal policy are used in an attempt to counter downward forces in the economy. There is further discussion on this topic at the end of this Lesson.

EASY MONEY AND TIGHT MONEY

Fed tools are used to control the money supply in various ways. As discussed above, when the Fed wants to increase the money supply (easy money), it buys Treasury securities. The securities held by the public are exchanged for cash (the transfer of funds from the Fed to the bank). These funds are held by banks that can then extend more loans and this increases the money supply by a multiple of the original amount.

The money supply is also expanded when a commercial bank purchases securities from the public because the funds move from the commercial bank "vault" into the public's hands. Remember that only depositor funds (not the bank's funds) are counted as part of the money supply.

The money supply decreases (tight money) when bank reserves decrease. Once again, when the Fed sells Treasury securities or when a bank sells Treasury securities, the reserves will decrease. The public decreases checking account balances in order to buy the Treasury securities.

The Reserve Ratio

As noted at the start of this Lesson, the money supply is affected through changes in the reserve ratio. When the Fed decreases reserve requirements, banks are required to "hold back" less legal reserve on depositors' accounts and can, therefore, make more loans. Once again, as more loans are made, the money supply expands by a multiple amount. Increasing the reserve ratio decreases the ability of banks to create money (make loans).

The Discount Rate

The Discount Rate, as noted above, is the interest rate that the Fed charges banks to borrow funds to meet the reserve requirement. The discount rate is, in effect, the "wholesale cost" of funds. A higher discount rate tends to decrease bank reserves because the price of loans increases. Higher interest rates result in less borrowing as fewer projects become viable for a business profit. Conversely, a lower discount rate tends to increase bank reserves and encourages business expansion.

Enacting Monetary Policy

Basic concepts of the Fed's use of tools:

Easy Money

1. Easy money (money is readily available)
   a. Federal Reserve buys securities
   b. Reserve ratio could be reduced
   c. Discound rate could be reduced

"Easy" money (expansionary) chain reaction:

Fed buys securities and/or decreases reserve ratio and/or decreases the discount rate, which:

- Causes an increase in the money supply
- Results in a decrease in interest rates
- Causing an increase in aggregate demand because business investment increases
- Causing an increase in employment, output and income

Tight Money

2. Tight money (money is not readily available)
   a. Federal Reserve sells securities
   b. Reserve ratio could be raised
   c. Discound rate could be raised

Fed sells securities and/or increases reserve ratio and/or increases the discount rate, which:

- Causes a decrease in the money supply
- Results in an increase in interest rates
- Causing a decrease in aggregate demand because business investment decreases
- Causing a decrease in employment, output and income

Policy Tools Impact

Each of the major tools of the Fed varies in the amount of its use and its impact. Open market operations are the most important because they are used most frequently and most effectively. The effectiveness of a change in the discount rate depends on commercial banks' reaction to the change. Banks may or may not change their lending practices in reaction to a change in the discount rate. The reserve ratio is too powerful to be changed very often because even a small change can be magnified in a large way throughout the banking system.

MINOR CONTROLS

The Federal Reserve has other tools that are less influential than the three major tools.

Minor Controls Include

- Margin requirements
- Credit controls
- And moral suasion

Margin requirements set the minimum amount of a buyer's own cash that must be invested to purchase securities. The margin requirement as of this writing is 50 percent. The purpose of margin requirements is to lessen speculation in the securities markets. If you purchase Ford Motor Company stock today, you would be required to have at least half of the funds in cash. If you purchase $10,000 of stock, you must have at least $5,000 of your own funds invested, but you could borrow up to $5,000 from a broker or bank to complete the purchase.

The Fed also has **credit controls** that set the length of time and the amount of down payment on consumer credit purchases. During a recession, the amount of time allowed to repay a loan can be extended and the amount of the down payment decreased to encourage consumer purchases. During an inflationary period the amount of time allowed to repay a loan can be decreased and the amount of the down payment increased to discourage consumer purchases.

Finally, the Fed can suggest bank loan funding that would benefit the national economy. The activity is called **moral suasion** and is the application of "positive influence" and not force to encourage banks to increase or decrease loan activity as is appropriate for the national economy. In periods of inflation, restraint on loans is encouraged, whereas in periods of recession, loan growth might be encouraged. Banks are normally reluctant to increase loans in a recession because of increased risk of non-payment by consumers/businesses and are more likely to increase loans in inflationary periods because of increased business activity/profits. A "suggestion" from the Fed can help move things along in a better direction.

The Advantages and Disadvantages of Monetary Policy

Monetary policy is a powerful tool that has a direct effect on the equilibrium level of GDP as well as Net Domestic Product (NDP) and on the aggregate price level. The financial markets can be strongly influenced by the Fed, but ultimately it is these markets that determine interest rates. In turn, these interest rates are critical in determining the amount of business investment because of their effect on costs and, therefore, profits. The level of GDP/NDP is directly affected by the amount of aggregate demand that includes business investment. Interest rates are obviously a critical link in this economic process.

When there is an **easy money policy** (expansion), the Fed helps increase the money supply, and interest rates are reduced. Business investment increases because the cost of doing business is reduced. This in turn increases aggregate demand as well as GDP/NDP.

When there is a **tight money policy** (contraction), the economic relationships work in the opposite direction. A reduction in the money supply growth increases interest rates, which decreases business investment. This in turn decreases aggregate demand and decreases GDP/NDP.

Advantages (Benefits) of Monetary Policy

The effectiveness of monetary policy is widely believed to be very significant because of three basic advantages:

ADVANTAGES OF MONETARY POLICY

Speed and Flexibility
Isolation from Political Pressure
Equal Impact

Speed and Flexibility

The ability of the Fed to react very quickly to influence economic conditions is a major advantage. This phenomenon was witnessed on several occasions but especially with the attack in New York on 9/11/01. The Federal Reserve immediately intervened to reverse the dramatic loss of funds from the money supply caused by the panic within the financial markets. If you recall, speed of implementation was a major disadvantage with fiscal policy.

Isolated from Political Pressure

Second, monetary policy is considered effective because it is largely isolated from political pressure. The members of the Board of Governors do not have to answer directly to the President or Congress. This was one of the reasons for structuring the Fed with some level of independence. The Fed was created by Congress and must periodically report back to Congress, but it maintains its independence on a day-to-day basis.

Equal Impact

Finally, monetary policy is thought by many to be effective because its operations equally impact all citizens without regard to income, location or politics, but this may not be the case with fiscal policy.

Disadvantages of Monetary Policy (Costs, Risks and Limitations)

As with all economic activities, the implementation of monetary policy does have some costs and risks as well as its critics.

DISADVANTAGES OF MONETARY POLICY:

Recession
Contractionary Monetary Policy
Unequal Impact

Recession

Critics argue that monetary policy is more effective in controlling inflation, but it is ineffective in moving the economy from recession to growth. Clearly the impact of monetary policy is greater in reducing inflation by increasing interest rates, but it is less successful at inducing businesses to expand in a recession. It might be more accurate to say that in a recession, the Fed can induce businesses to contract less than they would have had the Fed not intervened.

Contractionary Monetary Policy

Another criticism is that implementation of contractionary monetary policy can result in a reduction in the private sector through the crowding-out effect. Contractionary monetary policy with higher interest rates can actually expand government relative to the private sector.

Unequal Impact

Some critics also argue that monetary policy does not impact all individuals equally because real estate and construction (for instance) are significantly more affected by interest rate changes than other areas of the economy.

Velocity Debate

A final problem of monetary policy is the difficulty in controlling the **velocity** of money (velocity is the average number of times a dollar is spent during a year). With the complexity of economic activity, the turnover (velocity) of money is not directly controlled by the Fed. The speed of money turnover is determined by spending pressure in the economy.

As you would expect with a relatively fixed supply of money, during periods of growing GDP, the velocity of money increases as money is spent more rapidly. In a recession, velocity will slow down.

Money Supply Growth Targets

Monetary policy is often targeted on a particular variable as a guide for monitoring the effects of policy changes. In the past, the Fed has specifically targeted the growth in M1 and M2—at other times, it has targeted changes in specific interest rates. Although money supply growth ultimately affects interest rates, each target is somewhat different. At the time of this writing, the Fed was actually targeting the **federal funds rate** (interest rates banks charge each other on overnight loans to meet reserve requirements).

The Fed funds rate is highly sensitive to money market factors and well exemplifies the interaction of supply and demand for banking funds. The **prime rate** (the rate banks charge their best customers) tends to follow the Fed funds rate. See Figure 19.3 below.

The Federal Open Market Committee (FOMC) usually directs its open market operations to target the federal funds rate. The effectiveness of the Fed operations is then measured by its effect on the federal funds rate. In 2009, the target for federal funds was 0.25 percent for most of the year. This rate is very low in nominal terms—and even a negative number in "real" (inflation-adjusted) terms. This was a very "easy money" (expansionary) position for monetary policy. As mentioned previously, the actual implementation of OMO occurs through the Federal Reserve Bank of New York with its close proximity (geographic and virtual) to the major financial markets.

Monetary Policy and Global Economics

The implementation of monetary policy is made additionally complex by the international position of the U.S. dollar. The dollar is widely used throughout the world and, in a closely related matter, the United States currently has a substantial deficit between exports and imports. This creates an outflow of American money to pay for the greater amount of imports. The net outflow of dollars is often returned to the United States for purchase of Treasury bonds that pay an attractive market interest rate (to a foreign investor) with low risk. The challenge is this: If interest rates are low, American firms are more likely to expand—but if interest rates are low, foreign investors also will trade dollars gained through trade for investments in other nations (instead of the United States), forcing down the value of the dollar. In order to balance these factors, the Fed must consider a higher interest rate to attract foreign investors to U.S. debt instruments (Treasury bonds)—but such a rate may slow the American economy.

An **easy money policy** (low interest rates) will decrease the value of the dollar and increase exports from the United States, but reduced interest rates will also discourage

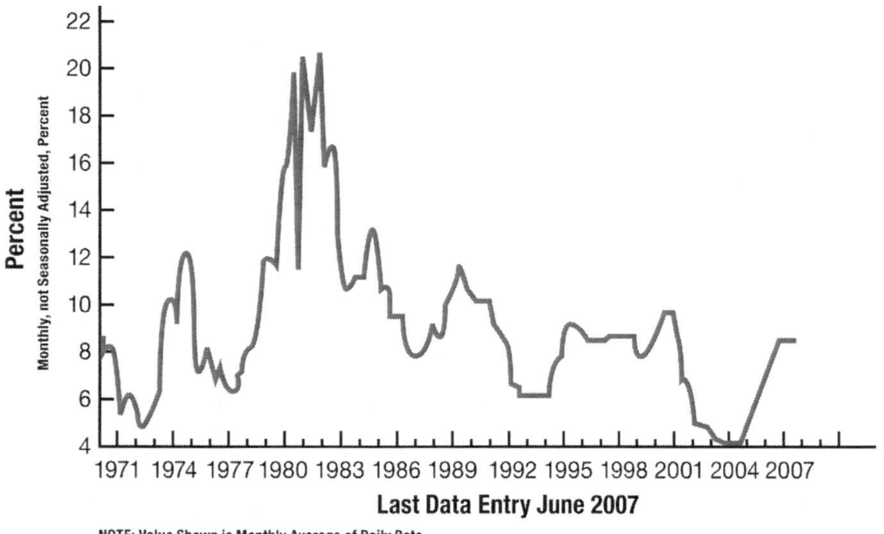

FIGURE 19.3
The Prime Interest Rate from 1971 to 2007

foreigners from investing in America. A tight money policy (high interest rates) will increase the value of the dollar, reduce exports and slow the American economy, but it also will attract a return of American dollars spent for imports. There is a podcast discussion of international trade at http://dallasfed.org/video/index.html with various global titles.

EQUATION OF EXCHANGE

For more than 200 years, economists have studied the relationship of money supply to inflation. In early economic history, John Stuart Mill recognized the importance of the money supply to prices, although at that time national income data were not available to accurately quantify the relationship. However, Irving Fisher formulated the equation of exchange in mathematical terms using modern national income data created during the 1940s. In modern economics, his equation is shortened to:

$$\mathrm{M} \times \mathrm{V} = \mathrm{P} \times \mathrm{Q}$$

This formula is a truism, meaning that the values are true by definition. If you multiply the number of dollars in circulation by the average number of times that each one is spent during a year, the result will equal the average price of an item times the quantity of items purchased (or produced). Another view of this relationship is that the amount of money times the number of times it is spent is equal to GDP (P times Q).

$$M \times V = P \times Q$$

M is the average amount in circulation
V is the velocity of the money that is described as the annual frequency with which a dollar is spent
P is the average price level
Q is the quantity purchased (or produced)

THE QUANTITY THEORY OF MONEY

The **quantity theory of money** is based on the equation of exchange. This theory assumes that V and Q tend to be relatively stable during a year. Therefore, there is a strong relationship between the quantity of money and the price level. The new Classical Theory discussed in Lesson 7 began with this **Monetarist Theory.** The Monetarist school of economics (not to be confused with Monetary Policy) uses the quantity theory of money (equation of exchange) as a basis of theory. Monetarists emphasize changes in the money supply as the most important determinant of employment, output and prices. According to this theory, the money supply is a critical causal force yielding the nominal GDP.

Critics of the Monetarist Theory, such as Keynesians, argue that V and Q are not stable. Keynesians further assume that the velocity of money varies directly with the interest rate. The unstable nature of V (in their view) can cause a significant effect on GDP. The view of some critics of the Monetarist Theory is that changes in the level of prices correlate to changes in the money supply, but they are not caused by changes in the money supply. Having a full moon the night before may correlate with your favorite team winning its game the next day but it may not cause the team to win (then again maybe it does—these are interesting questions).

A POSTSCRIPT: THEORY VS. REALITY—OUR RECENT ECONOMIC PROBLEMS

Dealing with the recession of 2008–2009 was an interesting experiment in the use of both monetary and fiscal policy to counter business cycles. This recession began with a mortgage debt crisis that resulted from poorly collateralized real estate loans and speculation in mortgage-backed securities and the insurance products generated for these securities. Risky loans were made for houses (called subprime mortgages) with the assumption that housing prices would continuously increase and, therefore, even if a borrower did have a problem, he could always sell the property to cover the loan.

The U.S. economy, however, entered a recession. This was initially driven by a financial crisis that was generated by those same mortgage-backed securities and their derivatives mentioned above. The price of housing in many markets began to fall significantly. This forced buyers into foreclosure and banks took possession of houses valued at less than the balance on their mortgage loans. These houses were often unsaleable in the short term. The mortgages were often insured, but due to the large scale of the defaults, insurance firms were not able to provide the funds.

With the slump of the housing and insurance industries, the financial markets continued to encounter problems because they were part of the structure of securities backing the original mortgages. As a number of banks as well as insurance and financial firms faced bankruptcy, President Bush requested a "bailout" for these institutions. Their collapse would potentially have caused a problem for the entire U.S. economy as well as many international banks holding U.S. mortgage-backed securities. Eventually Congress approved and the president signed a bill authorizing funds for banks as well as several insurance and financial firms. This represented an unprecedented modern use of fiscal policy on the part of the U.S. government.

In order to facilitate movement away from the risk of an even larger recession, the Federal Reserve began expanding its loan operations. The Fed made funds available for credit markets through extensive loan increases and nominal interest rates were reduced to almost zero. The Federal government, through the U.S. Treasury, bought stock in many banks and financial institutions in a coordinated effort with the Fed.

President Obama continued the federal bailout movement by purchasing controlling interest in Chrysler (Fiat) and General Motors. A second stimulus package was passed by Congress and signed by President Obama to use fiscal means to bolster the economy through tax cuts and increasing government funding for projects across the nation. This was intended to provide a major stimulus to aggregate demand.

These are very extraordinary actions within both fiscal and monetary policy. There are many arguments both for and against such government and Federal Reserve action. However, most economists agree that the recession of 2008–2009 was potentially the worst threat since the Depression in the 1930s.

Conclusion

A fundamental knowledge of economics would seem to be crucial to survival and prosperity in today's world. Most economists agree on the basic principles that you have studied in this course. There are, however, a number of different perspectives on the policy actions that can be taken by the federal government and the Federal Reserve (recall "normative economics"). You should now be well aware that the Classical, Monetarist and Keynesian views often differ on "what to do and when to do it."

There are many debates between Monetarists and Keynesians over the use of monetary policy. Monetarists argue that fiscal policy is weak due to the crowding-out effect. Keynesians believe that there is only a small amount of crowding-out.

Monetarists argue that requiring the Fed to operate with a "monetary rule" (money growth at the same rate as potential increases in real GDP) is wise. Such a rule, according to Fiscalists (Keynesians), would be very constraining for the Fed and would only increase the severity of business cycles.

The debate continues between these different schools of thought. While the approaches vary, the basic goals for the economy are the same. The Monetarist school was influential during the Reagan administration and continues to be an important part of monetary considerations. A presentation of this view is well documented by the Dallas Federal Reserve in the discussion with Economics Nobel Laureate Milton Friedman at http://www.dallasfed.org?video?index.html. Under the Economic Education tab, you will find videos with a recording titled "Cooperatives not Competitors" and "Trading Freely."

Monetarist Theory, the Supply Side Theory and Keynesian (Fiscalist) Theory are all widely held (and widely debated) today and each is slowly evolving. The fundamental relationships previously described have held, with some "evolution," since the 1930s. All three schools actually provide analytical frameworks for helping to understand the nature of our economy today and in the future. Most credible discussions of our economy will include some elements of all three theories.

Economic Growth

It is very important to remember (as you saw in Lessons 6, 8 and 9) that "real growth" in the economy depends on relatively slow, evolving rightward shifts in the aggregate supply. As your instincts might tell you, the presence of a steady (but not too rapid) expansion in the supply of money is very important to the real growth of the economy. On the opposite side of the coin, the lack of a balanced expansion in the money supply can certainly inhibit real growth and result in a stagnant (or even backsliding) AS curve.

It is critical for the health of an economy that expansion of the money supply (as well as long-term savings) be well balanced with the potential for rightward shifts in aggregate supply and the resulting expansion of production capacity (growth in the PPF). The Federal Reserve faces many challenging choices and trade-offs in trying to provide a balanced approach that considers the short-term health of the U.S. economy as well as its long-term growth.

Regarding "challenging choices" and the expansion of the AS and PPF, we should not forget what ultimately underlies our material standard of living. As long as our legitimate creativity, innovation and productivity as individuals and as a society continues to expand, then we can continue to grow in a sustainable way—and a strong standard of living can be shared by all. It really is about trying to make those good choices. If each of us individually, in our own microeconomy, can follow such an approach, then as a community (and as a larger society) we can all share in a strong standard of living—and a good quality of life.

SUMMARY

The Federal Reserve is responsible for monetary policy and working with the federal government to facilitate (assist) economic growth, stability and full employment (but remember that it cannot actually create those conditions—this can only be done at the "micro" level). The Federal Reserve uses both major and minor tools to assist in the pursuit of our economic goals. The Fed's major (or quantitative) tools include open market operations, the discount rate and reserve requirements. The minor tools include moral suasion, consumer credit controls and **margin requirements.**

ADDITIONAL THOUGHTS ON "GROWTH" AND THE AS/AD MODEL

There is some mutual ground on the topic of "economic growth" among the views noted above (the "schools of thought"). Each view does acknowledge the AS/AD model and its relevance to growth. In each of these views, a rightward shift in both the AS and AD curves represents growth in employment, output and income. The means of facilitating these shifts may center on the supply side forces of capitalism and lower taxation and regulation or on the demand side forces with increased access to education and training. Some economists advocate increasing AS by decreasing government spending while others advocate increasing government spending for education and training; changes in government spending are eventually tied to changes in government taxing. In our economic future, we will most likely see an emphasis on a number of different approaches to facilitate the "rightward shifts" of both AS and AD.

KEY TERMS

Monetary Policy: Actions taken by the Federal Reserve to influence the availability and cost of bank credit in order to promote economic stability.

Reserve Requirement: The percentage of a bank's deposits that must be retained by the bank or deposited with the Federal Reserve.

Discount Rate: The interest rate paid by a commercial bank if it borrows from the Federal Reserve.

Open Market Operations: The buying and selling of government securities in the open market to influence bank reserves.

Tight Money Policy: If the Fed restricts the money supply (M1), usually in response to inflationary pressure, it is called tight money.

Easy Money Policy: If the Fed makes more money available (M1) for lending, usually in response to recessionary pressure, it is called easy money.

Margin Requirement: The amount of down payment required when you buy stock. Currently 50 percent of the total purchase must be paid when you complete the transaction.

Moral Suasion: The informal influence associated with the importance of the Federal Reserve.

Credit Controls: A seldom-used Fed control device, but it gives the Fed the authority to dictate any interest rate of terms of any loan.

Velocity: The speed at which money is spent.

Federal Funds Rate: The rate that banks charge each other for short-term (usually overnight) loans.

Prime Rate: The interest rate banks charge their best (usually corporate) customers. It is the benchmark for most other loans.

Monetarist Theory: One of the major schools of contemporary economics which asserts that controlling the money supply is the key to maintaining a stable economy. Monetarists are usually associated to a more conservative political viewpoint.

Equation of Exchange: This equation (MV5PQ) is a way of analyzing not only the growth of the money supply but also the speed at which money is turning over in our economy and the effects that follow.

Keynesian Theory: Sometimes called Neo-Keynesian economics, this school of thought is based on the aggregate demand/aggregate supply theory first developed by John Maynard Keynes. It sees the control of the money supply of secondary importance to Fiscal Policy. Keynesians are typically associated with a more liberal political viewpoint.

Name ______________________ Date ______________

Applied Exercises

1. Given the following Bank Y balance sheet, complete the questions below.

Commercial Banking System (in billions of dollars)

Assets		Liabilities and Net Worth	
Cash and Deposits with Fed	$100	Checkable Deposits	$200
Loans	20	Net Worth	100
Investments	50		
Bank Property Assests	130		

Answer the following questions assuming a 20 percent required reserve.

a. From the information above, how much do banks have in excess reserves?

b. How much is the additional maximum quantity of money that could be created?

c. If the Federal Reserve buys $5 billion in securities from the public and it is deposited in commercial banks, how can the supply of money change?

2. The quantity theory of money argues that the long-run price levels move in proportion to changes in the money supply. Answer the following questions based on that assumption.

a. Money Supply (M) $2,000
Price Level (P) 10
Quantity (Y) 500
Calculate the velocity of money given the above information.

b. Based on the quantity theory of money assumptions, what would happen if the money supply increased to $2,200?

Applied Exercises: Answers

1. a. **Required Reserves are 20 percent of checkable deposits or .2 times 200 = 40. The system has 100 in reserves (cash and deposits with the Fed) therefore there are 60 in excess reserves.**
   b. **The banking system can expand the money supply by the amount of excess reserves times the money multiplier. The money multiplier is 1/reserve requirement or 1/.2 = 5. The money creation possible is 60 times 5 or 300.**
   c. **If 5 billion is deposited into the banking system then banks will have 5 billion more in checkable deposits and 20 percent must be held in reserve or 5 times .2 = 1. Banks would then have 1 billion more in excess reserve applied to the money multiplier to determine the amount of money that can be created. Given the money multiplier is 5 as in B, and then 5 billion more of money can be created.**
1. a. **MV = PQ, therefore $2,000 times V = 10 times 500, resulting in a V = 2.5.**
   b. **MV = PQ, therefore $2,200 times 2.5 = $5,500, therefore the market cost of the economy has increased by 10 percent from $5,000 to $5,500.**

CHAPTER TWENTY

International Trade

> If a foreign country can supply us with a commodity cheaper than we ourselves can make it, better buy it of them with some part of the produce of our own industry, employed in a way in which we have some advantage.
>
> ADAM SMITH

WHAT IS ALL THE FUSS ABOUT?

Economists joke about how we don't agree on much. In fact, even when two economists are in agreement about some issue, one of them is bound to pretend to disagree just so a good argument can break out.

Photo courtesy Jack Chambless

That is why it is so nice that there is at least one topic where you will get near-universal agreement among professionals in the dismal science. The agreement surrounds our view of the importance of international trade in furthering the progress and happiness of mankind.

You might find yourself wondering how there can be a near-consensus among economists that trade is a wonderful thing when every time there is an international trade conference rioters and protesters take to the streets claiming that trade is so horrible that it must be dramatically reduced in order to save workers and the planet. As it turns out, there is a good reason why the rioters feel this way. It is either because they are stupid or because economists have done a terrible job of educating the masses on the benefits of international commerce.

It is more likely the latter is true. When we consider the fact that an increasing number of Democrats and Republicans (including Tea Party types) think that international trade is doing more harm to the U.S. than good,[1] well, somewhere the economics community has dropped the educational ball . . .

Rising Anxiety

Q: Do you think free-trade agreements have helped or hurt the U.S.?

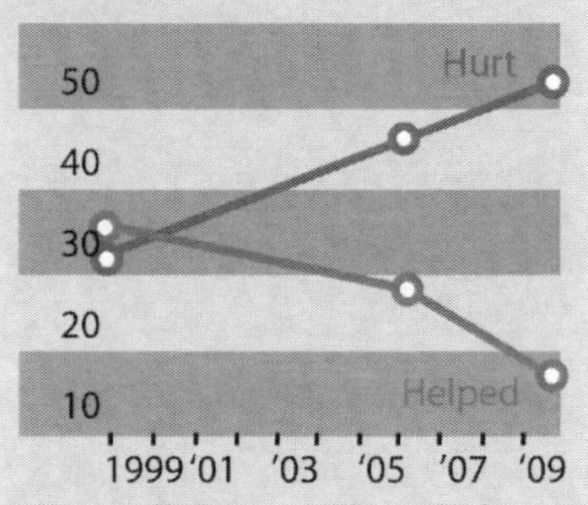

Hurt
50
40
30
20
10
Helped
1999 '01 '03 '05 '07 '09

Source: WSJ/NBC News poll. Margin of error in Sept. 2010 poll is ±3.1 percentage points.

Republished with permission of Dow Jones & Company, Inc., from *Wall Street Journal,* October 2, 2010; permission conveyed through Copyright Clearance Center, Inc.

A REFRESHER ON THE PRINCIPLE OF COMPARATIVE ADVANTAGE

Oregon is one of the leading hops-producing states in the U.S. Hops is the plant used to give beer a spicy flavor. Louisiana is one of the largest oil-producing states in America.

What if residents of Oregon decided to boycott oil from Louisiana, and at the same time, brewers in Louisiana began refusing to buy hops from Oregon? Furthermore, suppose Oregon decided to become self-sufficient in oil production, while down on the bayou, an attempt was made to grow hops.

What would it take for each state to become self-sufficient? First, it would require that each state *ignore the concept of opportunity cost.* If Louisiana shifted into high gear on hops production, more and more of the states resources would have to be allocated to growing hops.

The same is true for Oregon. Imagine all of the hops farms that would have to be destroyed as the state cleared the land to make room for petroleum exploration and drilling. More resources devoted to hops growing in Louisiana and oil exploration in Oregon would mean less resources in each state to produce the most efficiently supplied product.

Residents of Oregon would be very upset to read geological reports indicating that there is little, if any, oil in Oregon. People in Louisiana—where the temperatures are not conducive to producing hops—would be equally upset to find out that a beer shortage is imminent because the state can't produce enough—or any—hops.

In the long run, each state will come to realize that, through trade, Oregon will realize a steady flow of high-quality oil from Louisiana while residents of Louisiana will be able to enjoy what might be America's finest hops. This is in addition to the fact that Louisiana and Oregon will enjoy a net increase in total jobs available. This takes place because Louisiana will produce more oil than it needs and simply sell off the excess to

Photo courtesy Jack Chambless

states like Oregon, while Oregon will do the same with the hops. Trade, therefore, is a positive-sum game—not the zero-sum game that enriches one party at the expense of another.

TRADE BETWEEN NATIONS

Since the beginning of human beings, trade has been a natural function of any economy. This is true at the individual level, state to state, and at the international level as well. For this reason, over the past several centuries people have looked outward to meet their wants and needs when their own economy lacked the resources to do so.[2] As far back as the time when people got around on foot, horseback, or small canoes, trading between tribes, villages, and nations has been viewed as the best way to avoid pervasive scarcity.

Today, most people are aware of the fact that it makes sense for Saudi Arabia to export oil and import computers. Honduras has no business trying to catch the United States in jet aircraft production, so Honduras buys jets from us and we buy bananas from Honduras. What is unclear to many students is why, for example, the United States would ever import cars from Japan when we have shown that we can effectively produce them here.

This question is not limited to cars. The mere mention of washers and dryers, televisions, VCRs, DVDs, stereo players, steel, bulldozers, clothing and assorted agricultural products will create an uproar among Americans who recall a time when America dominated the world market in the production of these and other goods and services. Over time, that dominance has faded to the point where you would be hard-pressed to find an American-made television or DVD player. How America lost these markets and why we are strong in so many new ones, like computer software, energy equipment, medical technology, and movie production is a critical lesson in comparative advantage. Let's look at it.

HOW AMERICA LOST THE AUTOMOBILE MARKET

While the automobile was not invented in America—the Germans actually beat us to it—the United States was the dominant nation in automobile production from the days of Henry Ford's Model T until the early 1970s. Mr. Ford got us off to such a great start by producing a high-quality affordable product on an assembly line that saved his company millions of dollars in production costs.

Over time, General Motors and Chrysler entered the arena—as did others with much less success—until by 1970 the world's automobile market was dominated by the "Big Three." Of course, Germany, Japan, Sweden, and Italy were also factors in the international marketplace, but the majority of cars sold in America were built in the U.S. by one of the three major companies.

In the early 1970s all of that changed. It started with the dramatic increase in oil prices that stemmed from the 1973 Arab Oil Embargo. With gas prices skyrocketing, all of a sudden the very large, gas-drinking cars of the U.S. were not as attractive. Americans had always had a love affair with speed and larger cars. Cheap gas helped fuel this market. However, with the days of inexpensive gas quickly disappearing, Americans began noticing the fact that Honda, Toyota, and other Japanese companies were producing much smaller, fuel-efficient cars.

As the demand for Japanese cars increased, the initial reaction in Detroit was one of indifference and some would say, arrogance. Former Ford and Chrysler Chairman Lee Iacocca even went so far as to say, "A true American will only buy an American-made car." What he and other American executives quickly learned is that a true American has a budget constraint to worry about and will be more loyal to her wallet than the origins of her car.

Eventually, the U.S. automakers woke up and realized that the Japanese were not going to go away. It was during the remaining years of the 1970s that the Americans responded with their own version of small cars. You may have heard of or seen such products as the Ford Pinto, the Chevy Vega, and the Gremlin. Not only were Americans not impressed with the rather hideous look of these cars, but the quality of these automobiles also left a great deal to be desired. As a result, the demand for American cars continued to fall.

Of course, the next response was predictable. With their market share eroding faster than they could fathom, the executives of the Big Three ran straight to Washington, D.C., and begged for protection from this "unfair" intrusion by the Japanese into our markets. It did not hurt that it was less than 40 years since the Japanese had bombed Pearl Harbor. The executives appealed to the consumers' sense of patriotism and residual resentment against our former enemy and Congress's sense of political savvy to help get very restrictive tariffs and quotas placed on the Japanese. At one point during the 1980s, things got so bad that Chrysler filed for bankruptcy.

Not only did the government use our tax dollars to bail out this firm that had been selected for extinction, but then the Reagan administration caved to the mounting pressure for protection and asked the Japanese to "voluntarily" reduce imports. The world "voluntary" actually meant "mandatory," lest the Japanese face even greater punitive measures.

It did not matter. The American consumers kept on buying the superior Japanese product. The Japanese, with the use of "Kan-Ban" or "Just-in-Time" inventory management, continued to turn out better and better cars at terrific prices.

In 1986 oil prices collapsed. As a result, the demand for larger cars began to increase once again. The Japanese were years ahead of schedule in meeting this change in the market. Figuring that oil prices would not stay high forever and recognizing that Americans prefer bigger cars, the Japanese rolled out such products as the Toyota Camry, the Honda Prelude and Accord, and the Nissan Maxima.

These larger cars proved to be a huge hit with Americans and another blow to the American carmakers that were begging Americans to believe that quality problems were dissipating. The consumers were buying it.

By the late 1980s the American economy was roaring, and consumers had plenty of money to spend. It was then that the Japanese made the final monumental step in their march toward taking over the American car market. Automobiles called Acura, Lexus, and Infiniti appeared in showrooms around the country. These cars, produced by Honda, Toyota, and Nissan, respectively, did not bear the names of the Japanese producers. The Japanese did not want car shoppers to think that these new luxury models were simply slight alterations of the other Japanese cars. They wanted the consumer to perceive them as being like Mercedes-Benz or BMW.

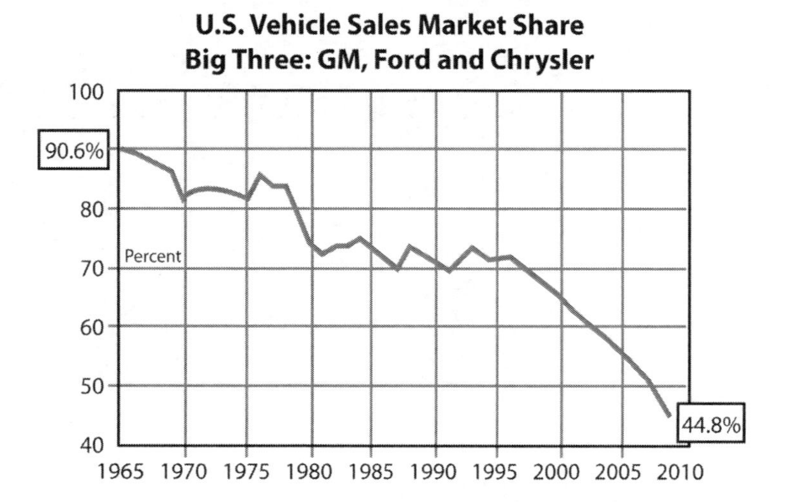

Today, the Big Three, for the first time in history, sell less than 45% of the vehicles bought in America. In 2008, General Motors saw its stock fall to below $10 per share. Eventually the company filed for bankruptcy and received billions of dollars in taxpayer money to stay afloat.

Foreign automakers who build cars in the United States pay an average of $30 per hour in wages and benefits to non-union workers while U.S. companies pay over $70.[3]

Given what you learned about the impact input costs have on supply and prices, you might be inclined to believe that such a competitive disadvantage in labor costs would lead to higher prices for American cars relative to what Japanese producers charge. That is not the case. Japanese cars are actually around *$2,500 more* than comparable American cars and still the American consumer prefers the Japanese brand.[4]

American companies have scrambled to improve the quality of the cars built in this country. The minivan, the SUV, and divergent types of pickup trucks have helped companies like Ford survive—and at times prosper—in the world automobile market, but serious cost pressures and quality issues remain.[5]

While similar events in electronics, steel, and other industries have contributed to the emergence of other nations as world leaders in production, the primary reason why America is not self-sufficient is simple.

Whether it is red wine from France, DVD players from Japan, vodka from Russia, or sugar from Haiti, there are some countries (for reasons associated with climate, technology, years of experience, or perhaps national priority) that do a better job producing certain goods than we do. However, as the table that follows clearly illustrates, the United States has no reason to worry about being "taken over" by the rest of the world. The good news is that we enjoy a tremendous advantage over the rest of the world in most categories of production.[6]

CONCEPT CHECK

Asia enjoys a tremendous comparative advantage in the shrimp business. Does this mean that Louisiana shrimpers should stop fishing? Should the U.S. government provide protection for American shrimpers? Why or why not?[7]

Photo courtesy Jack Chambless

THE ECONOMICS OF PROTECTIONISM

> The problem in a lot of our trade agreements is that the Administration tends to negotiate on behalf of multinational companies instead of on behalf of workers and communities.
>
> Barack Obama

Despite all of the evidence that trade creates a positive-sum game, there are still those who argue that the best use of public policy is to restrict trade—or even ban it under certain circumstances.[8] Where does this argument come from? Does it garner any support among economists? In this section, we will uncover the historical reasons for tariffs and quotas and whether or not trade restrictions make any economic sense.

A tariff is a tax on an imported good or service.

A quota is an artificial limit placed on the amount of a good or service that can be legally imported each year.[9]

If you are wondering how the government decides which products are hit with tariffs and quotas and what formula is used to determine the amount of the tariff, it is very simple. The system used can be found in the invisible manual called *Twilight Zone Economics*. Consider this:

The United States allows Jamaica to sell only 950 gallons of ice cream to hungry Americans each year. Mexico is allowed to export 35,292 bras per year to the U.S. Haiti—the world's most efficient producer of sugar—is allowed to sell only 7,730 tons to the U.S.[10]

Low-priced watch parts are hit with a tariff of 151.2%. Tobacco stem importers pay 458%. Shoe importers pay 67%. Pity the consumer whose watch breaks down the day he decides to take up smoking and cross-training.

A Healthy Share of the World Market Shares of Global Corporate Profits and Sales

Industry	U.S.		Japan		Europe	
	Profits (%)	Sales (%)	Profits (%)	Sales (%)	Profits (%)	Sales (%)
Energy equipment and services	99.6	92.7	0.8	1	*−0.4	6.3
Aerospace and military technology	81.6	75.8	0	0.4	18.4	23.8
Data processing and reproduction	65.1	73.2	10.7	22.2	24.2	4.6
Electronic components and instrument	65	61.8	30.5	35.8	4.5	2.4
Beverages and tobacco	63	63.4	3.6	16.4	33.4	20.2
Health and personal care	61.9	48.9	8.2	20.3	29.9	30.8
Leisure and tourism	60.3	45.7	7.4	16.3	32.3	38.1
Forest product and paper	59.7	51	7	17.4	33.3	31.6
Energy source	50.4	45.8	2.3	13.5	47	40.7
Metals-Nonferrous	45.7	30.2	11.9	30.8	42.4	39
Recreation and other consumer goods	44	33.2	46.4	60.7	9.7	6.1
Food and household products	42.6	32.6	7.8	21.7	49.6	45.7
Electrical and electronics	41.1	21.4	25.7	50.7	33.2	27.9
Chemicals	41	28.2	13.3	30.3	45.7	41.5
Industrial components	38.2	24.5	32.5	44.7	29.3	30.8
Automobiles	23.6	37	31	35.3	45.5	27.6
Machinery and engineering	19.2	18.9	34.3	46.3	46.3	34.9
Appliances and household durable	16.5	7.6	74.4	66.6	9.1	25.7
Metals-Steel	2.3	10.1	51.2	57	46.5	32.9
All industries	47.7	37.4	15.5	31.5	36.8	31.1

*Europe's businesses in the sector had a net loss.

Source: Morgan Stanley Captial International and Daniel Strickberger

If you eat food on occasion, keep in mind that the tariff on grapefruit juice is 41.3%. Carrot and dried prune importers pay 17.5%. Olives, dates, frozen chicken, cucumbers, watermelon, yogurt, garlic, and asparagus all are assessed tariffs of 20% or higher.[11]

Representative Richard Roe once proposed to reduce the 33% tariff on protective garments worn by firefighters. Even though no American companies make this garment, the American Textile Manufacturers Institute objected. ATMI argued that only if the tariff were kept high, would the price of these garments reach a level that *might* encourage some American firms to make this garment. The Bush administration followed the same logic when it imposed import quotas on Chinese brassieres to protect the totally nonexistent U.S. bra industry.[12]

In his second term, Mr. Bush approved billions of dollars in taxpayer-financed subsidies for American farmers. He indicated that unless India took steps to reduce assistance to Indian farmers, the U.S. would consider a tougher trade stance with India.[13]

In 1988, foreign ice cream makers "swamped" the U.S.; 576 gallons came from New Zealand and *12 gallons* from Denmark. With a whopping one-tenth of 1% of the domestic ice cream market dominated by foreigners, the United States government was outraged when Canada—banned from America's ice cream market altogether—imposed a quota on U.S. ice cream.

The first President Bush sent a letter to the U.S. International Trade Commission demanding an ice cream investigation, "telling the ITC to stop everything else and give ice cream imports their highest priority."[14] With over 30 people working on this project, a final report was submitted on August 28, 1989. The details of the report were never revealed for "national security" reasons.[15]

The U.S. recently complained about Australia's 12% tariff on almonds. The U.S. almond tariff is 14.8%. Also receiving criticism was Canada's 12.5% tariff on frozen peaches. The U.S. frozen peach tariff is 20%. We also do not like the 7% tariff Guatemala imposes on soybean oil. The Guatemalans are probably not thrilled with our 22% tariff on this product.[16]

Former U.S. Trade Representative Clayton Yeutter once noted, "The Florida Citrus Industry . . . believes that removal of Japan's unfair barriers could cut the price of oranges for Japanese consumers by one third." Interestingly enough, the price of orange juice would fall by an even larger amount in America if not for our *60%* tariff on Brazilian oranges.[17]

It is also interesting to note that Congress seems to have a great deal of concern for the plight of America's poor people. Mink furs are tariff-free. Polyester sweaters pay 34.6%. Lobster is duty-free. Baby food pays 17.2%. Orange juice pays 40%, so maybe a poor mom should give her baby Perrier water, which is taxed at 0.8%.

THE HISTORICAL "JUSTIFICATION" FOR TARIFFS AND QUOTAS

No analysis of protectionism would be complete without some exploration into the reason tariffs and quotas are used against our trading partners. The defense of protectionism is vigorous. Therefore, each reason will be fully addressed, along with what economists think about the justifications offered.

TARIFFS AND QUOTAS PROTECT DOMESTIC JOBS

On July 7, 1999, President Clinton announced that the U.S. would impose stiff new tariffs on lamb imported from Australia and New Zealand. While New Zealand has a population of approximately four million people, the New Zealand sheep population totals sixty million. In contrast, the U.S. has a sheep population of about seven million.

With a tremendous comparative advantage in lamb and wool production, Australia and New Zealand have been able to sell lamb meat and wool to Americans at a much lower price than American producers can. Since the price of foreign lamb and wool is lower (and the quality arguably better), the demand for American-made lamb and wool is fairly low. This means that the derived demand for American workers in this industry is fairly low.

The way Mr. Clinton's tariff was designed to increase employment in this industry is straightforward. The imposition of a 40% tariff forced the Australians and New Zealanders to increase prices in America to cover the higher cost of selling their products. If prices increased enough, the average American consumer would opt to start buying American lamb and wool. As the demand for American lamb and wool increased, the demand for workers in these industries would follow, and voila! Jobs are saved in our country.

This has been the key argument for tariffs in almost every instance tariffs are considered. The only problem is with the research that suggests this argument is largely void of any economic merit.

". . .THE SINGLE WORST DECISION OF HIS PRESIDENCY."

That is what the conservative editorial board of *The Wall Street Journal* called Mr. Bush's 2002 decision to dramatically increase the tariff on imported steel.[18]

> Every day we go without expanding trade is another day of missed opportunities to strengthen the economy.
>
> PRESIDENT BUSH, APRIL 27, 2002

Not long after these remarks, President Bush imposed a 30% tariff on foreign steel. Not only did the tariff lead to an increase in the price of goods made with steel (during a time when our economy was suffering the lingering effects of a recession), but the tariff led to a loss of $680 billion in national income and the elimination of 200,000 jobs in the steel-using industries![19] In California, 19,392 jobs were lost. Texas saw 15,553 more people lose employment, while Ohio, Michigan, and Illinois each lost nearly 10,000 jobs. The Consuming Industries Trade Action Coalition estimated that the steel tariff had led to a loss of $4 billion in wages.

At least the tariff helped our steel industry, right? Well, no. It did not. While President Bush hoped that the higher tax on foreign steel would buy our steel industry time to improve efficiency and gain market share, the opposite actually occurred.

Steel prices shot up by a much larger amount than the administration had expected. The price for hot-rolled steel increased from $210 a ton to $350 a ton.

Since, in the short run, the demand for steel is fairly inelastic (meaning that it is a necessary good) the higher prices did not lead to a very large drop in quantity demanded around the globe. As a result, foreign steel producers like Brazil, Russia, and Japan increased their production of steel—in some cases by as much as 36%![20] Moreover, the higher prices did not help the U.S. steel industry that much.[21] Old and inefficient, the U.S. steel mills were unable to effectively increase output as much as our more efficient foreign rivals could. The end result was a glut of steel coming in from foreign nations that, even with the tariff, were more cost-effective in their operations and in a better position to absorb the new tax.

Making matters even worse was a World Trade Organization ruling in November 2003 that found the Bush administration's steel tariff illegal under international trade law. The W.T.O. then gave Europe and other regions around the world the authority to impose up to $2 billion in sanctions on everything from U.S.-made orange juice to motor boats and sunglasses.[22]

The fact that our steel industry failed to expand is not surprising. Economists Robert Z. Lawrence and Robert E. Litan surveyed 16 major industries receiving protection from 1950 through 1986. They found that only one industry—bicycle making—expanded. How could this be true? It is very simple, as it turns out.

Suppose the Pittsburgh Pirates baseball team—arguably one of the worst in recent history—struck an agreement with Major League Baseball that allowed the Pirates to pitch to opposing teams from only 10 feet away instead of the normal 60 feet, 6 inches away. Would this encourage the Pirates to try harder at improving their baseball skills, or would it give them a false sense of security, and erode their work ethic and the quality of their product? The answer is pretty obvious, and the applications to protectionism are clear.

Even with protection, industries like steel are in decline because consumers and businesses are not going to flock to the company that has been insolated from the free market. The market makes people and industries work hard or die. When the government protects inferior competitors, the incentive to improve is truncated, demand continues to fall, and jobs vanish.

CONCEPT CHECK

The United States has a 60% tariff on cement from Mexico.[23] What would happen to the price of construction projects in the U.S. and unemployment in the U.S., if the tariff dropped to 6%? Why?

Another issue that comes up with respect to the protection of domestic jobs is the cost of such protection. Import quotas on Japanese cars during the 1980s cost American car buyers about \$4.3 billion. That's nearly *\$160,000 per year for each job saved.* According to the Federal Trade Commission study, tariffs cost the American economy \$81 for every \$1 saved. This should not come as a great surprise.

If you were asked to use your money to help improve the productivity of two students—one who had a 3.93 GPA and studied 30 hours per week or one who had a GPA of 0.93 and smoked crack 30 hours per week—who do you think would be more expensive to help? If you said the crack smoker, go to the head of the class. The ratio of \$81 per \$1 saved is merely a function of whom we are attempting to help. Microsoft, Nike, and Rolex don't need much help—these companies are good at what they do.

Protecting sugar producers in Florida costs American taxpayers millions of dollars every year. This is because America does not possess a comparative advantage in sugar growing.[24] Consequently, many American candy makers have left America in order to be able to buy foreign sugar at lower prices. This move has led to thousands of Americans losing their jobs in the candy industry.[25]

All told, tariffs and quotas not only make job protection a very expensive proposition for consumers (the London-based Trade Policy Research Center places the cost at about \$1,200 per year, per family), but the gains in terms of total job creation are illusory.

Shutterstock © Scott Richardson, 2011.

ANOTHER LESSON FROM BASTIAT

You will recall that we examined the views of the French economist, Frederic Bastiat in the area of government spending and taxation. Bastiat also held very strong views on the subject of economic liberty as it pertains to trade. What follows is one of his more famous works on the subject.

A PETITION From the Manufacturers of Candles, Tapers, Lanterns, Sticks, Street Lamps, Snuffers, and Extinguishers, and from Producers of Tallow, Oil, Resin, Alcohol, and Generally of Everything Connected with Lighting.

To the Honourable Members of the Chamber of Deputies.

Gentlemen:

You are on the right track. You reject abstract theories and little regard for abundance and low prices. You concern yourselves mainly with the fate of the producer. You wish to free him from foreign competition, that is, to reserve the *domestic market* for *domestic industry.*

We come to offer you a wonderful opportunity for your—what shall we call it? Your theory? No, nothing is more deceptive than theory. Your doctrine? Your system? Your principle? But you dislike doctrines, you have a horror of systems, as for principles, you deny that there are any in political economy; therefore we shall call it your practice—your practice without theory and without principle.

We are suffering from the ruinous competition of a rival who apparently works under conditions so far superior to our own for the production of light that he is *flooding* the *domestic market* with it at an incredibly low price; for the moment he appears, our sales cease, all the consumers turn to him, and a branch of French industry whose ramifications are innumerable is all at once reduced to complete stagnation. This rival, which is none other than the sun, is waging war on us so mercilessly we suspect he is being stirred up against us by perfidious Albion (excellent diplomacy nowadays!), particularly because he has for that haughty island a respect that he does not show for us.

We ask you to be so good as to pass a law requiring the closing of all windows, dormers, skylights, inside and outside shutters, curtains, casements, bull's-eyes, deadlights, and blinds—in short, all openings, holes, chinks, and fissures through which the light of the sun is wont to enter houses, to the detriment of the fair industries with which, we are proud to say, we have endowed the country, a country that cannot, without betraying ingratitude, abandon us today to so unequal a combat.

Be good enough, honourable deputies, to take our request seriously, and do not reject it without at least hearing the reasons that we have to advance in its support.

First, if you shut off as much as possible all access to natural light, and thereby create a need for artificial light, what industry in France will not ultimately be encouraged? If France consumes more tallow, there will have to be more cattle and sheep, and, consequently, we shall see an increase in cleared fields, meat, wool, leather, and especially manure, the basis of all agricultural wealth.

If France consumes more oil, we shall see an expansion in the cultivation of the poppy, the olive, and rapeseed. These rich yet soil-exhausting plants will come at just the right time to enable us to put to profitable use the increased fertility that the breeding of cattle will impart to the land.

Our moors will be covered with resinous trees. Numerous swarms of bees will gather from our mountains the perfumed treasures that today waste their fragrance, like the flowers from which they emanate. Thus, there is not one branch of agriculture that would not undergo a great expansion. The same holds true of shipping. Thousands of vessels will engage in whaling, and in a short time we shall have a fleet capable of upholding the honour of France and of gratifying the patriotic aspirations of the undersigned petitioners, chandlers, etc.

But what shall we say of the *specialities* of *Parisian manufacture?* Henceforth you will behold gilding, bronze, and crystal in candlesticks, in lamps, in chandeliers, in candelabra sparkling in spacious emporia compared with which those of today are but stalls.

There is no needy resin-collector on the heights of his sand dunes, no poor miner in the depths of his black pit, who will not receive higher wages and enjoy increased prosperity.

It needs but a little reflection, gentlemen, to be convinced that there is perhaps not one Frenchman, from the wealthy stockholder of the Anzin Company to the humblest vendor of matches, whose condition would not be improved by the success of our petition.

We anticipate your objections, gentlemen; but there is not a single one of them that you have not picked up from the musty old books of the advocates of free trade. We defy you to utter a word against us that will not instantly rebound against yourselves and the principle behind all your policy.

Will you tell us that, though we may gain by this protection, France will not gain at all, because the consumer will bear the expense?

We have our answer ready:

You no longer have the right to invoke the interests of the consumer. You have sacrificed him whenever you have found his interests opposed to those of the producer. You have done so in order *to encourage industry and to increase employment.* For the same reason you ought to do so this time too.

Indeed, you yourselves have anticipated this objection. When told that the consumer has a stake in the free entry of iron, coal, sesame, wheat, and textiles, ``Yes," you reply, ``but the producer has a stake in their exclusion." Very well, surely if consumers have a stake in the admission of natural light, producers have a stake in its interdiction.

"But," you may still say, "the producer and the consumer are one and the same person. If the manufacturer profits by protection, he will make the farmer prosperous. Contrariwise, if agriculture is prosperous, it will open markets for manufactured goods." Very well, If you grant us a monopoly over the production of lighting during the day, first of all we shall buy large amounts of tallow, charcoal, oil, resin, wax, alcohol, silver, iron, bronze, and crystal, to supply our industry; and, moreover, we and our numerous suppliers, having become rich, will consume a great deal and spread prosperity into all areas of domestic industry.

Will you say that the light of the sun is a gratuitous gift of Nature, and that to reject such gifts would be to reject wealth itself under the pretext of encouraging the means of acquiring it?

But if you take this position, you strike a mortal blow at your own policy; remember that up to now you have always excluded foreign goods *because* and *in proportion* as they approximate gratuitous gifts. You have only *half* as good a reason for complying with the demands of other monopolists as you have for granting our petition, which is in *complete* accord with your established policy; and to reject our demands precisely because they are *better founded* than anyone else's would be tantamount to accepting the equation: $+ \times + = -$; in other words, it would be to heap *absurdity* upon *absurdity.*

Labour and Nature collaborate in varying proportions, depending upon the country and the climate, in the production of a commodity. The part that Nature contributes is always free of charge; it is the part contributed by human labour that constitutes value and is paid for.

If an orange from Lisbon sells for half the price of an orange from Paris, it is because the natural heat of the sun, which is, of course, free of charge, does for the former what the latter owes to artificial heating, which necessarily has to be paid for in the market.

Thus, when an orange reaches us from Portugal, one can say that it is given to us half free of charge, or, in other words, at *half price* as compared with those from Paris.

Now, it is precisely on the basis of its being *semigratuitous* (pardon the word) that you maintain it should be barred. You ask: ``How can French labour withstand the competition of foreign labour when the former has to do all the work, whereas the latter has to do only half, the sun taking care of the rest?" But if the fact that a product is *half* free of charge leads you to exclude it from competition, how can its being *totally* free of charge induce you to admit it into competition? Either you are not consistent, or you should, after excluding what is half free of charge as harmful to our domestic industry, exclude what is totally gratuitous with all the more reason and with twice the zeal.

To take another example: When a product—coal, iron, wheat, or textiles—comes to us from abroad, and when we can acquire it for less labour than if we produced it ourselves, the difference is a *gratuitous gift* that is conferred up on us. The size of this gift is proportionate to the extent of this difference. It is a quarter, a half, or three-quarters of the value of the product if the foreigner asks of us only three-quarters, one-half, or one-quarter as high a price. It is as complete as it can be when the donor, like the sun in providing us with light, asks nothing from us. The question, and we pose it formally, is whether what you desire for France is the benefit of consumption free of charge or the alleged advantages of onerous production. Make your choice, but be logical; for as long as you ban, as you do, foreign coal, iron, wheat, and textiles, *in proportion* as their price approaches zero, how inconsistent it would be to admit the light of the sun, whose price is zero all day long!

JOBS AND NAFTA

This might come as a huge shock to many of you, but one of the first major economic decisions Bill Clinton made was associated with not telling the whole truth. Fortunately for America, his less-than-honest approach to trade helped America's economy tremendously during the 1990s.

When Mr. Clinton was running for president in 1992, he told union workers and environmental groups that he would not ratify the North American Free Trade Agreement with Mexico and Canada unless there were protections for union workers and adherence to environmental laws.

When he won the election he came into office and ratified NAFTA without any special protections for either group.[26]

Mr. Clinton also did not buy into the argument launched by Ross Perot and others, that NAFTA would kill jobs in America. Their argument was based on the simplistic theory that, since Mexican workers make so much less money than their American counterparts, once tariffs were lifted or even reduced, American companies would no longer be able to compete with the low wages paid to Mexican workers. Perot argued that the next event would be "a giant sucking sound of jobs leaving for Mexico."

When NAFTA was eventually ratified in 1993, America's unemployment rate was 7.5%. By May of 2000, the unemployment rate was 3.9%. While this is not all due to NAFTA, some interesting data has emerged about NAFTA's impact on the American economy.

On July 1, 1997, Congress issued a detailed "report card" covering the first three years of implementation of NAFTA. The data indicated that NAFTA had led to an increase in exports and imports by all three countries involved (U.S. exports to Mexico grew by 37%, to Canada by 33%) and the linkage of 2.3 million jobs in America to this agreement.[27]

By 2010, the data was even better. Trade between the U.S. and Mexico had increased from $40 billion in 1992 to $148 billion, while contributing to a 14.4% *increase* in the earnings of U.S. factory workers.[28]

Why did the dire predictions of net job losses to Mexico go unrealized? As it turns out, Perot is not totally off-base. Free trade has led to devastating job losses for manufacturers of toys, food, and textiles, to name just a few. The perception is that low wages in developing or third-world nations kill our jobs. The reality is that low wages are only a small part of the reason why some people lose jobs when tariffs and quotas are abolished.

REVISITING THE LOWWAGE FALLACY

Suppose you were the owner of a company that produced the guiding systems for orbiting satellites. You have three choices of where you are going to build your next plant: the United States, Mexico, or Rwanda. Suppose the average salary of a guidance system programmer would be $120,000 per year in America, $48,000 in Mexico, and $19,000 in the impoverished African nation of Rwanda. There is no question: You are going to move to Rwanda, right?

Before you depart, please consider the following questions. Are you concerned about the overall level of skill, education, and training of the Rwandan labor force? Are you concerned about the stability of the government there? Does potential language or cultural problems worry you? What about the quality and reliability of the phone, computer, and electric power delivery systems?

How about the highway system you will use to transport your guidance systems? What about the availability and location of suppliers? Are you starting to see the problem? The reason why most companies in America that employ highly skilled, educated workers do not leave for low-wage nations is because you get what you pay for. Low wages often mean low skills. Low skill means low productivity, and low productivity means very high labor costs.

In reality, it is actually cheaper to build many products in the United States than in nations with very low wages, simply because of the vast differences in labor productivity.[29] In fact, many American companies that left for Mexico when NAFTA passed have since *returned* to the U.S.

When companies do relocate to foreign nations, it is usually for one or more of the following reasons. One is to improve the *productivity-to-wage relationship.*

This means that in Malaysia, workers sitting at a sewing machine making bed sheets are performing a task that requires very little in the way of skill. Since this task can be done in a repetitive manner, the productivity of a 13-yearold girl in Malaysia would come close to that of an adult in a South Carolina textile mill. With the combination of high productivity and low wages, the average cost of the Malaysian worker makes them too cost-effective to keep the South Carolina plant open.

In this case—and others like it—people who oppose free trade have a point. Jobs will continue to be lost in American industries where foreigners have similar productivity but lower wages. This may seem horribly unfair, and certainly the person in South Carolina would have every reason to be angry, but let's consider the alternative.

Would you be willing to pay $15 for a cotton T-shirt made in America if it meant not being able to pay $7 for one from China? What about those Nike shoes you wear? How about a price of $159 rather than $99? You do have a choice.

If enough Americans decided to boycott all companies that use cheap foreign labor, the demand for their products would fall to the point that relocating back to America would be their only viable option. Once here, with the much higher wages being paid, we would then have to pay higher prices. Any takers?

THE REAL COST OF A NIKE SHOE

Suppose you go out to the mall and buy a pair of Nike running shoes for $70. Who gets the money? The answer might surprise you. The table below will help you overcome the belief that Nike earns ridiculously high profits by exploiting people in other countries.

As you can clearly see, the manufacturer, Nike, and the retailer each earn profit, but the retailer earns most of the profit. Nike earned 8.83% profit, the manufacturer earned 1.78% profit, and the retailer earned 12.86% profit out of the $70 price tag.

A second reason U.S. companies relocate to foreign nations is to *reduce their regulatory costs.* It is a fact of life that American companies face much higher regulatory costs than many other nations impose. Regulations stemming from worker safety, environmental protection, child labor, and other laws effectively increase the operating costs of doing business in the states. Moving to Indonesia and not having to worry about complying with thousands of pages of government rules and regulations can be enticing to many corporations.[30]

Increased regulations have also been the reason for many European companies leaving for the U.S. Laws that keep workers from working more than 40 hours (or even less) per week and mandating family leave and extended vacation time has made it very expensive for companies to survive in places like Spain and France.

Avoiding tariffs and quotas is another reason for the migration of U.S. and other nation's companies. If you drive a Japanese-brand car, chances are it was made in the United States.

According to the American International Automobile Dealers Association, over 50,000 American workers are employed in the building of cars like the Honda Accord

Manufacturer (Asia)		Nike (Beaverton, Oregon)		Retailer (Yourtown)	
Materials	$9.00				
Cost of labor	2.75	Cost of shoe to Nike	$20.00	Cost of shoe to retailer	$35.50
Cost of capital	3.00	Sales, distribution, and administration	5.00	Sales clerks' wages	9.50
Profit	1.75	Advertising	4.00	Shop rent	9.00
Shipping	0.50	Research and development	0.25	Retailer's other costs	7.00
Import duties	3.00	Nike's profit	6.25	Retailer's profit	9.00
Total paid by Nike for shoe	20.00	Total paid by retailer for shoe	35.50	Price paid by you	70.00

(Marysville, Ohio) and Civic (East Liberty, Ohio); the Nissan Sentra (Smyrna, Tennessee); the Toyota Camry (Georgetown, Kentucky) and Corolla (Fremont, California); and the M-Class Mercedes-Benz (Vance, Alabama).[31]

A major reason for this proliferation of "foreign" auto production in America, is based on the protectionist legislation that raises the costs of building a car in Japan or Germany, then shipping it to the U.S. as well as the strong productivity of U.S. workers.

Reducing transportation costs and *opening new markets* are also valid justifications for plant location in foreign markets. When PepsiCo built a bottling plant in Vietnam, a big part of the decision to do this was to bring down the costs of shipping Pepsi products to this market and to open up this market that was impenetrable before Bill Clinton lifted the embargo against our former enemy.

PUNISHING RIVAL NATIONS FOR CLOSED MARKETS

In more recent times, this argument has been widely used by administrations when imposing tariffs and quotas.

The Clinton Administration once threatened to impose a tariff of 100% on the Japanese in retaliation for not opening up their markets to more American cars and car parts.[32] Japan has also been a target in cases involving cellular phones, citrus, and semiconductors. The U.S. has threatened Canada with tariffs and quotas for perceived unfairness in our market penetration with respect to beer, lumber, and wheat.

This argument for tariffs and quotas is not without merit. For economists the test is very simple. *If* the United States has a comparative advantage in the production of beer, economic reasoning would indicate that Canadians should be allowed to drink our product without having restrictions on the supply or without having to pay artificially high prices. Therefore, if we were to tell the Canadians that we would not import hockey sticks from them until more Calgary residents can drink Bud Light, this would promote efficiency in both markets. The problem is that the United States has often been guilty of world-class hypocrisy when it comes to this argument.

The U.S. once charged Japan with not allowing Motorola to sell as many cellular phones as Motorola argued it should be able to. The only problem was that, at the time, Motorola was trying to sell the Japanese phones that were made for America's frequencies and were useless in Japan!

The first President Bush flew to Japan in the early 1990s to try to open up the Japanese car market to American cars. The Japanese drive cars with the steering column on the right side of the car. The American carmakers kept trying to sell them cars with the steering column on the *left-hand side.* In one of the most egregious examples of corporate arrogance ever, the U.S. carmakers informed the Japanese that building cars with the steering column on the right-hand side would impose higher costs of production on the Americans.

The Japanese were therefore told that when they had purchased enough left-side steering column cars, the Big Three would use that revenue to finance the production of the models with the steering column on the right-hand side . . .

HOW NOT TO MAKE FRIENDS IN FOREIGN LANDS

In 2001, Congress approved huge increases in agricultural subsidies for U.S. farmers. The average cotton farmer, for example, now earns half his income from government subsidies, rather than from the actual sale of cotton. Moreover, the approximately 25,000 cotton farmers in the U.S. have an average net worth of $800,000. What's the point?

Armed with roughly $3.4 billion in subsidy checks, the U.S. cotton industry produced a record crop of 9.74 billion pounds in 2001.[33] This level of production led to a huge increase in the global supply of cotton, which in turn suppressed cotton prices for vastly poorer cotton farmers in Africa, Asia, and other parts of the world.

Many of the farmers in Mali, and other countries where subsidies do not exist, ended up going out of business because of America's arbitrarily anti-free-market welfare program for wealthy cotton farmers. The U.S. response to the increase in poverty for these farmers was not surprising. To offset the $30 million in losses for Mali farmers, the U.S. government sent them $40 million in foreign aid—paid for by the same taxpayers who were called upon to subsidize U.S. cotton farmers.

For 2002, the $118 billion farm subsidy bill—which assured cotton farmers about 70 cents per pound—did not call for U.S. cotton farmers to leave any land idle, like past agreements had. The result was an even bigger surplus of cotton, even lower global prices, and more poverty for people in those nations.

Cotton is but one example of America's hypocritical stance on trade. From our recent steps to seek punitive damages against nations engaging in "unfair trade"[34] to rules that allowed the Export-Import bank to take U.S. taxpayer money and give it to wealthy corporations to promote trade,[35] America is often looked upon as a nation that believes in trade as long as the rules favor those with power and influence, rather than benefiting those that have a comparative advantage to begin with.

PUNISHING COMPETING NATIONS FOR PREDATORY PRICING, A.K.A. "DUMPING"

In 1997, the United States accused Chile of dumping salmon on American markets. This does not mean that the Chileans were piling up dead fish on our docks. It means we were piling up a rather smelly case against the Chileans for doing a great job of selling fish.

A threat to our prosperity?

Predatory pricing occurs when a company or industry drops the price of some product below the costs of producing that product in an attempt to run its rival out of business.

In the short run, predatory pricing exacts an economic toll on the predator as prices fall to levels where losses are incurred. In the long run, after the predator's rivals are gone—unable to stay in business due to below-cost prices—the predator will dominate the market.

This allows the predator to raise prices to a level that not only helps them recover their losses from the predatory act, but also confers upon them the ability to take advantage of monopoly power and charge very profitable prices indefinitely.

With constant mild ocean temperatures, lower labor rates, and freedom from burdensome regulations, the Chileans have a comparative advantage in the harvesting of Atlantic salmon, which farmers grow in pens sunk along bays in the ocean.[36] From 1994 to 1997, exports of Chilean salmon increased from $46.5 million to more than $111 million, and Chile captured about 45% of the American market at prices that were up to 25% lower than American companies were charging.

If you are a lover of salmon, you might say "Great, now I can eat more of the product I enjoy." Not so fast. In America, land of the litigious, this price advantage was not left unchallenged by fishermen hurt by the law of demand.

Led by international trade lawyer Michael Coursey, the U.S. charged that Chile had charged prices that were 42% below cost in America and the rest of the world. The solution? A 42% tariff on Chilean salmon.

For economists, this is a curious claim. Let's put on our critical thinking hats for a moment and reflect on what must take place for an industry to pull off a successful predatory pricing scheme.

First, the Chileans would have to *identify their rivals' cost of production.* In salmon fishing or farming, this might be easy to do, but this decision still carries two types of costs. The Chileans would have to willingly spend money to find out what it costs to harvest salmon in America. Without this information, they would not know by how much to lower prices. Spending this money raises their costs of production and therefore, causes profit levels to fall.

The Chileans would also incur an *opportunity cost* from this decision. Spending money on industrial espionage is money that could have been spent on the nextbest alternative, like better harvesting techniques, new nets, better marketing campaigns, and so forth.

Let's assume the Chileans are willing to fork over the money for this research. We come to step two. Once your rival's costs of production are identified, you must *lower your prices below their cost of production and keep the price there until they are out of business.* This is a sticky issue. Lowering prices to the point where your rival is gone may take a long time. In the meantime, your rival might merge with another company or be bought outright by a deep-pocketed investor.

The even greater problem is the issue of the Chileans' own profits falling from lowering prices to damagingly low levels. How smart can this strategy be when you have to inflict low profits or losses on your own firm in order to hopefully have long-run success?

Nevertheless, let's just assume the Chileans are willing to incur losses or that they have large profit reserves to support this venture. Step three takes place once your rival is gone. *When your rival is gone, you must increase prices* to a level that recovers your losses from the predatory act and ensures monopoly profit in the long run.

How likely is monopoly profit in the long run? Monopoly means the single seller of some good or service with no close substitutes. To make monopoly profit in the long run, you would have to make sure no one ever entered the industry to challenge your economically enviable position. Is that possible? Could the Chileans patent their salmon? Can they create a cartel like the Colombian drug lords and execute any fisherman who

Photo courtesy Jack Chambless

Should Canadian beef compete with Longhorns from Texas?

ever ventures out looking for competing salmon? Can they make sure no salmon ever swim anywhere away from Chile?

In reality, the Chileans have as much of a chance of monopolizing the salmon industry as George W. Bush has of being appointed to the United States Supreme Court.

If the Chileans can identify all the costs of production in America, and *if* they can afford to lower their prices, and *if* they can run all of the U.S. fisherman out of the market, there is no way they can keep one or more new firms from entering once they are raking in the profits from being the only country producing salmon. Profits act as a magnet to attract new competitors. This is always the case. This means that *in order to be a successful predator, you have to be willing to be a predator forever.*

It is not surprising that a growing number of economists not only question the merits of predatory pricing claims, but now argue that what appears to be predatory pricing is just good, old-fashioned competition that leads to lower prices for consumers and the rewards for a comparative advantage to the nation accused of wrongdoing.[37]

That is why economists became so fatigued sorting through the dumping claims levied by the Bush Administration against Canada and China.

For our neighbors to the North, the past few years have been frustrating ones. First, there was the accusation by the U.S. that "Mad Cow disease" was a threat from Canada. The U.S. government decided to temporarily create a quota of zero pounds per year in order to make sure now sick cows came in from Alberta and other provinces.[38]

Then we had the argument that the Canadians were dumping softwood lumber in our markets. With a red hot housing market already causing home prices to hit record levels, the 25% tariff on Canadian wood did not help consumers find much in the way of affordable housing in the last decade.[39]

China has not gotten off easy either. After years of protectionist tariffs and quotas on Chinese trousers, skirts, shirts and other clothing, China was finally allowed to export—with no quotas, various textile products. The lifting of the quota took place on January 1, 2005. In that year, exports from China increased by 60%.[40] Not surprisingly, the price of clothing in Wal-Mart and other stores fell as well.[41]

With such a huge increase in supply, many American textile manufacturers, already reeling from years of job losses and declining profit, lobbied the Bush Administration to stem the tide of low-priced imports from China.[42]

In the end, President Bush approved across the board increases in tariffs on Chinese textiles and the renewal of quotas as well. By some estimates the protection of American textile makers effectively raised taxes by $55 billion on consumers in our country.[43]

In the meantime, China is not standing still. While U.S. companies continue to seek out ways to avoid direct competition with the world's largest emerging market, the Chinese government has embarked on a policy of seeking out alternative countries that might be willing to sign free trade agreements that the U.S. shies away from. In 2003 China had formal free trade pacts with *zero* nations. By 2005 China had agreements with 25 countries—proving that there is more than one way—and one place—to sell underwear.[44]

The three previous "justifications" represent the primary rationale for tariffs and quotas. The last three arguments are not used as much, but from time to time can be a thorn in the side of free traders.

TO PROMOTE HUMAN RIGHTS AND ENVIRONMENTAL PROTECTION

When demonstrators showed up in Miami and Seattle to riot over the issue of trade, a great number of them were there to show their support for human rights in China and other nations and to argue for greater environmental awareness. These are certainly noble and valuable goals. I cannot think of too many people who rejoice over the conditions in which many people in Asian factories work. Not too many people seem to be hoping for the eradication of the sea turtle and the pollution of the oceans, either.

Opponents of trade argue that the globalization of markets has led to companies exploiting workers in slavelike conditions around the world while ravaging the environment in nations that do very little, if anything, to stop them or even slow them down. Let's look at it.

Nike has been at the crux of the firestorm of criticism for employing thousands of Asians at pay rates that Americans would never accept in conditions that OSHA would squash in about 30 seconds. We now know why Nike is in Asia. This Portland-based company feels it is too expensive to make shoes in Oregon and still make profit. Since Nike is a private company, it can produce shoes wherever it can secure the property rights to do so. The question is what would the lives of the Asian workers be like if Nike did move back to Oregon?

Is Nike forcing anyone to work for them in Asia? Are they using slaves held at gunpoint? Do the workers in those factories have alternatives to Nike that pay more? The answer to all of these questions is obvious—and no. If Nike pulled out of Asia, the workers who lost their jobs would have to turn to their next-best choice. As you might imagine, their next best choice is worse than what Nike offers.

We cringe at the thought of working for pennies an hour, but all wages are relative. Recall that actor Ben Affleck cringed at the "low wages" paid to custodians at his alma mater, Harvard.[45] Bill Gates might cringe at the "low pay" Mr. Affleck takes in. Who are we to say that the Asians don't want Nike there? If Nike and other companies continue to set up shop in those developing nations, over time the demand for labor will rise, and so will wages. This has already been observed in China, where more and more factory bosses are lamenting the growing pay rates that workers can command as the Chinese economy continues to grow.[46] With pay rates rising by nearly 20% per year in some cases, companies like Ann Taylor Stores Corp., Guess Inc., and J. C. Penney have been leaving for Vietnam and Bangladesh.[47] Ironically, it was companies like these that helped create rising wages, higher standards of living and economic development that made China a

SUGGESTED CLASSROOM DEBATE

In 2010 President Obama signed a trade agreement with South Korea that was designed to phase out tariffs on 95% of the trade goods coming into South Korea.[53] Will this agreement hurt South Korea? Will it do anything to help the American economy grow? Why, or why not?

more expensive place to do business. Thus, what some people call exploitation, is called opportunity by people in Asia.[48]

As for the issue of environmental protection, here is an interesting fact: The dirtiest nations in the world are the *poorest nations* in the world. In northern Bohemia in the Czech Republic, breathing the air is "like smoking 10 cigarettes a day" due to the smog created by antiquated coal-fired power plants.[49] In Mexico City, air pollution is so bad that cars are allotted specific times when they can be driven on the roads. In Africa, the chief source of energy creation is the burning of wood—one of the worst sources of air pollution. In the meantime, the quality of water in India and much of Africa, Asia, and South America would repulse the average American.

How can trade help these problems? As it turns out, trade is a two-edged sword. It is true that with increased trade comes development, and development can damage the environment. However, studies show that as a nation develops, it gains the economic and political resources to emerge as a net protector, rather than damager of the environment.[50]

The United States has cleaner air in many regions than ever before.[51] We have more trees than we did in 1900. Recycling programs flourish while we voluntarily buy environmentally safe products and insist on less pollution emanating from our cars and power plants. The Internet and other high-tech inventions continue to move us away from the old smokestack industries to industries that create virtually no pollution. All of this has been made possible by economic growth.

While it is true that more trade means more wealth, and more wealth can mean more malls and fewer trees—initially, it is a paradoxical truth that if you want to see a nation stay dirty, keep them poor. Poor nations do not care about buying unbleached cotton T-shirts. Nor do they have the money to fund an Environmental Protection Agency or to assist in the fight against global warming. Poor nations are simply trying to survive. That means big trouble when the choice is burning a rainforest to create farmland versus protecting the rainforests so wealthy Americans can go on nice vacations in South America.[52]

PROMOTING NATIONAL SECURITY

> Without steel, we cannot guarantee our national security. Without steel, we cannot rebuild from our national tragedy.
>
> SENATOR JOHN ROCKEFELLER, D-WEST VIRGINIA

Up until September 11th, one of the least-used argument in support of tariffs and quotas was the argument that trade jeopardizes the national security of our nation. The conjecture goes something like this:

Over the past several years the United States has imported approximately 67% of the oil that is used in this country. Suppose in the wake of the most recent increase in oil prices, the domestic petroleum industry begins lobbying Congress to put more restrictive tariffs or quotas on our Middle-Eastern trading partners, in order to be less dependent on foreign oil, and protect America from being hurt by OPEC policies. After all, oil is of vital interest to our national security, so why not protect the domestic suppliers?

The problem with this argument is twofold. *First,* it is not as if we are at the mercy of OPEC. We have reserves in America and access to even more oil in non- OPEC nations like Canada and Mexico. Therefore, a cry for national security tariff protection is a bit spurious if our national security is not actually at stake. *Second,* if we confer this status on oil, what is next? Why can't farmers claim that we cannot afford to lose agriculture to foreign concerns? What about jets, computer software, and toothbrushes? Why can't Boeing, Microsoft, and Oral-B argue that we must protect America from foreign planes, software, and toothbrushes that are not made by people with American teeth?

It is hard for economists to accept the argument that there are industries in our country that are of vital national security and are simultaneously threatened with extinction at the hands of foreign competition.

ONCE AGAIN, STEEL . . .

> Ask anyone if we should have a steel industry in America, and they will say yes!—unless they're economists.
>
> ANONYMOUS STEEL LOBBYIST

For years, the U.S. steel industry has sought protection from imported steel on the grounds that foreign steel makers were unfairly dumping cheap steel in America. From time to time, administrations from Reagan to Clinton bought this argument and provided relief in the form of tariffs and quotas. Yet the domestic steel industry never seemed to do any better in world markets. This led to some initial reluctance on the part of the Bush administration to offer even more protection for this floundering industry. That is, until the steel beams of the World Trade Center melted and sent the icons of American capitalism crumbling into the streets of New York City.

Immediately after September 11th the steel industry junked its call for tariffs on the grounds of predatory pricing and adopted a new strategy for gaining artificial protection from competition. The new argument was simple. Steel is needed to build tanks, guns, and jets, and steel will be needed to rebuild the World Trade Center if that should occur.

If the steel industry in America dies, so say the steel unions and steel executives, Osama bin Laden or some other enemy of America would eventually attempt to disrupt the supply of foreign steel coming to America and the U.S. would be at greater risk of losing the war on terrorism.[54] Thus began the lobbying efforts to impose tariffs on foreign rivals.

Not only that, but the steel industry sought a $12 billion bailout—specifically asking the Bush administration to use taxpayer dollars to take over the retiree pension and health insurance obligations of the major steel producers.[55]

President Bush finally caved into the political pressure to do something about the weakened steel industry. With steel-producing states being key battleground states in the 2002 Congressional elections and the 2004 presidential campaign, Mr. Bush felt the politically rational thing to do was capitulate to the calls for help. His help came in the form of the aforementioned 30% increase in the tariff on flat-rolled steel that is used to make cars and appliances. Steel rebar—used in construction and highways—got a 15% tariff, while other products like hot rolled

CONCEPT CHECK

Go online and research the "Golden Arches Theory of International Conflict." Does it appear to be a theory that supports free trade? Why, or why not?

What should this cost?

steel, stainless wire, tool steel, stainless flanges, and slab got tariffs ranging from 8% to 24%.[56] Do you remember the law of unintended consequences? This law came into effect about three seconds after the Bush announcement.

First, the European Union announced the possibility of increased tariffs on U.S. motorcycles, fruit juices, handguns, and textiles. Russia then banned the importation of all U.S. poultry—costing chicken producers over $600 million. Canada then imposed a 71% tariff on U.S. tomatoes. Canada also imposed a tariff on lumber from the U.S. that impacted our $6 billion market[57] and announced that a tariff on U.S. steel was being considered.[58]

Of course, well before President Bush imposed this tariff, steel-using companies and economists howled in protest. The Bureau of Labor Statistics pointed out that while approximately 160,000 people work in the steel industry, over *12 million* people work in steel-consuming jobs. This means companies like Whirlpool, Ford, John Deere and many other giants of industry would face much higher prices for steel. This would translate higher prices on consumers of washing machines, cars bulldozers, and so forth or a push to cut costs somewhere else—like labor hours, wages, benefits, or capital expenditures.[59]

Perhaps the greatest fear in the economics community was summed up by Gary Hufbauer of the Institute for International Economics, who said that the danger of the precedent-setting steel tariff was that, "the first big Faustian bargain on steel will be followed by a lot of mini- Fausts" in order to satisfy various constituencies.

For those of you who are unfamiliar with the famous story by Johann Wolfgang von Goethe, a "Faustian deal" is one where you give up a lot to gain a little. For President Bush, his deal with steel could cause other struggling industries to line up and look for a hand-out instead of looking into ways they can be more competitive in the global arena. As we saw in the section on job losses, the steel tariff ultimately led to higher prices, less job creation, and a questionable use of taxpayer dollars just as the economy was struggling to rebound from the recession of 2001.

PROTECTING INFANT INDUSTRIES

An infant industry is one in its earliest stages of development. In some countries, this gives rise to the argument for government-induced insulation from competition. To economists, there is some merit to this type of protection under limited circumstances.

If Costa Rica—a nation rich in botanical wildlife—decided to create a biotechnology industry and protect it with tariffs and/or quotas on foreign pharmaceuticals, this would receive tepid support from a good number of economists if Costa Rica could rationally be expected to develop a comparative advantage in this relatively new industry. It would also be important to have some assurances that, once a comparative advantage was acquired and Costa Rican companies could compete head to head with U.S. and European drug companies, that the protectionist measures would be eliminated.

The fact that once support is given it may be lobbied for indefinitely is one reason why most economists would have trouble extending the hand of government to fledgling industries. Temporary support has a way of becoming permanent welfare very quickly.

TO PUNISH CHINA FOR "CURRENCY MANIPULATION"

A significant portion of this book has touched on China's rising economic power—and the factors that have precipitated this amazing occurrence.

What has not been broached is the question concerning the degree to which China has achieved some of this magnificent progress by artificial means. Specifically, many critics of China's economic policies point out the Chinese government places controls on the value of the Yuan—the Chinese currency.

The table below illustrates some of the various exchange rates when converting foreign currency into dollars, and vice versa. This data is from January 28, 2011, but will be useful for our purposes even if the data has changed by the time you are reading this section of the book.

Currency	1 U.S. Dollar	in U.S. Dollars
Australian Dollar	1.00746	0.992595
Brazilian Real	1.68522	0.593394
British Pound	0.631439	1.58368
Canadian Dollar	0.999	1.001
Chilean Peso	484.481	0.00206406
Chinese Yuan	6.58103	0.151952
Colombian Peso	1863.81	0.000536535
Danish Krone	5.47998	0.182482
Euro	0.734991	1.36056
Hong Kong Dollar	7.79318	0.128317
Hungarian Forint	202.063	0.00494895
Iceland Krona	116.597	0.00857655
Indian Rupee	45.8467	0.0218118

Suppose a citizen of China wanted to buy a GMC Yukon SUV that retailed for \$38,000 in the United States. \$38,000 × 6.58103 = 250,079.14 Yuan. By the same token, a new king-size bed sheet produced in China and sold for 444.71 Yuan, would mean a customer in a mall in Utah would pay \$67.57 (444.71 × .151952).

The value of the dollar is determined by the same forces that create the value of anchovies and parachutes—the forces of supply and demand.

When people around the world are confident in the strength of the U.S economy and the economic policies of our government, the demand for our dollars typically rises. This causes the value of the dollar to rise. When the value of our dollar rises, our products become more expensive to folks in China and other nations; while Chinese, and other foreign goods, become cheaper in America.

Recently, as America has gone deeper into debt and has experienced a lengthy economic slump, the demand for dollars has fallen while government borrowing has increased the supply of dollars. This has lowered the value of the dollar, helping our exporters fare better in international markets while making the price of foreign goods rise in the U.S.

It is widely argued that if China allowed its currency to "float" with the forces of supply and demand, that the price of the Yuan would increase. Now each Yuan would be able to "purchase" fewer dollars. Let's say that a floating exchange rate would mean \$1 (U.S) equals 4.24 Yuan. Therefore, each Yuan would now be worth \$.235849. That GMC Yukon would now cost only 161,120 Yuan, while the bed sheet would cost \$104.88 (444.71 × .235849).

The result, critics charge, would be greater exports of American goods to China, a falling trade deficit with this nation, and more economic growth for American industries that have a comparative advantage but are simply shut out of China's market.[60]

There are some problems with this argument that many economists have pointed out and can be discovered by you, if you are willing to take the time to do proper research.

For example, China has not officially pegged its currency to the dollar since 2005. During that time the value of China's currency has risen, but we continue to buy more from China than China buys from us. Among the many reasons for this reality is rising productivity in China; improvements in technological progress in China that has given it a growing share in world metals and equipment markets; a strong educational system that is turning out far more mathematicians, engineers, and scientists than America; and a continued move toward lower taxes and greater property rights.

While it is certainly possible that China has engaged in "unofficial" limits on the Yuan-to-dollar ratio, our problems with China extend well beyond currency markets. Quite often political realities overcome economic ones, when facing economic realities would get politicians in trouble.

FINAL THOUGHTS

> Free and open trade creates new jobs and new income. It lifts the lives of all our people. It spurs the progress of economic and legal reform, and open trade reinforces the habit of liberty and sustains democracy.
>
> President George Bush, speaking during the Summit of the Americas, April 2001

Yes, that was one year before the steel tariff decision. During this semester, you have been exposed to a great number of topics that not all economists agree on. As you can see, not even the president agrees with his own statements from time to time. Hopefully, it is somewhat comforting to end this chapter with a consensus view from the economics community.

The *winners* from international trade are fairly obvious.

Nations with a comparative advantage, skilled workers in America and other developed nations, unskilled workers in developing nations, the environment in the long run, and governments in terms of increased tax revenue and economic prosperity make up the beneficiaries of trade.[61] This is the case even with more and more whitecollar jobs being "outsourced" to India, Russia, and China.

As we saw early in the textbook, there are actually more jobs coming in to American than there are going out. India's technology industry employed over 800,000 people in 2006. In America, over 10 million people had similar jobs.[62]

As long as America continues to achieve high levels of productivity, there will always be jobs that pay very well and that stay within our borders. The outsourcing of jobs was inevitable as India opens up to international trade.[63] However, this should be seen as an opportunity for Americans to increase our competitiveness rather than to run into the unproductive hole of protectionism. As the great economist David Ricardo taught us long ago, trade leads to shared gains, not gains for one at the expense of another.

It should also be noted that the United States has benefited from international trade in a less obvious manner—a slower rate of illegal immigration. Increased trade with Mexico has created greater prosperity in Mexico. Greater prosperity has led to a lessened need of many Mexicans to try to enter the U.S. illegally. While 2007 saw a tremendous debate about illegal immigration, there would be even more immigrants if not for NAFTA.

It is also somewhat interesting that as the value of the dollar fell in 2008, the demand for American goods increased dramatically overseas. From 2007 to 2008 exports increased by $115 billion and made up 13.5% of the gross domestic product—the highest level since World War II.[64] 2011 saw further movement upward in America's presence overseas.

Many of the winners during this time frame were small regional economies like Greenville, South Carolina, Waterloo, Iowa, and Kingsport, Tennessee, where the production of everything from turbines and forklifts to tractors and chemicals help propel much of the country forward while housing, banking, and other sectors faltered.

The *losers* from international trade have been many of America's unskilled workers in manufacturing industries, lower-skilled jobs in the technology sector, as well as industries that cannot stand up to the pressure of global competition.

One thing is certain: As technology continues to develop and the goal of economic freedom continues to be embraced around the globe, markets will become ever more interconnected. As that occurs, Adam Smith's treatise on the value of self-interest and liberty will be the standard-bearer for the global economy. As long as people desire more goods and services than can be found in their own nation, free trade will be rationally pursued.[65]

THE FUTURE OF TRADE—RELATIVELY FREE MARKETS?

In 2002, Congress voted to give President Bush five years of greater latitude to pursue expanded free trade opportunities. This agreement did not come without a potentially high price, however. In the narrowly passed legislation, U.S. union members stood to gain $1.2 billion from the newly created Trade Adjustment Assistance Program.

This taxpayer-financed program was designed to provide help to workers who lose their jobs to foreign competition. For example, people over 50 who lose jobs due to trade would qualify for $5,000 a year in "wage insurance" if they end up taking a job that is lower-paying than the one they had before trade eliminated their job.

Farmers also gained—at the expense of taxpayers—by authorizing subsidies of $100 billion over ten years. This particular feature was particularly galling to many of our foreign trading partners that have been trying to crack our agricultural markets for years. The subsidies give American farmers an advantage in global markets and thwart the progress toward more open markets.

During the 2004 presidential campaign, John Kerry moved away from the policy stance of Bill Clinton by advocating a much more interventionist role of government in international trade matters.[66] He advocated overhauling the U.S. tax code to raise taxes on corporations that outsource jobs and indicated that he would take a harder look at trade policies that did not provide more protection for labor union workers but did not advocate getting rid of agreements like NAFTA.[67]

In the 2008 campaign John McCain voiced support for free trade and said he would continue to work toward agreements with Columbia, South Korea, Panama and other nations. Barack Obama did not seem as enthusiastic about free trade—contending that he would renegotiate NAFTA and not pursue new trade agreements without more protections for union workers and the environment.[68] In the Ohio debate between Mr. Obama and Hillary Clinton, Mrs. Clinton repeatedly claimed that Ohio had suffered greatly because of free trade. When Tim Russert, the debate moderator, produced data showing that Ohio had seen more jobs created because of trade Mrs. Clinton struggled to defend her position that free trade was working to our detriment.[69]

Mr. Obama and Mrs. Clinton are not alone in their reluctance to support the reduction of tariffs and quotas. Former Senator Robert Byrd from West Virginia was successful in getting legislation passed that has hurt the cause of freer trade. Under what is known as the Byrd Amendment, US companies that win anti-dumping and anti-subsidy cases against foreign rivals not only get higher US tariffs imposed on those competitors' goods but they also *receive the revenues* from those tariffs. This has led foreign governments to protest that the law unfairly punishes non-US suppliers not only with tariffs but also with subsidies for US rivals. In 2007 alone, companies received $264 million in compensation for not being an effective competitor.[70]

In this decade, we now face new challenges. As aforementioned, more and more Americans of all political persuasions and income brackets have come to believe that free trade is bad for our country. It is a bit odd that despite all of the things we wear, eat, and use every day from other nations, we still think somehow trade is harming us.

In "The Fatal Conceit" (1988), Friedrich Hayek wrote that, "man's instincts were not made for the kinds of surroundings, and for the numbers, in which he now lives." According to Hayek and modern-day evolutionary psychologists, it is man's natural instincts to believe that the world is a zero-sum world with a fixed number of jobs and a static amount of wealth.[71] Hence, if you get more, I must get less.

Recessions and 10% unemployment rates help magnify what may very well be our natural inclination to believe that one must lose if another person gains. The recent "Great Recession" therefore has quite possibly created a "Great Misunderstanding," that America can only regain her prosperity by closing off products from China and other nations.

Two final notes: First, the last time America bought into the wholesale notion that avoiding trade would rescue our economy, was in 1930 when we let our government pass the Smoot-Hawley Tariff Act. This Act led to enormous increases in the tariffs we required other nations to pay. Retaliation by those nations ensued, world trade collapsed, and the U.S. lurched even closer to entry into World War II.[72]

Second, as the United States continues its war against terrorism, it should be noted that there is a direct causeand- effect link between open trade and economic wealth. The poorest nations—and the nations most plagued with terrorist activity—are the nations that are the most closed off from the rest of the world.[73]

ENDNOTES

[1]See "Americans Sour on Trade" by Sara Murray and Douglas Belkin, *The Wall Street Journal,* October 4, 2010.

[2]See "Aid is Good; Trade is Better" by Supachai Panitchpakdi, *The Wall Street Journal,* January 17, 2005; "Progenitor of the Paper Millionaires," *The Wall Street Journal,* July 19, 2000; and "We Want Trade, Not Aid" by Yoweri K. Museveni, *The Wall Street Journal,* November 6, 2003.

[3]See "The Decline of Detroit" by John Schnapp, *The Wall Street Journal,* July 14–15, 2007.

[4]See "Detroit's automakers lose ground to imports" by Tom Krisher, *The Orlando Sentinel,* August 2, 2007.

[5]See "Why Toyota Won" by James P. Womack, *The Wall Street Journal,* February 13, 2006; and "Behind GM's Slide: Bosses Misjudged New Urban Tastes" by Lee Hawkins Jr., *The Wall Street Journal,* March 8, 2006.

[6]The last year such comprehensive data was available was 1992. However, individually, the numbers have not changed dramatically from 1992 through 2011.

[7]See "Shrimp Gets a Makeover, as Foreign Imports Rise" by Katy McLaughlin, *The Wall Street Journal,* August 19, 2004; and "Trade and Aid Clash over Shrimp Tariffs" by Greg Hitt, *The Wall Street Journal,* April 25, 2005.

[8]This is not a new sentiment. During the time he was emperor of France, Napoleon implemented tariffs on farm products to aid French farmers. Source: Museum of Florida History, Tallahassee, Florida.

[9]More than 8,000 products have tariffs attached to them when they arrive in the U.S.

[10]See " 'Fair Trade' is Unfair" by James Bovard, *Newsweek,* December 9, 1991, p.13.

[11]See *The Fair Trade Fraud* by James Bovard, St. Martin's Press, 1991.

[12]See "The Great Brassiere War," *The Wall Street Journal,* November 19, 2003; and "U.S. Moves to Limit Textile Imports from China" by Edmund L. Andrews, *The New York Times,* November 19, 2003.

[13]See "Bush Seeks to Use Backlash on Jobs as Lever in India" by Michael Schroeder and Jay Soloman, *The Wall Street Journal,* March 8, 2004.

[14]See "A U.S. History of Trade Hypocrisy" by James Bovard, *The Wall Street Journal.*

[15]See "The Great Ice Cream War" by James Bovard, *The Wall Street Journal,* September 14, 1990.

[16]See *The Fair Trade Fraud,* Bovard, p. 66.

[17]See "U.S. panel order tariffs on Brazilian OJ" *The Orlando Sentinel,* August 18, 2005.

[18]See "Steeling Our Wealth," *The Wall Street Journal,* September 23, 2003.

[19]See "The Steel Tariffs' Costs," *The Wall Street Journal,* February 25, 2003; "Bush's Steel Opening," *The Wall Street Journal,* November 11, 2003; and "Lessons of Steel," *The Wall Street Journal,* December 2, 2003, p. A18.

[20]See "So Far, Steel Tariffs Do Little of What President Envisioned" by Neil King Jr. and Robert Guy, *The Wall Street Journal,* September 13, 2002.

[21]Arthur T. Denzau of St. Louis's Washington University found that restrictions on imported steel in the 1980s saved 17,000 jobs in the steel industry and among its suppliers. However, the higher prices that resulted led to the loss of 52,400 jobs in American steel-using industries. For every job saved, three were lost.

[22]See "U.S. Tariffs on Steel are Illegal, World Trade Organization Says" by Elizabeth Becker, *The New York Times,* November 11, 2003; and "The White House Steel Trap" *The New York Times,* November 11, 2003.

[23]See "U.S. Nears Mexican Cement Pact" by Jim Carlton, *The Wall Street Journal,* August 29, 2005.

[24]See "Clinton's Sugar Daddy Games Now Threaten NAFTA's Future" by Mary Anastasia O'Grady, *The Wall Street Journal,* December 20, 2002.

[25]See "A Saga of Politics and Candy Canes" by Sean Mussenden, *The Orlando Sentinel,* December 24, 2002.

[26]See *The Commanding Heights* by Daniel Yergin and Joseph Stanislaw, Simon & Schuster, 1998.

[27]See The Heritage Foundation's: NAFTA's *Three-Year Report Card: An "A" for North America's Economy* by John Sweeney.

[28]See "The Triumph of NAFTA," *The Wall Street Journal,* January 12, 2004 p. A14; and "Free Trade Accord at Age 10: The Growing Pains are Clear" by Elizabeth Becker, Clifford Krauss, and Tiem Weiner, *The New York Times,* December 27, 2003. May 16, 1997.

[29]See "We're # 1 And It Hurts" by George C. Church, *Time,* October 24, 1994.

[30]See "Is Free Trade Immoral?" *The Wall Street Journal,* February 26, 2004, p. A10.

[31]Source: http://www.aiada.org/

[32]Source: May 16, 1995, edition of the *CBS Evening News.*

[33]See "Hanging by a Thread" by Roger Thurow and Scott Kilman, *The Wall Street Journal,* June 26, 2002.

[34]See "Come on, America, Play By the Rules!" by Pascal Lamy, *The Wall Street Journal,* March 3, 2003; "Why Can't America Be More Like Us?" by Franz Fischler, *The Wall Street Journal,* February 19, 2004; and "Brave New World" by Supachai Panitchpakdi, *The Wall Street Journal,* February 26, 2004.

[35]See "A Guardian of Jobs or a 'Reverse Robin Hood' " by Leslie Wayne, *The New York Times,* September 1, 2002.

[36]See "The U.S. Builds a Fishy Case Against Chilean Salmon" by Greg Rushford, *The Wall Street Journal,* September 26, 1997.

[37]See "Predation: The Changing View in the Economics and the Law" by James C. Miller III and Paul Paulter, *Journal of Law & Economics,* vol. XXVIII (May 1985); "Not So Fast: The Myth of Predatory Pricing—Exposed" by Rob Norton, *Fortune,* February 7, 2000, p. 49.

[38]See "The errors in closing the border to our beef," *The Globe and Mail,* June 27, 2005.

[39]See "It looks like it's time to play let's make a deal in the softwood dispute" by Barry McKenna, *The Globe and Mail,* July 26, 2005.

[40]See "Deal expected on textile imports," *The Orlando Sentinel,* August 18, 2005.

[41]See "Tension rises over textile exports" by Lorrie Grant, *USA Today,* June 1, 2005, p. 5B.

[42]See "How the Textile Industry Alone Won Quotas on Chinese Imports" by Greg Hitt, *The Wall Street Journal,* November 10, 2005; and "Bush trade nominee talks tough on China" by Christopher Swann and Edward Alden, *Financial Times,* April 22, 2005.

[43]See "Protect Us From Protectionists" by Richard W. Fisher, *The Wall Street Journal,* April 25, 2005.

[44]See "China Irks U.S. as It Uses Trade to Embellish Newfound Clout" by Peter Wonacott and Neil King Jr., *The Wall Street Journal,* October 3, 2005.

[45]See "Prime Numbers," *The Chronicle of Higher Education,* May 19, 2000, p. A14.

[46]See "Rising Wages will Burst China's Bubble" by Peter Tasker, *Financial Times,* January 10, 2011.

[47]See "U.S. Apparel Retailers Turn Their Gaze Beyond China" by Elizabeth Holmes, *The Wall Street Journal,* June 15, 2010.

[48]See "The Left Should Love Globalization" by Francis Fukuyama, *The Wall Street Journal,* December 1, 1999; and "U.S. Trade Law Gives Africa Hope and Hard Jobs" by Marc Lacy, *The New York Times,* November 14, 2003.

[49]See "Czech Republic's air pollution sickens and enrages citizens," *The Orlando Sentinel,* February 15, 1993.

[50]See "Does Helping the Planet Hurt the Poor?" by Bjorn Lomborg, *The Wall Street Journal,* January 22–23, 2011, p. C1.
[51]Source: The American Lung Association.
[52]For more on this issue, see "NAFTA: Part of the Trade-Environment Solution" by Kathryn S. Fuller, *The Wall Street Journal,* July 16, 1993.
[53]See "Obama and Trade" *The Wall Street Journal,* December 6, 2010, p. A18.
[54]See "Steelmakers Say They Are a Key Component of Security" by Robert Guy Matthews, *The Wall Street Journal,* September 19, 2002, p. B4.
[55]See "Big Steel Still Enjoys Outsized Clout on Trade" by David Wessel, *The Wall Street Journal,* December 6, 2001; and "Steel's Shakedown Attempt Will Test Bush's Resolve" by George Melloan, *The Wall Street Journal,* January 22, 2002.
[56]See "Imposing Steel Tariffs, Bush Buys Some Time for Troubled Industry" by Robert Guy Matthews and Neil King Jr., *The Wall Street Journal,* March 6, 2002.
[57]See "So Far, Bush's Gamble on Steel Tariffs Isn't Paying Off " by Neil King Jr. and Michael M. Phillips, *The Wall Street Journal,* March 27, 2002, p. A20.
[58]See "Canada Weighs Imposing Tariffs on Steel," *The Wall Street Journal,* March 28, 2002, p. A2.
[59]See "Bush's Steel Trap: Tariff to Aid Producers Anger Users" by Neil King Jr., *The Wall Street Journal,* February 11, 2002, p. A24.
[60]See "China Trade and American Jobs" by Daniel Ikenson, *The Wall Street Journal,* April 2, 2010.
[61]See "Human Betterment Through Globalization" by Vernon L. Smith, speech before the Foundation for Economic Education, September 2005; and "We Grow, They Grow" by David Malpass, *The Wall Street Journal,* November 3, 2004.
[62]See "An Outsourcing Giant Fights Back" by Saritha Rai, *The New York Times,* March 21, 2004.
[63]See "Creative Jobs Destruction," *The Wall Street Journal,* January 6, 2004.
[64]See "Second Thoughts on Free Trade" by Charles Schumer and Paul Craig Roberts, *The New York Times,* January 6, 2004; and *Open World: The Truth About Globalization* by Philippe Legrain, Ivan R. Dee, 2004.
[65]See "Trade Keeps Growing, Despite Stalled Global Talks" by John W. Miller, *The Wall Street Journal,* January 31, 2011.
[66]For more on the Clinton administration's trade policies, see "They Support Free Trade, Except in the Case of . . ." by David E. Rosenbaum, *The New York Times,* November 16, 2003, and *The Commanding Heights: The Battle between Government and the Marketplace that is Remaking the Modern World* by Daniel Yergin and Joseph Stanislaw, Simon & Schuster, 1998.
[67]See "Kerry Targets Job Outsourcing With Corporate-Tax Overhaul" by Bob Davis and John Harwood, *The Wall Street Journal,* March 26, 2004; and "Free Trade becomes hot campaign issue" by Tom Raum, *The Associated Press* (appearing in *The Tallahassee Democrat),* February 22, 2004, p. 6A.
[68]See "Trade: What Exactly is a Free Trader, Anyway?" *The Wall Street Journal,* August 25, 2008.
[69]To see this exchange between Mr. Russert and Mrs. Clinton log on to: http://www.youtube.com/results?search_query=february+26+ohio+debate&search_type=&aq=f
[70]See "An expensive Byrd," *The Wall Street Journal,* September 11, 2008, pg. A14.
[71]See "The Protectionist Instinct" by Paul H. Rubin, *The Wall Street Journal,* October 7, 2010.
[72]See "Goodbye, Free Trade?" by Douglas A Irwin, *The Wall Street Journal,* October 9–10, 2010.
[73]See "The Map that Predicted the Terrorist Attacks" by Mark Skousen, *FEE Today,* 2002.

Name ______________________ Date ______________

CHAPTER REVIEW

1. What is the principle of comparative advantage? How does this principle explain the benefits of open trade between states and nations?

2. Fully explain four of the major reasons given for tariff protection and what most economists think about the justification given.

3. What are two reasons for tariffs and quotas that economists sometimes support? Why is the support given?

4. What is predatory pricing? Does it work? Why, or why not?